The Sirius Connection

Murry Hope is one of the foremost authors on esoteric wisdom, ancient magical religions, parapsychology, paraphysics and related subjects and, as a proponent of the 'field' theory (see Introduction), she has spent many years endeavouring to effect a meeting point between these studies and the disciplines of mainstream science. She has run lectures and seminars and appeared on radio and television worldwide in her capacity as an expert in these fields. Several of her twenty published books are available in twelve different languages.

By the same author

The Greek Tradition
The Psychology of Healing
The Psychology of Ritual
Time: The Ultimate Energy
The Lion People
The Paschats & the Crystal People
The Way of Cartouche
Atlantis: Myth or Reality?
Practical Atlantean Magic
Practical Greek Magic
Practical Celtic Magic
The Gaia Dialogues
Cosmic Connections
Olympus: An Experience in Self-Discovery

THE SIRIUS CONNECTION:

Unlocking the Secrets of Ancient Egypt

Murry Hope

ELEMENT

Shaftesbury, Dorset • Rockport, Massachusetts
Brisbane, Queensland

Text © Murry Hope 1996

Originally published as *Ancient Egypt* in 1990
by Element Books Limited

Published in Great Britain in 1996 by
Element Books Limited
Shaftesbury, Dorset SP7 8BP

Published in the USA in 1996 by
Element Books, Inc.
PO Box 830, Rockport, MA 01966

Published in Australia in 1996 by
Element Books Limited
for Jacaranda Wiley Limited
33 Park Road, Milton, Brisbane 4064

Reprinted August 1996

Cover design by Max Fairbrother
Page design by Roger Lightfoot
Typeset by Plejaden Publishing Service, Boltersen, Germany
Printed and bound in Great Britain by
Hartnolls Limited, Bodmin, Cornwall

British Library Cataloguing in Publication
data available

Library of Congress Cataloging in Publication
data available

ISBN 1-85230-818-4

Contents

To Her Grace Sekhmet Montu (LHS)
Who still observes the Old Ways

Acknowledgements

My gratitude and sincere thanks to the Scribe, Historian, and those members of the Ammonite Foundation in Cairo, Egypt who, with the permission of Her Grace Sekhmet Montu (LHS), made certain information from their private records available to me.

Acknowledgements and thanks are also due to the following publishers and authors who have kindly granted permission to use illustrations and quotes from the following books:

Thames & Hudson: *The Egyptians* by Cyril Aldred
Element Books: *The Great Pyramid Decoded* by Peter Lemesurier, and *The Psychology of Ritual* by Murry Hope
Souvenir Press Ltd: *Colony Earth* by Richard Mooney
JR-T Publications: *The Sons of Re* by John Rose
Sidgwick & Jackson: *The Sirius Mystery* by Robert K. G. Temple
Penguin Books Ltd: *Archaic Egypt* by Prof. W. B. Emery
Inner Traditions International Ltd, Rochester, Vermont, USA: *Sacred Science* by R. A. Schwaller de Lubicz, line drawings by Lucie Lamy (distributed by Harper & Row, Hagerstown, Maryland, USA)

Additional artwork by Martin Jones.

Introduction

It has been postulated that, prior to the rise of the historically acknowledged cultures of Sumeria and Ancient Egypt, a great civilization existed, the science and technology of which exceeded even our present-day achievements. However, when a freak of nature conspired to obliterate its homeland, all that remained were folk memories which slowly degenerated into legendary myths and superstitions. In *The Sirius Connection* I have explored the significance of the binary star Sirius on the growth and culture of dynastic Egypt. For example, was this association purely concerned with the inundation of the Nile during the Dog Days, which were reckoned from its heliacal rising, or were the ancient Egyptians aware of a deeper, more profound significance? Sirius is believed by many mystics and metaphysicists to hold the evolutionary key to Earth's development and, this being the case, it is likely to play an important role in the future of our planet. Perhaps the ancient Egyptian priests who had received their knowledge from the aforementioned technologically advanced pre-Flood civilisation were only too aware of this, which was why they sought to conceal its true significance within their most secret and powerful rites. Over the many centuries which spanned the Dynasties of ancient Egypt, however, the original knowledge and true meanings behind such practices slowly degenerated into the hocus-pocus of superstition, eventually succumbing to the inevitable 'power syndrome', their original meanings (and ethics) being long since forgotten.

However, this book is not primarily concerned with the Egypt of old and the religious faiths and customs favoured by this ancient people, but rather an investigation into those aspects of ancient Egyptian belief that were inherited from a much older and more profound tradition, which combined an understanding of general science, astronomy, astrophysics and psychology comparable to anything we know today, and in some aspects even more advanced. The multi-faceted knowledge contained in these cosmic truths included the role of our planet and solar system in relation to the galaxy, the evolutionary pattern designed for humankind and those other species with which we share the Earth, and the true nature and ultimate potential of the hominid mind/consciousness.

What I have therefore tried to do is to sever the bonds of historical orthodoxy and render a picture of Egypt, from archaic times, which concentrates on the origins of its metaphysical beliefs, for therein lies the plan of the labyrinth of ignorance from which we must needs escape if we are to align the ancient knowledge with modern science and psychology. For example, it was not by coincidence that Sirius was always depicted as a five-pointed star, the significance of those five points lying in their representation of what are known in metaphysics as *The Primary Four* – fire, air, water and earth – with Time at the fifth or overseeing point.

Over forty years of research into the origins of ancient magical and mystical beliefs have led me to conclude that what is popularly labelled 'occult' or 'magical' power can be easily accommodated and accounted for in recent studies of para-psychology and theoretical physics. All energy sources within the *known* Universe would appear to fall into four distinct cate-gories – the weak and strong nuclear forces, electromagnetism and gravity, with the possible existence of a fifth, or reconciling force which I have proposed to be Time. (See *Time: The Ultimate Energy*). Two of these (the weak nuclear force and electro-magnetism) I designate chaotic and two (the strong nuclear force and gravity) orderly, with Time carrying both aspects in equal proportion. As with the other four, Time has its corresponding primary particles at the quantum (microscopic) level, but it would also appear to carry more metaphysical connotations, which were obviously acknowledged and accorded due respect by the earliest known centres of civilization and their prehistoric predecessors.

I would therefore define much of the occult/magical/religious material which has seeped through the historical sieve as a body of knowledge concerned with natural cosmic laws which, due to an overemphasis on the worlds of physical matter, has become severed from the scientific mainstream. So-termed 'occult' mysteries, having supposedly originated in either prehistoric, or Sumerian, Egyptian, Babylonian, times, are therefore nothing more or less than ancient scientific facts that have become encoded into terms of reference easily understood by the unlettered, many of which, over the centuries, degenerated into superstition, their true meaning having been long since forgotten.

But I must return to archaic and ancient Egypt and the source from which its people obtained this knowledge. There has been much debate as to whether their teachers actually came from the region of Sirius itself – in other worlds they were extra-terrestrials as Robert Temple and other researchers have suggested – or whether their origins were nearer home, in Atlantis, for example, or Antarctica as recently proposed by Graham Hancock in his bestseller *Fingerprints of the Gods*. My own premise, which combines both empirical research and inborn 'memory', is that this solar system was seeded from the binary stars Sirius A and B, the archetypes of which pre-programmed their knowledge into the genetic structures of the few among those aforementioned highly advanced prehistoric people who were capable of comprehending it and applying it to both their spiritual understanding and technology. The Scriptural episode concerning the 'Sons of God and Daughters of Men' therefore relates to a genetic infusion, orchestrated by more advanced minds (fields of consciousness) rather than a coupling with extra-terrestrials! Thus implanted, the relevant gene was then passed to certain individuals within those areas colonized, and has surfaced from time to time down the ages – among the few labelled 'genius', perhaps, to whom we are all indebted for their contributions to the sciences, arts and humanities, but more often among those unsung heroes and heroines whose job it has been to simply ensure its perpetuation, either genetically or via the avenues of knowledge.

Let us, for a moment, consider the problems faced by that aforementioned advanced race when trying to convey their great fount of knowledge to an unlettered people deeply enmeshed in the shrouds of superstition, who still functioned mainly in the instinctive mode, the rational and intuitive aspects of their brains, lacking the appropriate stimulation, being incapable of comprehending the advanced technology in common use by their tutors. To them, their gods and goddesses were the ruling mystical archetypes of their existence, those metaphysical forces to which they turned for help and understanding when the contingencies of everyday life so demanded. So, what better way for their tutors to convey their knowledge of cosmic energies and principles than to personalize those five forces which they knew to be the driving energies behind this Universe? The five epagomenal Neters, perhaps? Many other interesting (and to the paraphysicist highly obvious) characters also make their appearance, Time Lords Thoth/Tehuti and Anubis, for example, while the knowledge of the alternating currents of chaos and order is surely exemplified in the cyclic tales of the continual battle between Horus and Set, which will be highlighted in the ensuing pages.

Although, in presenting the relevant Egyptological data, I shall accord full credence to known facts and accepted scholarship, I also intend to extend the panorama to include some of the views and interpretations extant in current metaphysical/paraphysical belief such as the nature of consciousness which is defined by the 'field' theory, as 'a field of active particles begging organisation'. All information should therefore be assessed within each of the following categories: Actual, Astronomical, Allegorical and Archetypal. So, enjoy your trip through the labyrinthine past and form your own conclusions accordingly, as I know you will.

Part 1

Egyptian Background

CHAPTER 1

Origins and Anomalies

Although archaeology may be seen to have unearthed a considerable amount of information regarding the origins of dynastic and predynastic Egypt, much of its early history is still shrouded in the mists of uncertainty. These many unanswered questions have naturally given rise to a great deal of speculation. How did a flourishing civilisation suddenly appear in those parts in defiance of what many scientists believe to be the natural process of evolution? And then there is the question of the many myths, legends, and classical writings that have come down to us which appear to be at variance with the views held by orthodox Egyptologists. The ancient Egyptian preoccupation with the binary star Sirius is one example.

It has recently been discovered that tribal peoples in remote parts of Africa also possess ancient and accurate astronomical information regarding this luminary, which could have only come from a highly advanced civilisation, the question arises – from whom or where did they obtain their knowledge? In 1976, the American scholar Robert K. G. Temple published his revolutionary theory that the quantum leap from primitivity to civilisation resulted from a contact with the inhabitants of a planet in the system of the binary star Sirius, prior to 3000 BC. Citing evidence from knowledge possessed in Egypt and Sumer, which percolated into other parts of Africa, he presented a convincing case for the appearance of extraterrestrials prior to the rise of dynastic Egypt.

However, there are other, equally plausible, explanations for both the sudden appearance of a mature Egyptian culture and the

early Egyptian's preoccupation with Sirius which also demand
attention. According to the information we do have from those
early times, the Siriun influence is indisputable, but whether the
indigenous population of those parts actually experienced a
contact with aliens or simply received their information from
another highly technologically and scientifically advanced
civilisation *here on Earth*, who either gleaned it via their technology
or were the original recipients of the extraterrestrial visitation, we
can but speculate. The sheer antiquity of our subject matter and
the time-scales involved may be evidenced in the fact that those
whom we look upon today as 'ancient Egyptians' were themselves somewhat preoccupied with their own history, being as
much intrigued (and probably mystified) by their origins as many
of us are today. For example, King Nefer-hotep (c. 1750 BC), in
deciding to fashion a statue in the likeness of the god Osiris, had
his scribes search among the ancient archives in the library of
Heliopolis for a pristine representation of that divinity to ensure
its accuracy. Rameses IV, whose reign was some 600 years later,
showed similar antiquarian leanings – and we think of *them* as
ancient! Several of the buildings around the Step Pyramid contain
evidence to the effect that the monument was open to sightseers
for over 1000 years before the time of King Neter-khet, who
reigned in the early part of the third dynasty, c. 2660 BC.

It was during the reign of Ptolemy II, Philadelphus, that the
Egyptian Manetho (Beloved of Thoth), who lived in the last
years of the fourth and first half of the third century BC, wrote
his famous *History of Egypt*. Manetho was High Priest at
Heliopolis, and a historian of veracity and reliability. Not only
did he write on historical subjects, but also on the mystic
philosophy and religion of his country, and it is generally
believed that his books were the fountain-head of knowledge on
all things Egyptian, from which Plutarch and later writers
derived their information. It is to Manetho that we owe the
scant writings and other fragments contained in *Thrice Greatest
Hermes* that were assembled and published by the great Theosophical scholar G. R. S. Mead in the early part of the twentieth
century. Unfortunately, Manetho's work has not survived intact
but exists in fragmentary and garbled summaries, preserved in
the writings of Josephus, and other classical authors, whose
quotes are usually by way of support for their own views rather
than as a precise historical reference. No doubt people have

been using ancient texts in this way since writing was invented, just as I, in turn, shall be leaning on texts from antiquity to aid my enquiry.

According to Manetho, Thoth, the Egyptian god of letters, produced 36,525 books of ancient wisdom – *a figure identical to the number of Primitive Inches in the Great Pyramid's designed perimeter.*[1] Manetho is believed to have derived his information from the hieroglyphic inscriptions in the temples and other priestly records. Of the fragments of his original writings that have come through to us, Mead considers the most important to be that preserved by the Byzantine historian Georgius Syncellus (c. AD 800), from a work by Manetho entitled *Sothis* that has otherwise disappeared. The passage with the introductory sentence of the monk Syncellus runs as follows:

> It is proposed then to make a few extracts concerning the Egyptian dynasties from the Books of Manetho. [This Manetho,] being high priest of the Heathen temples of Egypt, based his replies to [King Ptolemy] on the monuments that lay in the Seriadic country. [These monuments,] he tells us, were engraved in the sacred language and in the characters of the sacred writings of Thoth, the first Hermes; after the Flood they were translated from the sacred language into the then common tongue, but [still written] in hieroglyphic characters, and stored away in books by the Good Daimon's son, and the second Hermes, father of Tat – in the inner chambers of the temples of Egypt.[2]

The King, it seems, had been acquainted with Manetho's vast knowledge of the past and asked the priest if he could see some of the records, and whether, in fact, Manetho's powers of perception could equally be applied to probing the future? Mead continues the story:

> In the *Book of Sothis* Manetho addressed King Philadelphus, the second Ptolemy, personally, writing as follows, word for word:
> 'The letter of Manetho, the Sebennyte, to Ptolemy Philadelphus.
> 'To the great King Ptolemy Philadelphus, the venerable: I, Manetho, high priest and scribe of the holy fanes of Egypt, citizen of Heliopolis but by birth a Sebennyte, to my master Ptolemy send greeting.
> 'We must make calculations concerning all the points which you may wish to examine into, to answer your questions concerning what will happen to the world. According to your commands, the sacred books, written by our forefather Thrice Greatest Hermes, which I study, shall be shown to you. My Lord and king, farewell.'[3]

From the aforegoing we may deduce the name 'Thoth' or 'Hermes' to be purely titular, and relating to an order in the priestly castes that dealt with history and records. We may also be permitted to conclude that the first Hermes, or earliest order of priesthood, used a sacred language – possibly archaic Egyptian, but more likely the old Atlantean tongue. Two successions of priests and prophets were separated by a Flood which was, no doubt, one and the same inundation that the priests of Sais mentioned to Solon years earlier. All in all, Manetho's text would appear to be inferring that the archaic civilisation of Egypt, that was apparently badly hit when Atlantis went down, was regarded as one of great excellence – the time of the gods, divine kings or demi-gods. There were, as is to be expected, the usual flock of scholars who loudly proclaimed the *Book of Sothis* as a Neoplatonic forgery, but the apology subsequently rendered by Mead and other later authorities more than satisfies all but the deliberately biased.

For those unfamiliar with the story of Atlantis, the 'Old Country', it was believed in ancient times that an island continent once existed in the region of the north Atlantic ocean, the exact location of which is debated by scholars to this day; alternative theories have also been proffered by researchers to account for the many myths and legends concerning this fabled land. However, the best-known treatise on Atlantis is contained in Plato's *Timaeus* and *Critias* in which the philosopher describes its advanced technology, the grandeur of its architecture, its unusual social structure, and the factors that contributed to its final downfall, which coincided with the biblical Flood and similar legends world-wide. The original teller of the tale was Solon (639–559 BC), one of the Seven Sages of Greece and generally considered the wisest. From Solon the story was passed to the family of Critias the Elder and thence to his grandson, Critias, who related it to Plato (427–347 BC). However, this is by no means the only account of Atlantis to be found in ancient writing, and for those interested there is a fount of supporting evidence from other sources both ancient and modern. So popular, in fact, has the subject of Atlantis proved over the years that when Ignatius Donnelly's (1831–1901) book *Atlantis: The Antediluvian World* was published in the last century, a poll undertaken by the British press at the time accorded the news value of Atlantis as second only to the coming of Christ! There are many theories as to what caused Atlantis to sink, most of which have received detailed analysis in my book *Atlantis: Myth or Reality?*

Manetho arranged the reigns of the various kings into thirty-one dynasties, which Egyptologists have grouped into the Old, Middle and New Kingdoms and the Late Period, (See *Appendix*), each characterised by a homogeneous civilisation and divided from each other by interludes of political confusion. Exact lengths of the various reigns are not given in all cases, however, which tends to give rise to perplexities as far as the change-overs are concerned. Scholars have tended to tackle the chronology of Egypt by working backwards and forwards from certain fixed points determined from chance records of astronomical phenomena. For example, the heliacal rising of the star Sirius, recorded in the seventh year of the reign of Sesostris III, can be calculated to have occurred in 1872 BC. Prehistoric ages have been identified purely from archaeological investigations at various sites in Upper and Lower Egypt, the recent advent of radio-carbon dating helping to render a more accurate picture of these early times.

Following the generally accepted archaeological beliefs concerning pre-dynastic times, Cyril Aldred informs us in his book *The Egyptians* that in late Palaeolithic times the retreating ice cap affected the climate of North Africa, causing it to become progressively drier. The Nile, formerly a vast inland lake, had shrunk to assume its present contours, which necessitated the scattered inhabitants of the region to congregate on the verges of the great river in their search for water. The early pre-dynastic period, calculated from around 5000 BC and verified from archaeological finds in the Faiyum depression, and Mosta Gedda in the north, and Deir Tasa in the south, encompassed the Neolithic and Chalcolithic periods. These early predynastic times are allocated to the period from 4000 BC to 3600 BC, the main sites being those at el-Badari, Merimba, el-Amra, Nagada, el-Ballas, Hu, Abydos and Mahasna. The Middle and Late predynastic period is reckoned to be from 3600 BC to 3200 BC, after which we enter the realms of recorded history. What we do know, however, is that during the Amration Period between 4000 and 3600 BC, named after the archeological site at el-Amra, near Abydos in southern Egypt, there was an influx of a race of broad-headed (brachycephalic) people, while the indigenous population of

Hamites belonged to the long-headed (dolichocephalic) type. In fact, all the evidence points to the fact that this spread of foreign influence in the fourth millennium BC, like that of the second, came from the north.

Now, let us compare the aforegoing with the information available from other sources. According to Herodotus, who received his material from the Egyptian priests, their written history dated back 11,340 years before his era, or nearly 14,000 years prior to the present. A degree of support for this can be found in Ignatius Donnelly's quote of the following extract from Professor Winchell's *Preadamites:*

> 'At the epoch of Menes,' says Winchell, 'the Egyptians were already a civilized and numerous people. Manetho tells us that Athotis, the son of the first king, Menes, built the palace at Memphis; that he was a physician, and left anatomical books. All these statements simply imply that even at this early period the Egyptians were in a high state of civilization. In the time of Menes the Egyptians had long been architects, sculptors, painters, mythologists, and theologians.' Professor Richard Owen says: 'Egypt is recorded to have been a civilized and governed community *before* the time of Menes. The pastoral community of a group of nomad families, as portrayed in the Pentateuch, may be admitted as an early step in civilization. But how far in advance of this stage is a nation administered by a kingly government, consisting of grades of society, with divisions of labor, of which one kind, assigned to the priesthood, was to record or chronicle the names and dynasties of the kings, the duration and chief events of their reigns!' Ernest Renan points out that, 'Egypt at the beginning appears mature, old, and entirely without mythical and heroic ages, as if the country had never known youth. Its civilization has no infancy, and its art no archaic period. The civilization of the Old Monarchy did not appear with infancy. It was already mature.'[4]

Diodorus Siculus, writing in the first century, tells us:

> The Egyptians were strangers who, in remote times, settled on the banks of the Nile, bringing with them the civilisation of their mother country, the art of writing, and a polished language. They had come from the direction of the setting sun and were the most ancient of men.[5]

These comments were to receive confirmation in much more recent times by Professor W. B. Emery in his book *Archaic Egypt,* who states:

... towards the end of the fourth millennium BC we find the people known traditionally as 'The Followers of Horus' apparently forming a civilized aristocracy or master race ruling over the whole of Egypt. The theory of the existence of this master race is supported by the discovery that graves of the late predynastic period in the northern part of Upper Egypt were found to contain the anatomical remains of a people whose skulls were of greater size and whose bodies were larger than those of the natives, the difference being so marked that any suggestion that these people derived from the earlier stock is impossible. The fusion of the two races must have been considerable, but it was not so rapid that by the time of the Unification it could be considered in any way accomplished, for throughout the whole of the Archaic period the distinction between the civilized aristocracy and the mass of the natives is very marked, particularly in regard to their burial customs. Only with the close of the Second Dynasty do we find evidence of the lower orders adopting the funerary architecture and mode of burial of their masters. The racial origin of these invaders is not known and the route they took in their penetration of Egypt is equally obscure.[6]

There would appear to be no suggestion here that the remains Professor Emery refers to were anything but hominid and belonged to a species indigenous to Earth.

Aside from the family of Horus, other deities were obviously involved in the prehistory of Egypt. The legends of the Phoenicians, preserved by the ancient Phoenician writer Sanchoniathon (fourteenth/thirteenth century BC), speak of Taut or Thoth as being the inventor of the alphabet or art of writing. A passage in Manetho confirms this, telling of how, prior to the Deluge, Thoth (or Hermes Trismegistus), inscribed on stelae, or tablets, in hieroglyphics, or sacred characters, the principles of all the old knowledge. After the inundation his successor translated the contents of these stelae into the language of the common people. Likewise, Josephus reports:

> The patriarch Seth, in order that wisdom and astronomical knowledge should not perish, erected, in prevision of the double destruction by fire and water predicted by Adam, two columns one of brick, the other of stone, on which this knowledge was engraved, and which existed in the Siriadic country [Egypt][7]

L. Filipoff, astronomer of the Algiers University, claims to have discovered new facts in old fifth- to sixth-dynasty pyramid texts, which connect the god Thoth or Tehuti with the zodiacal sign of Cancer. Filipoff assumes Thoth to have been a culture bearer from a land in the west, who made his appearance when the vernal equinox was in Cancer on or around 7256 BC. When Thoth (referred to in later texts as Hermes) arrived on Egyptian soil he was greatly moved by the people's lack of education and law, so he and his companions set about teaching them science, religion, art and music. This suggests that the world was into the 1256th year (or thereabouts) of the Age of Cancer at or around the time of Thoth's visit, the intimation being that Thoth and, no doubt, those people who came from 'a land in the west' who were later deified, were missionaries and colonists from Atlantis rather than extraterrestrials.

The Denderah zodiac, one of the features of the Temple of Hathor at Denderah, may also be seen to have some relevance to the Thoth story.

This is a circular map of the heavens showing the signs of the zodiac as they were seen and understood by the Egyptians in ancient times, with particular emphasis on the signs of Cancer and Leo. The Egyptians also added their own secret meanings to the picture (note the figure of Thoth beside the sign of Virgo), the original meaning of which is still being debated by researchers and Egyptologists. *(See Fig 1.1 opposite).*

Not all authorities are in agreement when it comes to its interpretation, and it has been suggested that the real meaning of certain hieroglyphics might well have eluded Egyptologists. John Anthony West, for example, commenting on the observations of Schwaller de Lubicz, apropos of certain anomalies in the Denderah zodiac, writes:

> The Zodiacal constellations are arranged in an irregular circle around the center. Note the curious placing of Cancer, well within the circle described by others, or perhaps intended as the inner point of a spiral ... Schwaller de Lubicz thought the signs of the zodiac disposed about an eccentric circle with one center at the pole of the ecliptic (nipple of the female hippopotamus) and the other at the pole star (jackal or dog). This does not seem to me entirely convincing. Note the placement of Libra, for example. But whatever the scheme directing the arrangement, it is certain that the sign of Cancer has been singled out for special treatment.[8]

The Temple of Denderah was erected by the Ptolemies in the first century BC upon the site of an earlier temple. Its hieroglyphics declare it to have been constructed 'according to the plan laid down in the time of the Companions of Horus', that is to say well before the beginnings of dynastic Egypt. The learned Thoth, so often equated with Hermes or Mercury, and the watery sign of Cancer seem unlikely bedfellows, however, although the second line of Gaius Manilius' (48 BC–AD 20) well-known poem, which allocates the Greek/Roman gods to the zodiacal signs, runs: 'Apollo has the handsome Twins and *Mercury the Crab*', hinting at a tradition known to both cultures. Before supposedly leaving Earth and returning to the stars from whence he came, the winged Hermes (Thoth/Mercury?) is believed to have bequeathed to mankind the so-called 'Emerald Tablets' of

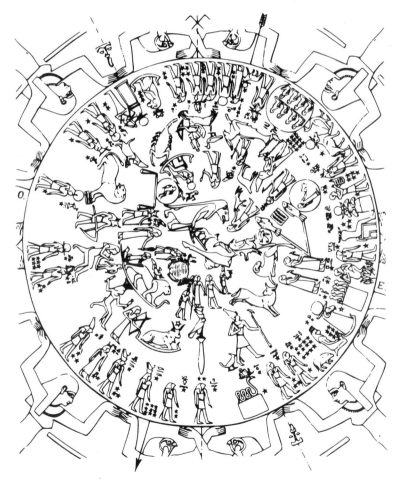

Fig. 1.1 The Denderah zodiac from the Temple of Hathor.

Hermes Trismegistus. Although often viewed as purely a product of the Middle Ages, these tablets have, on the basis of research by the eighteenth-century scholar Dr Sigismund Bacstrom, been traced to c. 2500 BC.

The philosopher Proclus (AD 412–485) mentions the travels of a Greek named Crantor, who visited Sais and was shown a certain column in the temple of Neith, complete with hieroglyphics, which recorded not only the history of predynastic Egypt, but also that of the country from which those people hailed who brought their culture to the shores of Egypt in those distant times – Atlantis! The Egyptian priests effected a translation for Crantor, and their account was in full agreement with that quoted by Plato in the *Timaeus*, with which they were familiar. Although Egyptologists claim that they know of no such pillar, or of the existence of any texts relating to the Atlantis episode, this is hardly a conclusive argument; Atlantis could have been mentioned many times in the innumerable documents that were lost when the vast libraries were burned and pillaged by the fanatical zealots of the new faiths that were ultimately to take hold in Europe and the Middle East. Dare we hope that some priceless scroll, which will supply us with the necessary details, may yet be found in the archaic ruins of some ancient mud or sand-covered temple or tomb? If there is any truth in the time-capsule theory so beloved of modern metaphysicists and fringe scientists, the answer must be, 'Yes'!

Regarding this theory the Roman historian Ammianus Marcellinus (AD 330–400) wrote:

> There are also subterranean passages and winding retreats, which, it is said, men skillful in the ancient mysteries, by means of which they divined the coming of the Flood, constructed in different places lest the memory of all their sacred ceremonies should be lost.[9]

In more recent times, the Alsatian philosopher, R. A. Schwaller de Lubicz, assembled a great deal of material over a period of ten years, following a sojourn of fifteen years at Luxor (1936–51). His step-daughter, Lucie Lamy, effected detailed measurements and drawings of the stones and statuary of the great temple at Luxor which served to show that the ancient Egyptians possessed a hitherto unsuspected knowledge of mathematics and cosmic form; these she later incorporated in her book *Egyptian Mysteries*. Schwaller de Lubicz himself was the author of several published works, notably, *Le Temple de l'Homme*, which also deals with the more esoteric aspects of early Egyptian culture.

Schwaller de Lubicz disagrees with orthodox historians in their classification of the Badarian, Amration and Gerzean sites as 'predynastic' merely on the grounds of their burial procedures, since, as Emery suggests, it seems obvious that they existed side by side with a more advanced race for several centuries before such customs were standardised. Schwaller de Lubicz also states that ethnological studies have revealed four racial types as composing the predynastic population: the Cro-Magnon type, a Negroid type (such as the famous specimens at Menton), a Mediterranean type corresponding to the contemporary white races and a mixed type. With rare exceptions, he tells us, 'there are no *blacks* properly so called'.[10] With regard to the Shemsu-Hor, Schwaller de Lubicz has this to say:

> The term *Shemsu-Hor*, incorrectly translated as 'Companions of Horus', literally means *Followers of Horus* in the precise sense of 'those who follow the path of Horus', that is, the 'Horian way', also called the solar way or *paths of Ra*. This epithet applies to superior beings who produced the race of pharaohs, as opposed to the majority of people who follow the common way, the way of Osiris. These *Followers of Horus* bear with them a knowledge of 'divine origin', and unify the country with it.[11]

Note how Schwaller de Lubicz refers to the indigenous population as worshipping Osiris, whereas Emery is of the opinion that the worship of Set was the religion in current vogue at the time of the arrival of the Shemsu-Hor, the Horus-Set confrontation presenting nothing more esoteric than the takeover of Egypt by the newcomers. This and similar ideas are to be expected since the events that take place on Earth are simply reruns of cosmic dramas, which is why it behoves us, as Jung advises, to examine the myths at more than one level. In like manner, we could also view Isis, Osiris and Horus as Atlantean colonists, but more of these aspects later.

The ancient Egyptians possessed solar, lunar and Sothic calendars. In fact, the binary star we know as Sirius (Sothis to the Egyptians) features strongly in their earliest history, suggesting that its significance must also have been known to those people who originally brought civilisation to their shores – the Atlanteans. Schwaller de Lubicz tells us:

The Sothic cycle is established on the coincidence every 1,460 years of the *vague year* of 365 days with the *Sothic (or Sirian) year* of 365¼ days. All civil acts were dated according to the vague year, composed of exactly 360 days plus the five epagomenal days consecrated to the *Neters:* Osiris, Isis, Seth, Nephthys and Horus.

The Sirian, or *fixed year,* was established according to the heliacal rising of Sirius, yet the interval between two heliacal risings of Sirius corresponds neither to the tropical year, which is shorter, nor to the sidereal year, which is longer. For it is remarkable that *owing to the precession of the equinoxes, on the one hand, and the movement of Sirius on the other, the position of the sun with respect to Sirius is displaced in the same direction, almost exactly to the same extent.*

Calculations established by astronomers have demonstrated that between 4231 and 2231 BC, the approximate duration of the reign of the Bull, *Hap,* the Sirian year was almost identical to our Julian year of 365¼ days. This period would cover the entire Ancient Empire, and we cannot but admire the greatness of a science capable of discovering such a coincidence because *Sirius is the only star among the 'fixed stars' which allows this cycle. It can therefore be supposed that Sirius plays the role of a center for the circuit of our entire solar system*[12]

Sirius was known to the ancient Egyptians as *The Great Provider* and, as such, was constantly invoked in pyramid texts:

Isis comes to thee [Osiris] joyous in thy love;
Your seed rises in her, penetrating [*spd.t*] like Sirius [*spd.t*, Sirius].
The penetrating [*spd.t*] Horus comes forth from thee in his name of Horus-who-is-in-Sirius.[13]

The Pharaonic calendar is established as being introduced in 4240 BC. The five epagomenal days are related to the birth of the five Neters, and since the whole arrangement revolves around Sirius, the only star to return periodically every 365¼ days, does this infer that whatever energies were responsible for the tilt of the Earth's axis which precipitated the Flood, the loss of Atlantis, and the acquisition of the five epagomenal or intercalary days – was orchestrated from Sirius? Should this prove to be the case, it would be reasonable to enquire as to whether the five Neters were, as Donnelly and others suggest, Atlantean leaders, priests/priestesses, or leading personalities on the Atlantean political scene. Or were they from *somewhere else?*

When I wrote my epic poem, *The Story of Isis and Osiris* (Cesara Publications, Eire, 1974), I referred to the Egyptian Ra as relating to the Siriun system rather than our own sun, the latter being represented by Ra's legendary Eye. (Note that it was the goddess Sekhmet who carried the Eye to Earth. Are we perhaps being told that our own sun is, in fact, feminine or yin and therefore not the masculine or yang entity that some would have us believe?) It was not until I encountered the following statement and other aspects of Schwaller de Lubicz's work that many of my own 'memories' began to fall into place:

> It took our own discoveries in atomism and astronomy to suggest yet another characteristic of Sirius which coincides with what we are beginning to know about the atomic nucleus, made up of a positron (a giant star of very weak density) accompanying a neutron whose volume is exceedingly small in relation to the atom, but where all its weight is concentrated (a dwarf star of incredible density) ...
> The double star of Sirius – which for Pharaonic Egypt played the role of a central sun to our entire solar system – today suggests the existence of a cosmic system of atomic structure whose *nucleus* is this 'Great Provider', the Sothis [*spd.t*] of the ancients. There might well be a need to revise our cosmology in the not-so-distant future[14]

Details of my own studies of Sirius are to be found in my books *The Lion People* and *The Paschats and the Crystal People*, while my latest book, *Cosmic Connections*, covers the relationship between Sirius, our Sun and her planetary family.

The fact that during the whole historical period of Pharaonic Egypt – the heliacal rising of Sirius, which always took place when the sun was in the constellation of Leo – serves to confirm my suspicion that there is some connection between those enigmatic colonists, probably Atlanteans, the lion motif, and the fixed star Sirius, the longitude of which is 13 degrees 24 minutes of Cancer. Is there not a hint of the Thoth-Cancer connection to be gleaned from this? It is my belief that the Egyptians derived this information from the Atlantean priests, which hints at the standard of technical knowledge which the scientific community of the Old Country had attained. Of the Sphinx and pyramids I shall have much to tell later, but suffice it to say that it is no coincidence that the former is portrayed partly in leonine form.

Schwaller de Lubicz also sees Sirius as having some bearing on the climate of our planet and comments on the fact that climatological variation, if only a few degrees, can affect all life on Earth. A drop in temperature drives people towards other less hostile zones, while warmer temperatures witness the birth of new plant and animal life. Some of the principal movements within our solar system are well known, others not so, and since climatological modifications appear to obey sidereal variations, he sees Sirius as being responsible for both our climates and those of the entire solar system. *These points should be borne in mind in view of the changes in weather conditions that have been experienced globally over the past few years.*

It may be deduced from a study of the Siriun (Sothian) calendar that the precession of equinoxes, the discovery of which was hitherto attributed to Hipparchus, was known to the ancient Egyptians (and Atlanteans), the heliacal rising of Sirius being associated with the beginning of the Nile's flooding and the birth of Ra in the zodiacal sign of Leo. Schwaller de Lubicz tells us:

Yet it was always *Nun,* the primordial, indeterminate state (or ocean) which receives the characteristic impulse of the celestial influence, and this influence varies according to the precessional month.

Thus it is that Pharaonic prehistory was dominated by The Twins *Shu* and *Tefnut,* whose nature consists in separating Heaven from Earth. This has been interpreted as representing the two crowns of the Empire, as yet dualized. At that time there existed the kingdom of the South with its double capital, *Nekhen* and *Nekheb,* and the kingdom of the North with its dual capital, *Dep* and *Pe.* The vestiges of this period show a pronounced double character and it is certainly at this time that the Heliopolitan mystery of primordial dualization was revealed.

At Memphis, under the Ancient Empire, there was the domination of Hap, the Bull, who precipitated celestial fire into terrestrial form. The Bull, the great *Neter* of the historical period extending from 4380 to 2200 BC commands the Cretan civilization as well.

From the Middle Empire to the beginning of the Christian era, we see the domination of Amon, the Ram. It is in Thebes, under the predominance of Amon, that the generating fire is 'extracted', so to speak from its terrestrial gangue-matrix, Khonsu, by the grace of Djehuti (Thoth), master of Heliopolis.

Nun is invariable, while the receptive milieux, or environments, are generative, and hence feminine. They are successively: *Nut* in Heliopolis, *Sekhmet-Hathor* in Memphis, and then *Mut* in Thebes.

What was elaborated at Heliopolis was Shu and Tefnut as creation; in Memphis it becomes Nefertum, issue of the couple Ptah-Sekhmet, while at Thebes, the product of Amon and Mut is Khonsu.

But succession means generation and not juxtaposition, although the philosophical legend must situate the principles as if coexisting personages were involved.

Finally, toward the year 60 BC, with the end of the political empire of Egypt under Cleopatra, our Christian era of Pisces begins.[15]

As I have proposed in my other works, the prevailing ethos colours the overshadowing influences, each respective culture responding differently and interpreting the *Neters*, or gods and goddesses, in their own image and likeness or according to their particular needs.

From the Schwaller de Lubicz list, it becomes possible to place the famous Emerald Tablets of Hermes Trismegistus in their appropriate historical position, which would be somewhere between the Memphian and Middle Empires. Plato's bull cults, as described in the *Timaeus* and *Critias*, also assume a new reality in the light of later datings, showing how either Plato himself, Solon, who supplied the information, or the Egyptian priests mixed up their historical facts somewhere along the line. I tend to suspect Solon, as the works of Schwaller de Lubicz and Lucie Lamy seem to confirm that the Egyptians had retained their earlier knowledge with some degree of accuracy.

Regarding changes which took place in past astrological ages which affected our planet on a large scale, my own researches have indicated that a major catastrophe – possibly a pole shift occurred towards the end of the zodiacal Age of Scorpio and resulted in the sinking of Mu, later referred to as Lemuria by the British scientist P. Sclater, after the Lemurs, and was also responsible for the vast alterations in the terrain of South America (ref. Codex Troanus). This caused large portions of land to break away from the original continental matrix and was possibly responsible for the formation of the island continent of Atlantis. The ensuing age, that of Libra, would have involved a rebalancing of evolutionary factors, both in relation to Gaia herself and those life-forms which dwelt thereon. By the time the Age of Virgo arrived all would have settled down, and an advanced civilisation such as that of Atlantis would have been afforded ample external energies for the discovery and development of medicine and the sciences. Worship of the feminine principle would probably have dominated during this period.

Since evolution seldom, if ever, stands still, the Age of Leo might well have precipitated a swing towards patrism, or at least equality between the god-forms and between the human sexes. Leo is well acknowledged as being the sign of kings, so it is little wonder that Plato was able to render such a vivid description of the Kingly Period of Atlantis, which obviously carried right through into the Cancerian Age, in much the same way that many people today still cling tenaciously to the slowly disintegrating remnants of the Piscean influence.

An opinion shared by many researchers is that major catastrophes inevitably occur *at the end* of zodiacal ages; the last one to effect a major change in the axial rotation of our planet occurring during the latter days of the Cancerian Age and being responsible for the Flood. As the sign of Cancer is ruled by the moon, the involvement of that orb is obvious, as is its connection with Homer's fabled Silver or Matriarchal Age, which persisted in parts of Europe and the Middle East until the arrival of the patrist onslaughts from the 'north'. The beginning of these invasions has been placed, according to many authorities, somewhere between 3000 BC and 1200 BC, the latter date seeing its end.

In the light of the aforegoing, we can safely place the long and varied history of Egypt into its appropriate astrological pigeon-holes, and the conclusions reached by Schwaller de Lubicz become perfectly clear. Early chronological tables have been found in the course of excavation which take the records of early Egypt back many thousands of years. Unfortunately, they contain too many inconsistencies to merit scientific credence, although there is obviously a grain of truth amongst them. For example, we are told that there was a very long period during which Egypt was ruled by the Neters, or gods, followed by an equally long timespan when it came under the rulership of the Shemsu-Hor, or 'Companions of Horus'.

Schwaller de Lubicz asserts the most valuable document concerning the prehistory of Egypt to be the *Royal Papyrus of Turin*, which gives a complete list of the kings who reigned over Upper and Lower Egypt from Menes to the New Empire, including mention of the duration of each reign. The first columns of the papyrus, however, were consecrated to the prehistoric period which preceded Menes and consisted of a list of ten Neters, each with name inscribed in a cartouche prefaced by the bulrush and bee – the royal symbols of Upper and Lower Egypt – and followed by the number of years in each reign.

Unfortunately, most of these numbers are missing. These were followed by a list of kings having reigned before Menes, and the duration of each reign, while the remaining fragments establish that nine dynasties were mentioned which, Schwaller de Lubicz tells us were:

> ... the (venerables) of Memphis, the venerables of the North, and finally the *Shemsu-Hor*, usually translated as the 'Companions of Horus'. Fortunately, the last two lines have survived almost intact, as have indications regarding the number of years:
> '... venerables Shemsu-Hor, 13,429 years
> 'Reigns up to Shemsu-Hor, 23,200 years (total 36,620) King Menes.'[16]

It has been speculated by Donnelly and others that the 'Neters' were the original Atlantean colonists, those enigmatic 'sons of God' who mated with the 'daughters of men' (that is, the indigenous population) producing the 'Nephilim' or the Shemsu-Hor, those giant demi-gods borne by daughters of men to the 'sons of God' mentioned in Genesis 6:4, unaltered by later editors, and probably preserved from a longer, very ancient fragment. One cannot help but feel that there are still a few pieces missing from the jigsaw, and evidence of a more tangible nature is needed to set the Egyptian predynastic books in order.

As regards the chronology, with so little to go on the tendency has been for researchers to adjust the figures that are available from various sources (some of which are highly suspect) to accommodate their own pet theories; this has resulted in a series of suggested dates for the commencement of the civilisation in Egypt and the arrival of those enigmatic 'colonists' on the soil of Khemu. These range from 30,000 BC to 15,000 BC. According to Herodotus, who was thus informed by one of his Egyptian guides, 'the sun had risen twice where it now set, and twice set where it now rises', a passage which is seen by subsequent scholars as relating to the precessional cycles. This would place the foundation circa 36,000 BC which is, no doubt, guaranteed to strain the credulity of many an establishment of orthodox learning. However, the carved body of a man – believed to be the world's earliest-known anthropomorphic figure, which pushes back in time evidence of the human ability to create symbols – has been excavated at a 32,000-year-old level in a cave at Hohlenstein, West Germany. Several years later, museum officials were presented with a beautifully carved ivory lion muzzle that had been found in the same cave, and it fitted the statuette perfectly![17] The excavation was executed under the direction of Elisabeth Schmid and the findings later confirmed by Joachim Hahn, H. Muller-Beck, W. Taute and R. Wetzel. For those interested in further details, a full write-up on the find is given in my book *The Paschats and the Crystal People*.

Until recently, the images of beings with the upright stance of a hominid, but with the head and figure of a leonid, were confined to various early mythological iconographies. Notably the early Egyptians, wherein goddesses such as Sekhmet and Tefnut made their appearances along with other animal-headed deities, while in the ancient Hindu texts the 'tawny one' or lion-man, was believed to be the fourth incarnation of Vishnu.

Whether the significance behind this find is purely shamanic, in that it was the custom for ancient shamans to wear a mask depicting their totem beast whenever they officiated at public or private rites, or whether more Siriun connotations could be read into it (there is a belief shared by many psychics, and supported by myth and legend, that two races of intelligent beings inhabited the Siriun system in those ancient times, one being hominid and the other of leonine appearance, as portrayed in the ancient Egyptian statues of Sekhmet, Bast, Tefnut, and other leonid-type deities) is open to conjecture!

However one particular comment within this which caught my eye was the reference to the body being too long in proportion to the head. If any of my readers keep cats I would suggest they take note of the ratio of the head to the body when their pets stand on their hind legs. Look, also, for the formation of the leg structure when the feline is in the erect position and I think you will find that the statuette figured in the photograph on page 53 does not relate to a hominid woman shaman as would be popularly supposed, but to an all-feline being *who has learned to stand and function in the upright position, just as we do!*

It should be borne in mind, however, that prior to the arrival of the Atlantean colonists and missionaries, Europe, Egypt (and indeed the whole of Africa) could have come under Muan (or Siriun?) influence.

With reference to the sun's different rising and setting points, this can now be substantiated in the works of such experts as Professor Charles Hapgood, John Ivimy, Jeffrey Goodman, Richard Mooney, and other scholars of repute. The fact that the poles and equator have changed position in epochs past is common knowledge among those specialising in the disciplines concerned. There is also evidence to suggest that at some point during the Age of Cancer we acquired the extra five days known as epagomenal, the Earth having previously taken only 360 days to complete its annual cycle. Mooney offers the following information:

> The Reverend Bowles, a nineteenth-century archaeologist and authority on megalithic monuments in Britain, says that the circles of Avebury represent a calendar of 360 days, and that an extra five days were added later.
>
> In all the ancient classical writings of the Hindu Aryans, there is a year of 360 days. The *Aryabhatiya*, the ancient Indian mathematical and astronomical work, says: 'A year consists of 12 months. A month consists of 30 days. A day consists of 60 nadis. A nadi consists of 60 vinadikas.'
>
> The ancient Babylonian year was of 12 months of 30 days each. The Babylonian zodiac was divided into 36 decans, this being the space the sun covered in relation to the fixed stars during a 10-day period. Thus the 36 decans require a year of only 360 days. Ctesias wrote that the walls of Babylon were 360 furlongs in circumference, 'as many as there are days in the year.'
>
> The Egyptian year was originally 12 months of 30 days each, according to the Ebers papyrus. A tablet discovered at Tanis in the Nile Delta in 1866 reveals that in the ninth year of Ptolemy Euergetes (237 BC), the priests of Canopus decreed that as it was 'necessary to harmonise the calendar according to the present arrangement of the world.' One day was ordered to be added every four years to the 360 days, and to the five days which were afterwards ordered to be added.
>
> The ancient Romans also had a year of 360 days. Plutarch, in his life of Numa, wrote that in the time of Romulus the year was made up of twelve 30-day months.
>
> The Mayan year was of 360 days, called a tun. Five days were later added, and an extra day every fourth year. The Mayans computed the synodal period of the moon as 29.5209 days, as accurately as we can calculate today with our sophisticated equipment. Their degree of accuracy would surely not have been less when they computed the 360-day year. 'They did reckon them apart, and called them the days of nothing; during which the people did not anything,' wrote J. de Acosta, an early writer on America.
>
> The Mexicans at the time of the Spanish conquest called each 30-day period a moon.

The Incan year was divided into 12 quilla, or moons of 30 days. Five days were added at the end, and an extra day for every four years. The extra days were regarded as unlucky, or fateful.

The ancient Chinese calendar was a 12-month year of 30 days each. They added $5^1/_4$ days to the year, and also divided the sphere into $365^1/_4$ days, adopting the new length of the year into geometry as well. [18]

The aforegoing has usually been explained away by scholars as representing errors that were latterly refined as mathematical knowledge increased. One is tempted to ask, however, why so many different cultures, from different parts of the world, would have simultaneously committed the same error. We have heard of the Law of Synchronicity, but surely this tends to stretch coincidence a little too far! An alteration in the Earth's orbit changing its proximity to the sun would, however, account for the difference in the length of the year. And if the Earth had been jolted out of its former position, the moon would also have been affected. As Mooney puts it:

Since the moon is a smaller body than Earth, and the distances between them much smaller than between the Earth and the sun, the differences would have been even more noticeable in the case of the Earth/moon system than in the case of the Earth/sun system.

This would appear to have been the case. In several ancient sources it has been found that there were four 9-day weeks to each lunar month, making a month of 36 days. This 9-day phase has been found in ancient Greek, Babylonian, Chinese and Roman sources, among others. As these lunar computations did not fit with a year of 360 days, the calendars were altered to a 10-month year. This was an attempt to regulate the 'new' year to fit the 'old' 360-day year. [19]

The ancient Celts, who were decidedly lunar orientated, ascribed magical powers to the number 9, associating it with the three aspects of the Triple Goddess – Maiden, Mother and Crone.

Presuming legend to be the embodiment of past deeds, no-where is the advent of the epagomenal days better described, albeit allegorically, that in the Egyptian myth of the birth of the five great gods, or Neters, of ancient Egypt. Shu and Tefnut, the Twin Lion gods of Time, were the children of the Solar Lord Ra (seen in this context, I feel, as the binary star Sirius rather than our own sun). They, in turn, gave birth to Geb and Nut (the Earth and the sky). But Nut, who was also believed to have been the spouse of Ra, offended her husband by cohabiting with her brother. Enraged by his wife's infidelity, Ra swore that she should not be delivered of a child on any of the 360 days of his year, which might have caused her considerable difficulty had not Thoth, god of science and mathematics, Keeper of the Akashic Records, divine Advocate and Lord of Time, played his famous game of draughts with the moon, from which he won one seventy-second part of her light (1/72 of 360 is exactly 5!) which he made into five new days called 'epagomenal'. Nut was then able to give birth to the five children she had been carrying – Osiris, Horus the Elder, Set, Isis and Nephthys, in that order. The legend is also reiterated in the Greek myth of Cronus (Time) swallowing five of his own children and disgorging them after taking a potion administered to him by Metis (Justice!).

Although various magical and mystical interpretations have been placed upon these stories by scholars, metaphysicists and romantics, what the myths are basically telling us is that as a result of some drama played out between the Earth, the moon and some solar energy external to our star system, the calendar had to be changed, and that it was Thoth, a *lunar* deity, who effected the alteration. In other words, a change in the Earth's orbit involving the moon, which precipitated a change in the Earth's axis, was responsible for the five extra days we now have in our calendars, and since, as the ancient Egyptians have been most careful to tell us, the five epagomenal Neters have strong connections with Sirius, we may presume that a bright blue-white star in the constellation of Canis Major was the third, and probably most influential, player in this celestial drama.

Endnotes:
1 P. Lemesurier, *The Great Pyramid Decoded*, page 15.

2 G. R. S. Mead, *Thrice Greatest Hermes*, Vol. 1, page 104.

3 Ibid., pages 104–5.

4 I. Donnelly, *Atlantis*, pages 131–2.

5 C. Berlitz, *Atlantis*, page 135.

6 W.B. Emery, *Archaic Egypt*, page 40.

7 I. Donnelly, *Atlantis*, page 125.

8 J. E. West, *Serpent in the Sky*, pages 113–14.

9 A. Tomas, *From Atlantis to Discovery*, page 109.

10 R. A. Schwaller de Lubicz, *Sacred Science,* page 110.

11 Ibid., page 111.

12 Ibid., pages 26–7.

13 Ibid., page 27.

14 Ibid., page 28.

15 Ibid., pages 177–9.

16 Ibid., page 86.

17 *National Geographic,* Vol. 174 No. 4, Oct. 1988. 'The Search for Modern Humans' by John J. Putnam, page 467.

18 R. Mooney, *Colony: Earth,* pages 95–6.

19 Ibid., page 97.

CHAPTER 2

Prehistoric Legacies

A picture of the early pre-dynastic days of ancient Egypt is slowly emerging from the information through which we have already sifted. What we appear to be dealing with are three separate issues:

1. The life and religion of the indigenous peoples of those parts;
2. The culture which appeared to have arrived via the agency of newcomers to those shores; and
3. The likelihood of an overseeing, extraterrestrial influence from the Sirius system which could manifest in any of several ways.

Let us start with number one. According to orthodox sources, the first settlers in the region of the Nile banks would have found the transition from their nomadic ways an easy one since there was game, fish and fowl to be hunted and trapped in the valley, and edible roots, such as the papyrus rhizome, or plants like the wild Abyssinian banana, were there for the taking. Later migrants brought with them the arts of cultivation and husbandry, and the slow process of domestication began.

Reference Chart

PALAEOLITHIC, or Old Stone Age, designating the cultural period beginning with the earliest chipped stone tools, about 2.5 to 3 million years ago, until the beginning of the *Mesolithic* or Middle Stone Age *circa* 12,000 years ago.
NEOLITHIC, or New Stone Age – of or defining the cultural period between 10,000 BC and 7,000 BC in the Middle East and later

elsewhere – characterised by the development of farming and the making of technically advanced, polished stone implements.

CHALCOLITHIC, a period in man's development when both stone and copper were in use.

BRONZE AGE, which brought the Stone Age to an end, is distinguished by the invention of Bronze, which is believed to have been c. 3000 BC.

IRON AGE, which followed the Bronze Age, typified by the spread of iron tools and weapons, beginning in the Middle East around the twelfth century BC, and in Europe around the eighth century BC.

It has been argued that from a survey of material remains it is easy to see how the Egyptians gradually adapted themselves to agrarian ways, so that by the end of 3600 BC their lifestyle probably differed little from what it does today. I do not see this as a valid argument in favour of a slow process of evolutionary development in those parts, however, as it is possible, even in present times, to find peoples living in stages of extreme primitivity only a comparatively short distance from some bustling metropolis. Archaeological finds from the Chalcolithic cultures of el-Badari and el-Emra, near Abydos in the south, evidence the use of animal skins that had been tanned and softened, needles of bone, bracelets of ivory and shell, green malachite eye-paint, cosmetic oils, and combs of bone. Tools and weapons were almost exclusively of stone or flint.

Orthodoxy ventures little more than a guess as to the spiritual inclinations of these people, although their obvious belief in some 'hereafter' may be evidenced by the fact that in burials of the period the body was placed crouched on its side as though awaiting rebirth, complete with its material possessions, such as pots and pans, cosmetic palettes and sometimes rudimentary bone figurines of women. In fact, the whole scenario is suggestive of a people whose beliefs were basically pantheistic and animistic, with strong sympathetic magic undertones. In other words, the culture of the indigenous inhabitants of archaic Egypt was essentially African. No doubt they had their shamans, whose totem animals and fetishes later became the emblems emblazoned on the standards of their nomes.

During the pre-dynastic period every village, town or settlement possessed its own god, whose worship flourished or faded according to the fortunes of the community at large. When the country was eventually sectioned off into *hespu* or 'nomes', one god, in particular, or group of deities, would be chosen to represent one or more nomes. There would seem to be little evidence as to when this division of the country into nomes actually took place, although it must have been at a comparatively early period, since in earliest dynastic times there is evidence that Neith was the principal deity of Sais, Osiris of Busiris, Thoth of Hermopolis, Uatchat of Per-Uatchat, Ptah of Memphis, Sebek of Crocodilopolis, Amen (Ammon) of Thebes, Nekhebet of Nekheb and Khnemu of Elephantine. Egyptian lists give the number of nomes as forty-two or forty-four, although the classical writers Strabo, Diodorus and Pliny are not in agreement with these figures. Strabo tells us that the Labyrinth contained twenty-seven chambers, each representing a nome. Two of these were in Upper Egypt, ten in Lower Egypt and seven in Heptanomis. Herodotus, on the other hand, claims that the Labyrinth contained twelve halls, and Pliny lists forty-five nomes, the names of which were obviously Hellenised (Bk v., chapter 9).[1]

How, then, does all this slow and obvious evolutionary process from comparative barbarism to organised society relate to the highly developed and knowledgeable Egypt about which the classical writers waxed so poetic? Both are correct, in their own way, since each refers to a different group of people. Over the centuries major empires have risen, conquered, ruled for a while, and then gone into decline. During their days of extensive colonisation, diplomats, princes and wealthy prospectors have occupied the same land as the poor and unlettered. Archaeologists excavating these sites in later years may well come across the shards of simple pots used by those who toiled in the fields for little or no reward, and whose reed huts scarcely compared with the grand mansions of the governor, plenipotentiary or whoever. The latter, however, upon being relieved of his post either upon retirement or for some political expediency, would be inclined to take his belongings with him on departure, rich people not being disposed to leave valuable artefacts around for someone to dig up years hence.

Two decades of study at the temple of Luxor convinced Schwaller de Lubicz that the accepted dogma of orthodoxy is either erroneous or hopelessly inadequate. In truth, his work overthrows or undermines virtually every currently cherished belief regarding the history of man and the evolution of what we refer to as 'civilisation'. Along with the classical writers of old, Schwaller de Lubicz saw Egyptian science, medicine, mathematics and astronomy as being considerably more advanced and sophisticated than many modern scholars would be prepared to acknowledge. He also noted that every aspect of Egyptian culture appeared to have been complete *at the beginning!* Scientific, artistic and agricultural techniques, along with the hieroglyphic system, show virtually no signs of a period of development. In fact, the earlier the dynasty the higher the achievement. Although this astonishing fact is readily admitted by Egyptologists, its implications seem to go unmentioned due, no doubt, to their inability to render a satisfactory explanation in accordance with the requirements of their discipline. As John Anthony West puts it, *Egyptian civilisation was not a 'development', it was a legacy.*[2]

In 3200 BC Upper and Lower Egypt were united under one king, the two crowns becoming incorporated into one, (see *Fig. 2.1*). The art of the earlier dynasties alone evidences a highly sophisticated culture. The famous statue of King Chephren of the fourth dynasty, successor to Cheops and alleged builder of the second largest pyramid and originator of the beautifully executed hieroglyphics and likeness of Hesire, Vizier to King Zoser of the third dynasty, shows faces and bearings which are anything but primitive. In commenting on the art technique

Fig. 2.1 The three crowns of Egypt. A: the white crown of Upper Egypt.
B: the red crown of Lower Egypt.
C: the Pschent *or double crown of the united Kingdom.*

used by the ancient Egyptians for producing inlaid eyes on their statuary, West brings to our attention that the very early examples found to date are blue or grey-eyed rather than brown-eyed. Strangely enough, I also noticed that the traditional Eyes of Ra which were later allocated to Horus, Bast and other deities were also depicted with a blue pupil. Considering the fact that the indigenous population of those parts was almost exclusively brown-eyed, the original art work which served as a model for later copies must have obviously represented a people whose eyes were predominantly blue or grey. The same applies to blood groups, of which I have made an extensive study in relation to the subject matter of Atlantis (see *Atlantis: Myth or Reality?*).

The most obvious legacies from the old pre-dynastic period, and therefore from those mysterious strangers who brought instant civilisation to the simple people of the Nile valley, are surely the Sphinx and the pyramids which have provided a source of dialogue and polemic between historians, scientists, mystics and alchemists over the centuries. Were these monolithic structures really erected by thousands of perspiring slaves, dragging the massive stone blocks up a series of pulleys, to be fitted with a convenient exactitude by sheer brute strength alone? Diodorus Siculus, the Greek historian from Sicily who was in Egypt during 60 to 57 BC, seemed to think so; 360,000 men, he tells us, were employed on the project for twenty years. Herodotus, however, claims it was 100,000 men who flexed their muscles in the arduous task over a period of some twenty years, and that the extravagant venture all but bankrupted Cheops (Khufu), who saw fit to expose his daughter to the rigours of a house of ill-repute in order to set his bank account right again! The lady must have been more than proficient at her allotted task, however, for not only did she obtain the sum needed by her father, but also collected a stone for her future memorial from each of her 'visitors', or so the legend goes. (One rather suspects that dear old Herodotus was either spun a tall yarn by the Egyptian priests, who no doubt chuckled to themselves as he left, or that he deliberately embroidered the incident to amuse his readers, which he was apparently given to do upon occasions.)

Several books have been written recently by experts which give the exact measurements of the great pyramid, the mathematical precision of which evidences an advanced knowledge of that discipline. The angle between each of the sides and the plane of the foundations is almost exactly 51 degrees 51 minutes and 14 seconds. The ratio of the base-perimeter to the height equals twice the quantity of 3.14159, or *pi (π)*. The original pinnacle being missing, the height was calculated geometrically – in other words, the pyramid's height is to its base perimeter as a circle's radius is to its circumference. Furthermore, the mean distance of the Earth to the sun is about 149.5 million kilometres. The height of the Cheops pyramid is 147.8 metres, which equals the astronomical distance to the sun reduced by a thousand million, with an error of only one per cent.[3]

The basic unit of measurement employed in the construction of this edifice was the 'pyramid cubit' which is equivalent to 635.66 mm. The radius of the Earth from the centre to the pole is 6357 km – the pyramid cubit multiplied ten million times. The length of the pyramid side at the base is 365.25 (365.242 to be exact) pyramid cubits, a figure identical to the number of days in the solar tropical year – and the same figure is also to be found in other features of the design. Peter Lemesurier, whose definitive work on the subject, *The Great Pyramid Decoded*, is simply packed with amazing facts and figures on the subject, points out another 'coincidence':

> Yet from the slightly indented shape from the base of the core-masonry alternative measurements of 365.256 and 365.259 of these units can be derived – figures which turn out to be the length in days of the sidereal year (the actual time the earth takes to complete a circuit of the sun) and of the anomalistic year (the time taken by the earth to return to the same point in its elliptical orbit, which is itself revolving slowly about the sun). Meanwhile further measurements appear to give exact figures for the eccentricity of that orbit, for the mean distance of the earth from the sun, and for the period of the earth's full precessional cycle (a period of over 25,000 years). If one wished to have an architectural symbol for the planet Earth itself one could scarcely do better than to take the Great Pyramid of Giza.[4]

The Great Pyramid is built on solid bedrock, which renders it virtually invulnerable to the severest earthquake. Furthermore, the shape of the pyramids suggest a function other than a tomb, being ideally suited to withstand almost any kind of natural shock. The presence of shell fossils around its base has been seen by some researchers as evidence that the structure has experienced one or more major inundations, although sceptics will probably counter with the suggestion that the shells were probably there when the pyramid was built. Another suggestion, much favoured by metaphysicists, is that were the base of the pyramid to be completely uncovered, a downward pointing apex would be discovered, which exactly matches the top section. If this were to be the case, the concealed part could well contain all that hidden knowledge we are constantly reading about, although the fact that the internal passages and chambers do not appear to have yielded up any clues in this direction does tend to strain the credulity somewhat. However, since I wrote the original text of this book in 1990, Bauval and Gilbert have published their bestseller *The Orion Mystery*, in which they produce evidence, that the Great pyramid is aligned with Orion and Sirius, as representing Osiris and Isis respectively. News of a hidden chamber at the end of a long shaft also served as titillation and I, for one, eagerly await further developments in that area.

The Great Pyramid is by no means the only evidence of a mathematical knowledge possessed by these ancient people. The Eye of Horus, far from being the pleasing artistic illustration it might appear at first sight, carries precise measurements which must doubtless have been highly significant to the originators and which West emphasises in his accompanying caption. (See *Fig. 2.2.*)

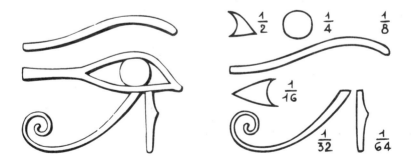

Fig. 2.2 The eye gives access to space, that is to say volume, and therefore to measure. In Egypt, the sections of the eye are the glyphs for the fractions 1/2 to 1/64. The parts total 63/64. (The sum of successive division will always fall short of unity except at infinity, which is perfectly consonant with Egyptian thought: only the Absolute is one)

The Eye of Horus was, of course, the left or lunar Eye; there was also a right Eye, traditionally the property of Ra, which his daughter Sekhmet hurled at those who saw fit to break the old god's covenants (cosmic laws?) (see Chapter 3). This right Eye later became the famous Uraeus, which featured in the head-dresses and ceremonial regalia of pharaohs, priests, and several popular deities. Regarding the dimensions of the Eye, Lucie Lamy has this to say:

> Egyptian arithmetic was based on dimidiation – halving – rather than on addition, and the eye plays a part in the notation. The *hekat*, the unit of volume used in the measurement of grain, is represented graphically by the Oudja Eye, and its fractions by the individual strokes of the glyph.
>
> Thus the lunar Eye is at the basis of the measurement of both time, because of the lunation which defines the month, and volume, because of its fractioning. It is interesting to recall that while vision through one eye is sufficient for the perception of distance, it is only when the ocular axes of both eyes converge that we are able to form the notion of three-dimensional space and therefore of volume.[5]

Since Egyptologists appear to be so sure that there is no evidence of an advanced technology in pre-dynastic Egypt, from where or from whom did the ancient Egyptians cull their knowledge of mathematics and astronomy? Another point that merits consideration is that although many of these figures could have been arrived at by normal mathematical processes, they could also be seen to suggest that our planet had at some time in the past *been viewed from outside of its orbit!* Now, we can go along with those psychics and mental time-travellers who suggest that the Atlanteans were the brains behind these structures, despite the Sumerian tale of Oannes (see pages 80–3) with his scale-like apparel (which could just as easily have been somebody dressed in a space suit or Atlantean diving gear as an alien Fish-Man), or we can favour the extraterrestrial connection, that is that beings from Sirius were the teachers.

One is inclined to think that if a Siriun connection was effected at some distant period in the past history of our planet, it occurred during the time of the early formation of the Atlantean civilisation, and it was to the Atlantean scientists that the Siriuns imparted their information concerning all matters cosmological. There is a third, and perhaps more scientifically acceptable explanation which came my way: one of the Timeless Ones, the Creators of Universes, in taking human form, effected a genetic mutation which was then passed on to his own children as a sleeper gene (allele?). This gene, which has now spread across the planet, will be the deciding factor as to who is destined to survive the anticipated pole shift (quantum leap), the shadow of which is slowly eclipsing our planet (see *The Gaia Dialogues* and *Cosmic Connections*).

Psychicists, explorers, science fiction writers and others curious about the enigmatic past have speculated as to how the pyramids were erected, assuming the slaves and trolleys concept to be an erroneous one. A theory that sonics were used is among the most popular. Some Babylonian tablets affirm that sound could lift stones, while according to one ancient Arab source the huge stone blocks were wrapped in some kind of papyrus and then struck with a rod by a priest, which appeared to have the effect of rendering them weightless and they could then be moved through the air effortlessly and placed precisely in position! I recall reading an account rendered by an Amazonian explorer of a plant found deep in the forest, the juice of which, when applied to the hardest of stones, rendered them like putty! For the moment it is anyone's guess, although recent scientific experiments appear to confirm the fact that the Great Pyramid is no ordinary structure, as it possesses properties which are at variance with any known scientific phenomena. (See *Atlantis: Myth or Reality?*)

Another aspect of the pyramids that is hotly debated is whether they were constructed as tombs, places of worship, safe harbours during a cataclysm, or time capsules. There would, however, appear to be several snippets of information which have seeped through from the past which might serve to throw some light on this question:

● Herodotus claimed to have seen inscriptions on the sides of the pyramids in his time.
● Ibn Abd Hokm, a ninth-century Arab historian, stated that most chronologists agreed that the pyramids were built by Surid Ibn Salhouk, King of Egypt, who lived 300 years before the Flood. His action was prompted by a dream in which he saw the whole Earth turn on its axis, the stars falling and striking one another as they did, and all men prostrate in fear at the terrible

noise which accompanied these phenomena. Upon waking, he summoned his priests, the chief of whom was named Aclimon, and made haste to relate to them the fearful vision he had experienced. Taking both astrological and astronomical calculations into consideration, they foretold the Deluge and the resulting climatic changes which would destroy his kingdom. However, a few safe years yet remained, during which the King, under the guidance of his advisers, built the pyramids with vaults, filling them with talismans, strange objects, riches, treasures, cartouches made of precious stones, instruments of iron, vessels of clay, jars which did not rust and *glass which could be bent and yet not broken.*[6]

● Ibn Haukal, an Arab traveller and writer in the tenth century, claimed that the writing on the pyramid casings was still visible in his time.

● Abd el Latif, writing in the twelfth century, mentioned that the inscriptions on the exterior of the pyramids could fill 10,000 pages.

● Ibn Batuta, another Arab scholar of the fourteenth century, stated that the pyramids were erected to preserve the arts and sciences, and other knowledge, during the Deluge.

● The Dictionary of Firazabadi (fourteenth century) states that the pyramids were supposed to 'preserve the arts and sciences and other knowledge during the Deluge.'

● A passage from the Coptic Papyrus, from the monastery of Abou Hormeis reads: 'In this manner were the pyramids built. Upon the walls were written the mysteries of science, astronomy, geometry, physics, and much useful knowledge, which any person who understands our writing can read.'[7]

● The Egyptian Coptic historian, Masudi, writing during the Middle Ages, recounts a tradition that the Great Pyramid was built by a king named Surid, who lived 300 years before the Flood, to safeguard the ancient knowledge. His version accords with those aforementioned – that the king had been forewarned of the disaster, which was connected in some way with the constellation of Leo. The walls and ceilings in the pyramid were engraved with astronomical, mathematical and medical knowledge, and strange beings (elemental spirits?) were placed there by priests to prevent this knowledge falling into the hands of those unworthy to handle it. Another Coptic legend confirms this, but also adds that Surid ordered the inscription to be engraved in words together with 'other matters' on the pyramid casing. The casing having disappeared, however, we are denied the knowledge the worthy monarch saw fit to leave for posterity.[8]

Of course, it could be argued that all these reports were culled from the same Middle Eastern source, although there is usually no smoke without fire, as the saying goes. My personal opinion is that the Great Pyramid was built neither as a tomb, temple of worship nor safe haven. A time capsule? Now that is another matter!

Along with the Great Pyramid, the Sphinx has probably been the subject of more conjecture than any other antiquity. Schwaller de Lubicz maintained that the erosion of the Sphinx was due to the action of water rather than of wind and sand. Were this to be confirmed, however, the accepted chronological history of civilisation would be overthrown. As West succinctly points out:

> In principle, there can be no objection to the water erosion of the Sphinx, since it is agreed that in the past Egypt has suffered radical climatic changes and periodic inundations – by the sea and (in the not so remote past) by tremendous Nile floods. The latter are thought to correspond to the melting of the ice from the last ice age. Current thinking puts this date around 15,000 BC, but periodic great Nile floods are believed to have taken place subsequent to this date. The last of these floods is dated around 10,000 BC.
>
> It follows, therefore, that if the great Sphinx had been eroded by water, it must have been constructed prior to the Flood or floods responsible for the erosion.[9]

It has been proposed that because the sculptors of Egypt were past masters at producing the faces of the Pharaohs exactly and in all mediums, the original face of the Sphinx might well have been exchanged for the likeness of Khephren, a fourth-dynasty Pharaoh who reigned from 2631 BC to 2618 BC approximately, a deception which has continued to play its role down the pages of history. Some scholars have suggested that the Sphinx' human head and leonine hindquarters is prophetic in itself, the rear portion referring to the end of the Golden Age of Leo and the fall of Atlantis, and the head to Leo's opposite sign, Aquarius, when the Old Country is destined to rise again. Since we are just entering the Age of Aquarius, there might well be something in this theory, especially if we are to take the greenhouse effect, and other recent climatic inconsistencies seriously. On the other hand, what if the original face, like the rear, had also been leonine but conveniently changed to suit Khephren? Bearing in mind the aforementioned belief (see page 18) that one of the races that inhabited the Siriun system was of cat- or lion-like appearance, which I hope to support with further evidence from several sources in the ensuing chapters, then that, to me, would certainly suggest a strong first- or second-hand Siriun influence. However, since this book was first published, researchers using seismic testing at the site for the first time have concluded that an ancient civilisation carved the Sphinx between 5,000 and 7,000 BC – at least 2,500 to 4,500 years earlier than has been accepted. Its creation being traditionally attributed to the Pharaoh Kephren (Khafre). The new study, led by Boston University geologist Robert M. Schoch, suggests that Kephren merely restored the monument, possibly replacing the original leonine head with a likeness of his own face.

Endnotes:

1 E. A. Wallis Budge, *The Gods of the Egyptians*, page 96.

2 J. A. West, *Serpent in the Sky*, page 13.

3 P. Lemesurier, *The Great Pyramid Decoded*, pages 8–15.

4 Ibid, page 8.

5 L. Lamy, *Egyptian Mysteries*, page 16.

6 A. Tomas, *Atlantis: From Legend to Discovey*, pages 111–12.

7 Ibid, page 115.

8 R. Mooney, *Colony Earth*, pages 198.

9 J. A. West, *Serpent in the Sky*, pages 198–9.

CHAPTER 3

The Gods, or Neters

Although the polytheistic inclinations of the ancient Egyptians may appear to be abundantly clear, Wallis Budge, for one, sees the numerous gods worshipped in dynastic times as aspects of a single creative force, and the various animals venerated as the *abodes of the gods,* rather than as the gods themselves. However, as some distinctions are obviously called for, I have effected the following broad classification:

1. The indigenous or nome gods of pre-dynastic times;
2. God-kings or incarnate deities;
3. Divinities from foreign sources which became either super-imposed over, or integrated with, native Egyptian deities over the centuries;
4. The epagomenal Neters;
5. Extraterrestrial and stellar influences.

Let us commence with the first category: the indigenous or nome gods of pre-dynastic times. In his mammoth work, *The Gods of Ancient Egypt,* Wallis Budge gives a comprehensive list of nome gods and the cities or locations at which they were originally worshipped:

Upper Egypt

Nome	Capital	God
Ta-Khent	Abu (Elephantine)	Khnemu
Thes-Hertu	Teb	Heru-Behutet
Ten	Nekheb	Nekhebet
	Senit	
Uast	Uast (Thebes)	Amen-Ra
Herui	Qebti	Amsu, Min or Khem
Aata	Ta-en-tarert (Denderah)	Het-Heru (i.e. Hathor)
Seshesh	Het	Het-Heru
Abt	Abtu (Abydos)	An-Her
Amsu, Min or Khem	Apu	Amsu, Min or Khem
Uatchet	Tebut	Het-Heru
Neterui	Tu-qat	Heru (Horus)
Set	Shas-hetep	Khnemu
Tu-F	Nut-en-bak	Heru
Atef-Khent	Saiut	Ap-uat
Atef-Pehu	Qesi	Het-Hert
Un	Khemennu	Tehuti (Thoth)
Meh-Mahetch	Hebennu	Heru
Anpu	Kasa	Anpu
Sep	Het-suten	Anpu
Uab	Per-Matchet (Oxyrhyncus)	Set
Atef-Khent	Henensu	Her-shefi
Atef-Pehu	Ermen-hert	Khenmu
Ta-She	Shet	Sebek
Maten	Tep-ahet	Het-Hert

Lower Egypt

Nome	Capital	God
Aned-Hetch	Men-nefert (Memphis)	Ptah
Khensu	Sekhemt	Heru-ur
Ament	Nut-ent-Hap (Apis)	Het-Heru

Sapi-Res	Tcheqa	Sebek, Isis, Amen
Sap-Meh	Saut (Sais)	Net (Neith)
Kaset	Khasut	Amen-Ra
Ament	Senti-nefert	Hu
Abt	Theket	Temu
Ati	Per-Asar (Busiris)	Osiris
Ka-Qem	Het-ta-her-ab	Horus
Ka-Hesed	Hebes-ka	Isis
Theb-Ka	Theb-neter	An-her
Heq-At	Annu (Heliopolis, On)	Ra
Khent-Ab	Tchalu (Tanis)	Heru
Tehut	Per-Tehuti (Hermopolis)	Tehuti (Thoth)
Kha	Per-ba-neb-Tettu (Mendes)	Ba-neb-Tattu
Sam-Behutet	Pa-khen-en-Amen	Amen-Ra
Am-Khent	Per-Bast (Bubastis)	Bast
Am-Pehu	Per-Uatchet (Buto)	Uatchet
Sept	Qesem	Sept[1]

From the aforegoing it may be observed that each nome had a representative deity whose temple was situated in the capital city of that nome. These temples were the workplaces of priests who were responsible for the maintenance of the temple itself and its associated buildings, the religious education of the people, and other priestly crafts which included such services as healing, the conducting of both personal and state rites, and the mummification of the dead. Thus, the priesthood was divided into various branches: scribes, healers, libationers, magicians, seers, and those who represented the gods themselves. Both men and women served in these priesthoods.

The nomic religions may certainly be seen to display a highly shamanic content. Priests of Anubis, for example, would don the jackal mask when performing their rites, thus assuming the role of Anpu (Anubis) himself, or acting as a channel for his energies. Like the ancient tribal chieftains, the old nome gods carried sceptres, one end of which was forked while the other displayed the head of the totem animal appropriate to the nome. In time, many of the animals and fetishes of the prehistoric period assumed human characteristics and became firmly installed as divinities in their own right. Since the ancient Egyptians could not conceive of a god without a family, husbands/wives and sons/daughters were soon added and the famous triads made their appearance.

Some of the gods listed above can be traced back much farther than others: Neith, for example, about whom we shall have more to say later. Interestingly enough, in the Egyptian language the word 'sky' is feminine, thus the sky became the goddess Nut or Hathor, whose starry belly men saw suspended in the heavens above them. The Earth, on the other hand, the Egyptians saw as masculine, and represented it as a man lying prone, from whose back sprouted all the world's vegetation. This Earth god they called Geb. In view of the recent emphasis on the feminine or Gaia aspect of Earth, one cannot help wondering whether there has been a confusion of polarities, especially as the Egyptians also favoured lunar *gods* rather than goddesses. Pantheism and animism may be evidenced in the worship of the Nile and other natural phenomena and fetishes. Some of what later became the great Egyptian centres of learning originated in the temples of the old nome gods, Ptah of Memphis being a prime example.

As the number of gods worshipped in the Nile valley over the years was considerable – Thuthmosis III enumerates no fewer than 740, most of which were doubtless no more than *genius loci*, ancestral spirits, or the essences of departed priests or favoured rulers and local dignitaries – I intend to keep to those better-known deities whose energies could be interpreted as being relevant to our subject matter.

As regards category 2, god-kings or incarnate deities, for many centuries the Pharaohs were seen as the sons of the gods and revered accordingly. There are two possible explanations for this, the first of which is fairly straightforward: either the early chieftains themselves, or their shamanic (priestly) representatives, were believed to embody the essence of their local deity, a 'gift' which was naturally passed on to their progeny. This could be viewed as an archaic form of the 'divine rights of kings'. The second concerns the ancient legend of the Shemsu-Hor, or Sons of Horus, who in turn carried the gene of their divine ancestors, the Neters. Pharaohs of the early dynasties were thought to have carried this bloodline through, although in later times it became diluted and eventually disappeared. Or did it? A confirmatory hint might be taken from the story of Ra's visit to Reddedet, wife of the high priest, in the guise of her husband, and how from this union were born the first three kings of the fifth dynasty. In fact, each time a Pharaoh was conceived, Ra was believed to have been in some way responsible.

While conducting research for my book *Atlantis: Myth or Reality?* I came across some curious facts during the process of studying comparative blood groups in relation to possible Atlantean colonies and migrations prior to the Flood. Traces of the A blood group, with its appropriate genetic markers, were found in royal mummies up to the eighteenth dynasty. Now the normal blood group in those parts was, and still is, O. The A blood group usually goes with the type of fair skin and blue eyes normally encountered in the Scandinavian and other Northern European races. So what was it doing among the Pharaohs of ancient Egypt? Blood tests on five Inca mummies in the British Museum also showed that three out of four of them possessed traces of the A blood group, which is utterly foreign to the American Indian. None of these, from either side of the Atlantic, displayed the Rhesus negative factor dominant in the Basques and Berbers.

The inference is, therefore, that a people alien to the local inhabitants of those parts (on both sides of the Atlantic) carried a blood group and accompanying genetic markers that differed from those of both the Egyptian and South American natives. As Professor Emery and other experts have indicated, these newcomers kept themselves very much aloof from the ordinary people, and any unions that were contracted tended to be with the aristocracy of those parts, which would account for the A blood group appearing among the ruling classes only. Of course, we cannot be absolutely sure that this was always the case, as tests to date have tended to be limited to the remains of those able to afford costly burials.

The results of the search for genetic identification among short sequences of DNA that have survived 7000 years in a marshy bog in what is now Little Short Spring, Florida have recently baffled scientists. A portion of DNA extremely rare in modern world-wide populations was discovered, indicating that these people had an ancestry totally unknown in the New World! Why should this be relevant to ancient Egypt and the divine gene of the old kings? It is my own belief that if a genetic identification of the ancient Pharaohs could be effected, some equally surprising (and probably similar) genetic markers would be found.

Regarding category 3, divinities from foreign sources which became superimposed over or integrated with native Egyptian deities over the centuries, many Egyptian gods, notably those of the Middle Period, were evident among the beliefs and worship of surrounding nations, solar deities such as Ra and Ammon corresponding to the divinities of adjacent and even far distant cultures. Some foreign influences are seen as obvious by many researchers; Set, for example, contrary to Professor Emery's views, is believed by certain scholars to have been a Hyksos import, the Hyksos being the 'shepherd kings' referred to by Manetho and more recently identified by Egyptologists as wandering Semites. These will, however, become obvious as an analysis of the major deities of dynastic times is effected.

Although we tend to refer to the 'gods' of Egypt, the Egyptians had their own word to describe their deities, and that was *Neter*. Budge tells us. (See *Fig. 3.1*).[2]

We have already said above that the common word given by the Egyptians to God, and god, and spirits of every kind, and beings of all sorts, and kinds, and forms, which were supposed to possess any superhuman or supernatural power, was NETER, and the hieroglyph which is used both as the determinative of this word and also as an ideograph is. Thus we have "god," and, or, or, or, "gods;" the plural is sometimes written out in full, e.g.,. The common word for "goddess" is NETERT, which can be written, or, or; sometimes the determinative of the word is a woman, and at other times a serpent, e.g.. The plural is NETERIT,.

Fig. 3.1

There has been much scholarly debate as to whether this ancient Egyptian axe-shaped ideograph, if indeed it was meant to be an axe as even this is debatable, was seen in the context of a weapon or a tool. Some experts have tended to favour a more esoteric interpretation, while others view it as purely a Stone Age fetish which could be traced back to the Neolithic or even the Palaeolithic Age. Axes as emblems of divinity have appeared in other megalithic cultures, notably in Brittany, the prehistoric funeral caves of the Marne, Scandinavia and America. The axe would therefore appear to have been a symbol of power among the indigenous population of those parts long before the rise of dynastic Egypt.

Egyptologists seem unable to agree among themselves as to the meaning of the word *Neter:* guesses hazarded include 'renewal', 'strength', 'mighty power', 'divine', 'exquisite', or 'to become'. Dr Heinrich Brugsch, however, was convinced that the word means 'the operative power which created and produced things by periodical recurrence, and gave them new life and restored to them the freshness of youth.'[3] Budge spends several pages quoting the views of numerous eminent professors, endeavouring to effect a translation via a study of other languages extant at the time. This type of scholarly polemic can sometimes cause one to lose one's way in the labyrinth of confusion. A concentrated study of the use of the term in hieroglyphic texts over many years does, however, tend to suggest that it related to some quality of life or immortality, or the power to generate life.

Category 4 applies to the five epagomenal Neters – Isis, Osiris, Nephthys, Set and Horus – who merit a chapter to themselves in which their natures, deeds and significances as far as Sirius is concerned will be analysed and debated in the light of the many theories that have been put forward over the centuries. These five Neters may also be seen by many as category 5 deities, in that they have extraterrestrial connotations, along with Thoth and Anubis who formed a part of their retinue, and Ra/Atum, Shu and Tefnut, Hathor/Sekhmet and her husband Ptah, Thoth's wife Seshat, and Sa (Orion), whose legends would certainly seem to suggest galactic connections, as we shall see. But let us first turn our attention to a general consideration of the main deities favoured by the Egyptians.

Ra/Atum

According to an early Egyptian creation myth, Nun (or Nu) was the primordial ocean which existed before creation, and from which all life emanated. This has a scientifically sound ring about it and infers that someone, somewhere in the distant past, was acquainted with the facts, while also providing fuel for those goddess-orientated believers who view the feminine principle as the primary source of all life. However, one of the best known of the early Egyptian gods was probably Ra or Re, commonly seen as representing the risen sun; the dark or hidden sun – before it had risen or after it had set – was called Atum. Ra's principal sanctuary was at Heliopolis, and legend had it that he originally manifested himself at that place in the form of a stone obelisk named 'ben-ben', which was preserved for many years in a temple named Het Benben: 'the palace of the obelisk'. The story goes that Ra or Atum originally dwelt in the bosom of Nun until, by an effort of will, he arose from the abyss and appeared in the resplendent light we now see as our sun. All very logical in the light of what science now knows concerning the birth of a solar system and the early life of yellow stars.

Ra (or some say Nun or Neith) then begat Shu and Tefnut, the Twin lion gods, without the assistance of a mate, and who, in turn, gave birth to Geb and Nut, from whom issued the family of Isis and Osiris. The metaphysical concept in this allegory is obvious, the splitting of the androgyne into male and female, or yang and yin, and the corresponding cell division in the world of genetics. Shu, Tefnut, Geb, Nut (Neith), Isis, Osiris, Set and Nephthys, together with Ra-Atum himself, were the great gods of the Ennead of Heliopolis, which ranks them among the earliest dynastic deities. However, Ra also had a spouse or feminine aspect who was known as Rat, although according to some authorities Rat did not appear in the earlier texts.

Ra is said to have created a 'first universe', different from the present world. The legend tells us that as long as he remained young and vigorous he reigned peacefully over gods and men. However, as age overtook him, the people he had created sensed his weakening powers and plotted against him. Who these 'people' were or whence they hailed from we are not told, but they appear to be part and parcel of this 'first universe'. Being divine, however, Ra soon discovered their machinations and, after consulting with the other gods, he decided to hurl his divine Eye against his rebellious subjects in the form of the goddess Hathor/Sekhmet, which constitutes a tale in itself. This 'Eye' story is probably a folk memory of some cosmic catastrophe that could have occurred either here or in another solar system about which we know but very little.

The ingratitude of the beings he had created apparently gave the old god a distaste for his 'first universe' so he decided to withdraw himself beyond its reach. On the orders of Nun, the goddess Nut, or Neith, changed herself into a cow, took Ra on her back and raised him high in the vault of heaven, at which time *our present world was created*. What we are dealing with here would appear to be an allegory of a cosmological drama involving another star or stars that were responsible for the seeding of the system in which we now dwell. The legend continues: from the moment that Ra (or his progeny?) became suspended in our skies his life became immutably regulated. During the hours of light he rode his solar boat across the heavens from east to west, taking great care to avoid his old enemy, the serpent Apep, (the darkness of ignorance) who was later vanquished by his daughter the cat goddess, Bast or her animus, Mau.

Shu and Tefnut

The story of Shu and Tefnut we have already dealt with in Chapter 1 (see page 14). Shu is often portrayed in human form while Tefnut, his sister, was leonine. To the Sirius-minded this suggests that the old Ra refers to the star in another solar system which probably housed both hominids and leonids, a fact of which those early teachers who landed on the shores of prehistoric Egypt were only too aware. In later times, Shu and Tefnut became the Twin Lion gods of 'Yesterday and Today', implying that whoever or whatever they had originally represented had conquered time!

Nut

Nut, like Neith, was the Celestial Cow who gave birth to the sky when nothing else existed. Perhaps these two goddesses were originally one and the same, as both are said to have given birth to Ra in some way unrelated to childbirth as we know it. Although Nut was sometimes referred to as the daughter of Ra, older legends suggest that she was, in fact, his mother, which would equate her with the Great Mother or female god from whose bosom all things had proceeded.

Neith (The Lady of the West)

Neith, Neit or Net, the protectress of Sais, was an extremely ancient divinity. Her fetish, two crossed arrows on an animal skin, was carried on the standard of a prehistoric clan, while two first dynasty queens derived their name from her. Her epithet, Tehenut 'the Libyan' is seen as suggesting that she probably had her origins in the West. For many years she was the principle deity of Lower Egypt and is often portrayed wearing the old red crown which was also called 'Net', and clasping a bow and two arrows. Due to her double role as warrior goddess and a woman skilled in the domestic arts, she is frequently identified with the Greek Athene, who had similar attributes. Her weaver's shuttle, seen as an ideogram of her name, played a role in one of the early Egyptian creation myths, as it was said that she wove the world as a woman weaves cloth. Under the name Mehueret she was the Celestial Cow who gave birth to the sky when nothing else existed.

The *Oera Linda Book*, believed to be the chronicles of the ancient Frisian people, whose lands off the coast of Scandinavia sank sometime between 5000 and 2500 BC (opinions vary but the latest scientific findings support the earlier date), tells of a race of matriarchal warriors who were fair haired, blue eyed and about seven feet tall. According to the ancient Frisian tradition, one of these handsome and martially gifted ladies, whose name was Min-erva, was responsible for the birth and growth of the old Athens, and was later deified as the Greek Goddess Athene; early statues depicted her clad in the apparel and weaponry of the ancient Frisian female warriors. One cannot help wondering whether Neith was not another such character. Since it has been speculated that the old Frisian country of Atland was a colony of Atlantis, we are probably back to those tall, fair strangers who made their appearance on both sides of the Atlantic, were subsequently deified as the 'Sons of God', and eventually became superimposed over the resident divinities of those parts. According to some authorities, Neith and Net were two separate identities, the bow and arrows belonging to the former and the weavers shuttle to the latter, which rather tends to confirm the idea of a superimposition.

Just as Isis and Nephthys, and Nekhebet (the vulture-goddess of the South) and Uatchet or Buto (the snake-goddess of the North) were often featured in pairs, so Neith is frequently to be found in the company of Selkit, the scorpion-goddess, either as guardian of the mummy and viscera of the dead, or as the protectress of marriage. These bipolar or 'sister' relationships, into which modern psychologists tend to read conscious/ unconscious connotations, were to be found in most of the ancient pantheons, the Sumerian sisters Inanna and Ereshkigal being a notable example.

Khepera

The name Khepera is said to signify both 'scarab' and 'he who becomes'. To the Heliopolitans, Khepera represented the rising sun which, like the scarab beetle, 'emerges from its own substance and is reborn of itself'.[4] In other words, the scarab and its representative divinity epitomised the continuing cycle of birth, death and rebirth through which all living essences must inevitably pass. I am inclined to classify this deity as a theo- sophical concept with shamanic overtones, rather than a celestial energy or archetype as such.

Hathor

Budge identified Hathor with the four great goddesses of ancient times, Nekhebet, Uatchat, Bast and Neith. Hathor was a sky goddess who was originally acknowledged as the daughter of Ra and later as Het Heru the wife of Horus, the name Het Heru meaning 'The House or dwelling of Horus'. In common with Neith, she is also represented as a cow, which was her sacred animal, and when depicted in her human form her head is adorned with horns, between which the solar disk is set. Although essentially the attribute of Hathor, in later dynasties this headgear became superimposed on the goddess Isis, which does, however, facilitate datings in statuary and art. Budge tells us:

> At the time when the Egyptians first formulated their theogony Hathor was certainly a cosmic goddess, and was associated with the Sun-god, Ra, of whom she was the principal female counterpart. In the theological system of the priests of Heliopolis she became, as Brugsch says, the 'mother of the light', the birth of which was the first act of creation; her next creative act was to produce Shu and Tefnut, that is to say, certain aspects of these gods, for according to a very old tradition Temu was their begetter and producer.[5]

This rather suggests that Hathor could be equated with Rat, the feminine aspect of Ra, or with Nut or Neith in her role as Creatrix of the universe. As the great goddess of Denderah, she appears in the form of a lioness with a uraeus on her head, or as a woman carrying a sistrum or a sceptre. The Lady of the Sycamore, the Lady of Annu, the Goddess of Turquoise and Mistress of the Land of Punt were other titles by which she was known, the latter suggesting her foreign origin in very ancient times. As the protectress of women, Hathor was believed to preside over their toilet and help them in their quest for beauty. Her uniting with Horus probably came at a later period, when the Egyptians generously provided them with a son, Ihy or Ahi, 'the Sistrum Player'.

Let us return for one moment to the story of how the god Ra hurled his divine Eye, in the person of his daughter Hathor, at those who broke his covenants. But it was not as Hathor, the Celestial Cow, goddess of nourishment, beauty and patroness of women and astrologers that she effected the nemesis of the sun god, but as the lioness Sekhmet, a name which simply means 'the powerful'. According to the legend, Sekhmet attacked Ra's enemies with such fury that the sun-god, fearing the extermination of the whole of the errant race, (which was not, it seems what he actually had in mind), had recourse to a stratagem which involved placing convenient jugs of beer and pomegranate juice which the goddess, being thirsty, drank with such gusto that she soon fell asleep and further slaughter was thus avoided!

There is a great deal of confusion concerning the Hathor/Sekhmet association, however, since Sekhmet was also the wife of Ptah and mother of Nefertum (Imhotep) of the famous

Memphis Triad, while Hathor later appeared in the role of wife to Horus. They would seem to be two distinct deities, one of which became superimposed over the other at a comparatively early stage in Egyptian history, possibly in pre-dynastic times.

Sekhmet

Aside from her Hathor *alter ego*, Sekhmet is an interesting deity in her own right. Lioness-goddesses go back a very long way and are to be found in the earliest texts and pantheons. Although originally a divinity of Latopolis, Sekhmet merited the title 'beloved of Ptah' upon joining the Memphis Triad as the wife of the artisan god. She is essentially a goddess of demolition and renewal, and her association with Ptah, the Master Mason, is an interesting one, both philosophically and metaphysically. Goddesses of destruction and regeneration appear in many pantheons, thus we may equate Sekhmet with the Indian Kali, the Irish Morrigan, or the Scottish Cailleach. The fact that the priests of Memphis knew exactly what they were doing may be evidenced in the fact that they chose the Master Mason or builder as her syzygy, or consort. In other words, as she effects those changes which are essential to all healthy growth via the refiner's fire, so Ptah, her husband, rebuilds the shattered structures; and from the coupling of these two totally complementary energies a third, a god of healing and medicine is born – Nefer-Tem, later known as Imhotep! The repetitive symbology merely exemplifies the chaos/order principle. Note how the progeny, or 'reconciling force' is inevitably portrayed as a healer (balancing?) god. This pattern is repeated in the Theban triad of Amon, Mut and Khonsu, Mut often being portrayed as a feline while Khonsu – The Navigator – was renowned for his healing miracles.

I tend to see many of these ancient Egyptian gods and goddesses as the embodiment of principles, or archetypal energies relevant to life and experience on Earth. As such, they were (and still are) capable of personalising when the resonant note is struck in the heart of the suppliant or, to adopt a more modern approach, it is possible to access their energies (databanks) field to field, or via a practice known in the East as Samyama (fusion). (See Glossary.) So, while the gods and goddesses of

ancient times are seen by many modern-day scholars and
metaphysicists simply as aspects of the 'self', and there is a
degree of the truth in this theory, the remaining part of the
picture, or other facets of the jigsaw (fragments of the archetypal soul), can and do exist interdependently of us, as indivi-
dualized energies or essences.

Wallis Budge intimates a strong connection between Sekhmet
and Thoth, and even suggests that the goddess could be viewed
as an aspect of Thoth's anima, Maat, Goddess of Truth. Thoth
(about whom I shall have much to say shortly) was what could
be described in modern parlance as a Time Lord, so how does
Sekhmet fit in with this particular concept? In order to understand this we need to consider the many leonine deities that
permeated the religion of those ancient times. Here are a few of
them according to Budge: the god and goddess SHU and
TEFNUT; lion gods ARI-HES-NEFER, NEFER-TEM (son of Sekhmet and Ptah); HEBI, HERU-NEB-MESEN, MAHES (Greek –
Mihos) son of Bast, the Cat Goddess; lion goddesses PAKHETH,
SEKHET (Sekhmet); MENAT, RENENET, SEBQET, URT-HEKAU
and ASTHERTET, which are also forms of both Hathor and
Nekhebet. The Leonine theme was often interchanged with that
of a cat as in the case of Mut, wife of Amun, Bast herself being
viewed by some scholars as a later version of one of the old Lion
goddesses. Budge tells us that the name Sekhmet means 'mighty
one', and derives from hieroglyphics 'to be strong'. She is sometimes portrayed in triple form as Sekhmet/Ubastit/Ra, Ubastit
often appearing as a cat-headed woman. Her worship, along
with that of the Twin Lion gods Shu and Tefnut, is believed to
have been introduced into Egypt from Bugem, a country in the
Sudan. Budge comments: 'This extraordinary triad of Sekhmet-
Ubasti-Ra, mentioned in *The Book of the Dead* (chapter clxiv) is
probably of Sudani origin. Ubasti was in one character a
benevolent goddess and akin to Hathor.'[6] This final statement is
of particular importance when viewed in the light of information
received from private Egyptian sources which will be dealt with
in Chapter 4. (The different spellings of these various Egyptian
names can prove confusing to many, but since scholars fail to
agree among themselves regarding either the original
pronunciations or their conversion to modern parlance, the
reader is left to work out the comparisons for him or herself.) We
have already established the connection between the leonine

gods and Sirius, and since Sirius, like Thoth, is also associated with time, the pieces slowly start to fall into place.

Thoth

According to the theologians of Hermopolis, Thoth, or Tehuti, to give him his correct Egyptian name, was the true universal Demiurge, the divine Ibis who had hatched the world egg at Hermopolis Magna. This work of creation he had accomplished *by the sound of his voice alone* (shades of the opening phrase of the Johannine Gospel: 'In the beginning was the word ...'). His divine ancestry is certainly open to speculation. The Books of the Pyramids refer to him as the oldest son of Ra, the child of Geb and Nut, or the brother of Isis, although according to other records he was vizier of Osiris and his family, and scribe to the king. His feats of magic healing, usually achieved through the power of his voice – as when he cured the child Horus from a deadly sting by a scorpion – and his teaching of the arts and sciences, arithmetic, geometry, surveying, astronomy, soothsaying, magic, medicine, surgery, music and writing – are well recorded for posterity among the writings and monuments of the past.

Thoth certainly ranks among the most interesting of the Egyptian gods, pyramid texts indicating that he was regarded as a divinity who was self-begotten and self-produced; that he was One. As Budge tells us:

> ... he made the calculations concerning the establishing of the heavens, and the stars, and the earth, that he was the heart of Ra, that he was the master of law both in its physical and moral conceptions, and that he had the knowledge of 'divine speech'. From many passages we see that he was the inventor and god of all arts and sciences, that he was the 'lord of books', and the 'scribe of the gods', and 'mighty in speech', i.e. his words took effect, and he was declared to be the author of many of the funeral works by which the deceased gained everlasting life. In *The Book of the Dead* he plays a part which gives him a unique position among the gods, and he is represented as the possessor of powers that are even greater than those of Osiris, and even those of Ra himself.[7]

As has already been observed, the classical writers referred to Thoth as a stranger who had landed on Egyptian soil during the zodiacal Age of Cancer. The fact that he appears in an almost avuncular role, as far as the Osirian family is concerned, suggests that he may have arrived in Egypt some years ahead of them. Assuming many of the classical historians and subsequent scholars to be correct, he could well have been the first Atlantean priest to bring the civilising influences of the Old Country to those shores. As regards his fabled voice, this could refer not so much to the actual *voce* as to a knowledge of sonics and an ability to manipulate matter through the agency of sound. After all, voice-activated devices are commonly used in modern technology so, assuming Thoth to have been the agent of a scientifically advanced society, perhaps he was able to demonstrate something of this nature in a recognisable way.

Another interpretation of his famous 'words of power', or 'hekau', is that his original language probably differed considerably from that of the indigenous population of the old Khemu (Egypt), and since he was apt to converse with his colleagues on matters scientific or magical in his native tongue, this strange language became associated with those feats which his advanced knowledge allowed him to perform. As mentioned earlier, I have always been of the opinion that what is termed 'magic' is no more than a folk memory of an advanced science which, without the paraphernalia or technology appropriate to its manipulation, could be viewed by later generations as 'supernatural'. Given a situation such as a major world catastrophe which could deprive many nations of the technology essential to carry out those feats of medicine, engineering, chemistry and the sciences generally, stories of such inventions could appear as magic or superstition to ensuing generations to whom fables of operating tables, laser beams and jet aircraft were simply the Sinbad folk tales of their times – the works of evil spirits or vengeful gods, depending on the prevailing religious influence.

Since we have already referred to Schwaller de Lubicz' belief that Sirius can exert an influence over our climate (see Chapter 1) the connection between the energies of Sirius and all aspects of time such as time-slips, time-warps, time-capsules and evolutionary quantum leaps, (an observation that did not escape the ancient Egyptians, as may be evidenced in the importance they placed on their Sothic [Siriun] calendar) merits consideration. Both of these factors are totally relevant to the problems which face our planet as we approach the third millenium. Any externally induced acceleration of time that is calculated to speed up the growth of, or promote a quantum leap within our solar system, is naturally going to affect all life forms within the radius of its influence. If we are to assume the original Thoth or Tehuti to have been the conveyor of Siriun energies, either directly or indirectly, this would account for his association with time and the arrival of the five epagomenal days (movement of the Earth in relation to the sun and moon).

Although Thoth is frequently mentioned as having a consort, or syzygy, by the name of Maat, seen as the goddess of Truth, she is really no more than a theosophical concept representing Thoth's anima, for the ancient Egyptians were loath to see any god or goddess without a partner, and if a progeny could be added, then, so much the better. Thoth is credited with having a wife, however, the goddess Seshat or Sesheta. Seshat was a goddess of writing and history who, like Maat, could also be viewed in the *alter ego* context rather than as an entity in her own right. According to legend, she was also a stellar divinity who served to measure time, and her other appellations include 'mistress of the house of books', and 'mistress of the house of architects'. She was also mentioned as the 'mistress of scribes', 'patron of historians' and 'record-keeper for the gods'. Her stellar origins interest me and suggest that, like Thoth, she could have been an Atlantean who had received instruction from the Sirius system (either via Samyama telepathically or more directly), or actually hailed from the stellar regions herself. I rather suspect the former, although, no doubt, Temple and other writers may well see fit to favour the latter.

Although Thoth's totem animal was the ibis, the fact that the cynocephalus, or dog-headed baboon, is frequently shown as his companion is sometimes taken erroneously as a representation of the god himself, the idea having originated in southern Egypt where it was believed that Thoth had upon occasions adopted that disguise.

Anubis

Anubis (Anpu), the Egyptian psychopompus (conductor of souls), later became confused with Thoth, although the energies of both archetypes are quite distinctive, each having his own sphere of operation, as far as the myths and human psychology are concerned. Anubis was the patron deity of travellers, both in and out of the body! As the go-between of this world and the next, he is often portrayed either as a jackal or a dark-coloured hunting dog with a bushy tail; the former, according to Budge, being the more accurate. Anubis was granted *carte blanche* for safe travel through all regions of the Underworld, which naturally designated him the ideal companion for the spirit of the deceased who was anxious to land up in the right division of the afterworld.

Like Thoth, Anubis' associations with the Isian family are all too obvious. Although in the Pyramid Texts he is referred to as the fourth son of Ra, implying his antiquity, it is as the offspring of Nephthys and Osiris that he is more popularly known, and since we are again dealing with principles, the psychology behind the parable of the latter becomes all too obvious. Nephthys – the Hidden One and the Revealer – seen in psychological terms as the deep unconscious, was originally the wife of Set (Chaos), their relationship being a sterile one, which makes sound sense. The issue that resulted from her coupling with Osiris – Stability or Order – was Anubis, the Protector *of the soul in the dark regions* implying that chaos presents no fears to he or she who has mastered the hidden aspects of the deep unconscious, and can face the stark reality of the revelation of truth and harmony. Anubis was (and still is, should one care to invoke his energies) patron of anaesthetists, psychiatrists and psychologists, while he can also help find anything that is lost or missing. He is also known as 'the Opener of the Ways', in which capacity he is invoked as much for guidance out of the labyrinth of confusion or doubt as for practical considerations.

Bast (The Lady of the East)

Bast, Bastet or Pasht, is seen as an aspect of both Tefnut and Sekhmet, hence her connection with the Memphis Triad, in which Ptah's spouse is sometimes depicted with the head of a cat rather than that of a lioness. Although in her cat persona she is frequently associated with the moon, she was originally a solar deity and, according to information given to Herodotus by the Egyptian priests, the twin brother of Horus and, therefore, the daughter of Isis and Osiris. Although statues of cats are frequently sold as effigies of Bast, her correct representation is as a cat-headed woman holding in her right hand a sistrum, and in her left an aegis, composed of a semi-circular breastplate surmounted with the head of a cat, and a basket. Sometimes the basket contained kittens, while in other representations the kittens were shown seated at her feet.

The better-known legend of her origin, however, sees her as the daughter of Ra, or even his feminine half, or anima, Rat, who defended her ageing parent against his only real enemy, the serpent Apep.[8] Since Sekhmet is also referred to as a daughter of Ra, a degree of confusion has arisen regarding these two archetypes, although the Egyptians distinguished them by showing Sekhmet clothed in a red garment and Bast in green apparel. In addition to the symbols already mentioned,

Fig. 3.2 Bas, the Egyptian cat-goddess

Bast was also allotted one of Ra's divine Eyes in the form of the Uraeus, the Serpent of Wisdom. According to one version she acquired this from her brother Horus, but the more popular belief was that she was given charge of it by Ra for defending him against Apep. Although the Uraeus is considered to represent the right Eye, and the Horus Eye the left, there was some confusion, even in those ancient times, since Eyes facing either way were depicted in connection with Horus, Ra and even Osiris.

Budge ascribes to Bast a pre-dynastic origin along with the other Libyan deities, Isis and Neith, whose worship can be traced back to archaic times. As Goddess of the East, she was also ruler of one of the four cardinal points, the West being sacred to Neith, the South to Nekhebet and the North to Uatchat. Bast is sometimes confused with Pekhet, or Pakht, who also possessed attributes of the cat or lioness. Pekhet carried the title 'The Lady of Sept', that is the star Sothis (Sirius), and was identified with both Isis and Hathor.

It was not until 950 BC, when Sheshonk and the Pharaohs of the twenty-second dynasty elected Bubastis the capital of the Kingdom, that the worship of Bast received special emphasis. Horus and Bast could comfortably be equated with Shu and Tefnut. Both Horus and Shu were sky gods, while Bast, like Tefnut, originally appeared in lioness form. This would suggest that although Bast is not normally included among the epagomenal Neters, as the feminine aspect or anima of Horus, like all the other felines, she may be seen as having strong Siriun connections.

Ptah

Ptah of Memphis was certainly one of the most powerful and influential deities of ancient Egypt. This gentle artisan god was patron of builders and craftsmen, and his title, Architect of the Universe, speaks clearly of his masonic associations, even in those early times. Ptah, in his Creator aspect, was believed to have come from another universe beyond this solar system and, following the instructions of Thoth, he created our visible world, the sun, planets and all living things. This immediately places him in the category of gods who were older than the Osirian family, Thoth, Ptah's wife, Sekhmet, and her father, Ra. From a metaphysical viewpoint Ptah's energies are involved with the conversion of energy into matter, wheras Sekhmet's work reversely – by changing matter into energy. Their 'progeny', Nefer-tem, represents the reconciling factor which I have often likened to the earthing prong in a three-point electrical plug.

Many modern philosophers and scholars consider the religion of Memphis to have contained the finest metaphysical concepts of all the ancient Egytian beliefs and philosophies. Although this might well have been the case in earlier times, by the time Memphis held court as a major centre in Egypt, only fragments of the original teachings remained, and they were so well cloaked in allegory as to render their understanding by anyone but the initiated almost impossible. The 'Ren' or name being sacred to Ptah, I have often wondered whether anyone else has tumbled to the metaphysical significance of the word 'masonic'. To me it is MA-SONIC – as relating to a long-lost knowledge of sonics. In the Old Country there was a scientific branch of the priesthood devoted entirely to the study and use of sonics. Because of the extreme danger that could result from the misuse of this knowledge, the priestly order involved was sworn to complete secrecy. How do I know? Those interested would need to read the final chapter of my book *Cosmic Connections* in which a full explanation of the *modus operandi* I employ in my searches is outlined.

Nefer-tem

This son of Ptah (construction) and Sekhmet (destruction and regeneration), Nefer-tem, whose name actually means 'beautiful godling', was a gentle, healing divinity who was later named Imhotep. The Greeks equated him with Asclepius, their own demi-god of medicine. It would seem that many of these god-names were no more or less than titles which had been carried over from the archaic past, and which often incorporated the name of some earlier person who had shown exceptional skills in the calling in question. Nefer-tem also shares properties in common with Khonsu, the third member of the Theban Triad, who was also a healing divinity. Some Siriun significance could be read into the fact that he is frequently depicted with a lion's head.

Amon, Mut and Khonsu, the Theban Triad

Probably one of the best known of all the Egyptian divine triads, as a result of the famous eighteenth dynasty findings (the discovery of the tomb of King Tutankhamun by Howard Carter and his team, for example), these three deities are highly evocative of the period in which they were prominent. Amon, Ammon or Amen is often identified with the Greek Zeus on account of his title 'king of the gods'. He was almost unknown in the Old Kingdom; his name which derives from a root meaning 'hidden' – only appears four times in the Heliopolitan Texts of the Pyramids. It was not until the twelfth dynasty, when the Pharaohs incorporated his name in their title, that Thebes commenced to assume some importance in the religion of the land. However, although Amon is traditionally associated with the Theban nome, Wallis Budge assures us that Hathor was the tutelary goddess of the old Thebes. So, from whence did the great Amon originally hail?

In his book *Egyptian Belief and Modern Thought* the American scholar James Bonwick equates him with Baal of the Semites, later the Celtic Bel, who gave his name to the feast of Beltane, but other authorities have suggested that he arrived in Egypt with the Hyksos and is, therefore, one and the same as Yaweh or Jehovah. The ram-headed Amon certainly experienced difficulties in maintaining his supremacy, even at Thebes. In the reign of Amenhotep III there was a reaction in Ra's favour, although the Sun God never really abdicated his authority anyway, having enjoyed his own cult under the name of Ra-Harahkte. This was followed by much chiselling out of the Amon name in various hymns and texts, although the two deities eventually united under the name of Amen-Ra, which probably served to satisfy both camps.

Another curious circumstance which Bonwick points out is that repeatedly the hieroglyphics for the word Amon face the wrong way, and he comments: 'But then, that god is a peculiar mystery.'[9] Amon's main antagonist was Amenhotep IV, better known as Akhnaton, who instituted the monotheistic worship of Aten who was portrayed by a solar disc. Once again, there was much mutilation of all texts, carvings and objects associated with Amon, a persecution which continued until the final demise of Akhnaton, when the priests of Amon once again assumed the reins of religious control and wreaked their vengeance in similar vein on the Atenites.

Amon's consort, Mut, whose name signified 'mother', is one of those ill-defined but convenient wifely deities whose identity could be seen to encompass a multitude of previous maternal divinities. During the height of Amen-Ra's popularity, Mut herself was viewed as a solar deity, and sometimes identified with Bast, whose cat-form she was believed to assume, and with Sekhmet because of her leonine and solar qualities.[10]

Khonsu, who replaced Mont as the son of Amon and Mut in the Theban triad, is, to me, by far the most interesting divinity of this Triad. His name means 'the Navigator,' or 'he who crosses the sky in a boat'. Originally a lunar deity, little is known of him beyond the region of Thebes, and his skills as an exorcist and healer seemed to appear with his inclusion in the family of Amon and Mut. Many are the strange tales of healing miracles achieved by this god via the agency of some fetish or statue believed to embody the essence of his powers. He was also worshipped in Ombos, where he formed the third person in the Triad of Sebek, under the name of Khons-Hor, who was represented as a man with a falcon's head, surmounted with a disk in a crescent moon.

The falcon's head is reminiscent of Horus, who was also renowned for his healing powers, as was his sister, Bast. Mut and Khonsu would appear to share much in common with Horus and Bast, Shu and Tefnut, and Sekhmet and Nefer-tem. Perhaps these ancient archetypes were conveniently bestowed upon Amon to effect his falling in line with popular Egyptian demand for a family unit. Amon, Atum and Ra possibly originated from a single monotheistic concept, although there are aspects of Amon which, as general scholastic opinion suggests, are of foreign origin. Budge refers to Amen and his consort Ament as being among the gods known to the Egyptians in very early times, their names being found in the Pyramid Texts (*Unas*, line 558) in connection with the Twin Lion gods, Shu and Tefnut. As early as the fifth dynasty they were numbered among the primeval gods, if not as principal divinities then certainly as subsidiary forms of some of them.

Many of the lesser gods who have not already received mention in this chapter can be traced to the original nome gods: Mont; Wepwawet, who is often confused with Anubis; Khnum, the gentle old potter, sometimes depicted as a ram or goat, and his two wives Anukis (Anuket) goddess of cataracts, and Satis (Satet) the Archer; Min, seen as the Pan of Egypt; Hapi, the divine name for the Nile; Apet or Taueret, hippopotamus goddess of maternity; Renenet, nourisher of babies during the nursing period; Sebek, the crocodile goddess, Shai, goddess of destiny; Renpet, goddess of spring and growth; Bes, jester of the gods; Nehet, goddess of eternity; Harmarkhis, the god-name for the Sphinx; Heket, the frog goddess, patroness of midwives; Mertseger who, like Buto/Uatchet, was also a snake goddess. Selkit, the scorpion goddess, the serpent goddess Buto/Uatchet, and Nekhebet, the vulture-headed goddess of childbirth have already received coverage.

Larousse lists the following animals whose heads appear on Egyptian divinities:

Bull	–	Osorapis, Apis and Mont
Cat	–	Bast, Mut
Cow	–	Hathor, Isis, but only when wrongly identified with Hathor, Nut
Crocodile	–	Sebek
Dog-faced ape	–	Hapi, Thoth
Donkey	–	Set (in later times)
Falcon	–	Harahkte-Ra, Horus, Mont, Khons Hor, Qebhsnuf
Frog	–	Heket
Hippopotamus	–	Taueret
Ibis	–	Thoth
Jackal	–	Anubis, Duamutef
Lion	–	Nefer-tem
Lioness	–	Sekhmet, Tefnut, Mut, Renenet
Ram	–	Amon, Khnum, Hershef, Arsaphes
Scarab	–	Khepera
Scorpion	–	Selkit
Serpent	–	Buto, Mertseger, Renenet
Vulture	–	Nekhebet
Wolf	–	Upuaut (Wepwawet), Khenti Amenti
Indeterminate, but evil animal	–	Set[11]

Collective divinities included the Hathors, who were in no way related to the goddess of that name, but were a kind of fairy-godmother group which inevitably made an appearance at the birth of those destined for fame, and the Four Sons of Horus, who represented the four Elements, (See *Fig. 3.3*).

According to one legend the Four Sons of Horus were supposed to have been born to Isis, although another tale tells of how Sebek, on Ra's orders, caught them in a net and took them from the water in a lotus flower. They were designated responsible for the guardianship of the viscera: Imsety protected the liver, Duamutef the stomach, Qebhsnuf the intestines, and Hapi the lungs. These four godlings are also ritually associated with the cardinal points of the compass, but opinions as to their allocation are so varied (see Chapter 6) that one can only hazard a guess as to which version is correct.

A careful perusal of the aforegoing will serve to highlight those divinities which have stellar connections (Thoth, his wife

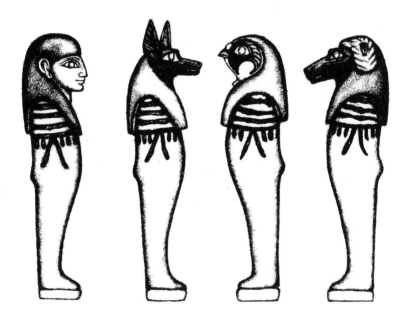

Fig. 3.3 The Four Sons of Horus, representing the four Elements: Imsety (with a human head) – Water; Duamutef (with a jackal head) – Fire; Qebhsnuf (with a hawk head) – Air; Hapi (with an ape head) – Earth.

Seshat, Sekhmet, Ra, Sah (Orion) and so forth – see category 5, page 35) who are either seen in the extraterrestrial context, in that they arrived from some elevated and unearthly realm, or as deities of stars or planets, as against the nome gods and goddesses, and those superimposed by surrounding cultures, conquerors, or visiting celebrities.

Endnotes:

1 E. A. Wallis Budge, *The Gods of the Egyptians*, Vol. 1, pages 96–100.

2 Ibid., page 63.

3 Ibid. page 67.

4 *The Larousse Encyclopedia of Mythology*, page 13.

5 Op. cit. Wallis Budge, page 429.

6 E. A. Wallis Budge, *Ancient Egyptian Theology*, page 29.

7 Loc. cit. Wallis Budge, page 401.

8 Author's note: Professor Stewart has recently suggested that the recurring serpent theme in ancient texts carries the encoded knowledge of superstring which, in the Ra/Apep context would make good sense, since it suggests the cycle from singularity to 'Big Crunch', or eventual demise of this Universe.

9 J. Bonwick, *Egyptian Belief and Modern Thought*, page 125.

10 Op. cit. Larousse, page 34.

11 Loc. cit. Larousse, page 48.

CHAPTER 4

Sirius and
the Five Epagomenal Neters

The idea that Thoth preceded Isis, Osiris, Nephthys, Set and Horus, the five epagomenal deities, poses several questions and possibilities. Let us suppose that the *original* Thoth, or Tehuti, had, in fact, visited Egypt a long time before the arrival of the Isian/Osirian group and set up a priesthood of healer/scientists who latterly bore his name in titular form. After many years had passed, learned men and women ascertained by astronomical observations and other scientific or intuitive means that a great calamity was due to befall the Earth, and in co-operation with their fellow priests from the Old Country, agreed to receive certain members of the royal families who had been advised to seek safe haven in the Atlantean colonies.

As the signs of the impending cataclysm made their appearance, Queen Isis, along with her husband Osiris and their son Horus, her sister Nephthys and her husband Set, duly presented themselves to the company of priests and officials in what was to be their new home – Egypt. But soon after their arrival, a massive interplanetary shake-up took place, involving the Earth, the moon, and, no doubt, some other bodies in the solar system, which served to alter our planet's position in relation to the sun, change the climate, and add five extra days to the calendar! The ordinary people of the time, and some of the priests, no doubt, immediately associated the arrival of the new royalty with those additional days.

However, the idea that these five royals arrived alone, without servants, guards, and the usual retinue that accompanies personages of such rank and fortune strains my credulity, so is there another explanation? Perhaps, but it is somewhat mind-boggling, although the American scholar Robert K. G. Temple was brave enough to publicise it in his controversial book *The Sirius Mystery*. But Temple was by no means the first to put forward the idea that beings from planets in the Sirius system visited Earth in the distant past. Several African tribes, notably the Dogon of Mali, have always maintained this to be a fact, as have the Hopi Indians of North America. Most researchers are, however, of the opinion that the African version of this know-ledge originated *from Egypt*.

The fact that the ancient Egyptians were aware of the fixed stars and the planets in our solar system may be evidenced in the adjacent illustration, (See *Fig. 4.1*). Schwaller de Lubicz comments:

> Here Isis holds the *wadj* scepter and the *ankh,* the dilation or spiritualization of life. Orion holds the *uas* scepter, the flow of sap, while facing Isis and presenting life with the left hand. In other words, Orion offers the life that he draws from Sirius.[1]

Isis appears to draw the power from Sirius (or is she herself Siriun?), from which star our solar system was seeded, and

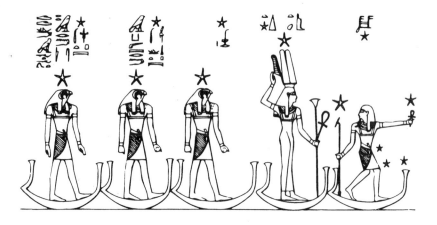

Fig. 4.1 Sirius (Isis-Seped.t) preceding Orion and followed by Jupiter, Saturn and Mars

transmits it via the agency of Orion to the children of our own sun. Could this energy possibly have become deviated somewhere along this subtle channel of communication? And, if so, who or which of the relay stations is the guilty party? I find myself saying Orion, but proof I cannot offer and I doubt whether anyone else could *at this moment in time*, although certain lines of research at present being pursued prompt me to opine that the transmission of subtle energies from one planetary or stellar body to another will soon be detected scientifically and any variations highlighted. After all, scientists are now aware that tiny particles can communicate with each other over vast distances, defying those two 'ring-pass-nots': time and space. If such minute structures are capable of intercommunication and interaction with each other, then why not the larger bodies? It is my contention that the ancients were perfectly aware of such things, but the knowledge became lost as our planet slowly declined into the backwaters of a temporary evolutionary regression.

The association between ancient Egypt and Sirius goes back many thousands of years. In order to established the fixed year, these ancient people deliberately chose the heliacal rising of Sirius, the only star to return periodically every 365¼ days during the entire Empire. Schwaller de Lubicz draws our attention to the fact that in the Pharaonic calendar, no attempt was made to concur with the seasons, in spite of the agrarian implications. He tells us:

> Indeed, while for us the summer solstice returns each year on June 21–22, thus determining a fixed reference point, *for the Pharaonic Sothic cycle of 1,460 years, the summer solstice advanced 11.5 days in relation to the rising of Sirius. That this fact was perfectly well known to the ancients is shown in the temporal correction brought to the celebration of the summer solstice or 'Birth of Ra '.*
>
> The essential facts are as follows:
>
> 1. The first day of the first month of the fixed year, or *festival of the New Year*, has always been determined by *the heliacal rising of Sirius*.
>
> 2. In the year 4240 BC the *summer solstice* fell six to nine days *after* the New Year, and was consequently celebrated under the name of *Birth of Ra* during the first month of the fixed year. But as the solstice advanced from five to six days each Sothic half-cycle, it happened that the *Birth of Ra* coincided with the *New Year* around the year 3400. In the year 2780, the solstice fell during the 'five days of the birth of

the *Neters'* (the 'epagomenae'). This remained in keeping with the calendar of celebrations as these days were considered 'the five days over the year ...'

It is significant also that tradition has already related the heliacal rising of Sirius with the beginning of the Nile's flooding and with the zodiacal sign of Leo; indeed, since the foundation of the calendar to the beginning of our era, *in Egypt the sun was always situated in the constellation Leo at the date of the heliacal rising of Sirius.* [Author's italics] This is the reason why, since the Ancient Empire, the temple gargoyles were carved in the shape of lion heads. In the zodiacal cycle, the sign of Leo is opposed and complemented by Aquarius, a sign represented on the Denderah zodiac by two vases from which water pours; this symbol is placed in the hands of the Nile god, Hapi. In the fifth millenium BC, the heliacal rising of Sirius took place in the constellation of Virgo; this could have motivated the attribution of Sirius to Isis, along with the mythical and vital significance of the character of Isis' star, Sothis (Sirius), which was also called 'the great provider'.

... The precessional cycle, therefore, is in theory that span of 26,000 years during which the vernal point travels through the twelve sites of the sky designated by their dominant constellations. This cycle is composed of twelve months, each with a duration of about 2,160 years; each month is subdivided into three decans of 720 years. These precessional months designate *the great Neter of the cult* whose influence colors all the other principles.[2]

During the course of writing this book, I have been privileged to become acquainted with some learned Egyptians who still follow the old beliefs, albeit secretly these days, since Islam, the state religion of modern Egypt, being intolerant of the old ways, can make the lives of 'heretics' or 'heathens' uncomfortable, to say the least! In answer to my sincere request for any information regarding Sirius, which may be concealed within their esoterica, I received the following missive. Sekhmet Montu is the reigning High Priestess of the goddess of that name, while Sau-Tahuti, her Astrologer/Mathematician, is believed to be over 100 years old. The missive was penned to me by their official scribe, whose name I may not mention for obvious reasons. The other names given are, as may be observed, purely titular:

Written in the name of The Great House (LHS), Her Grace, Sekhmet Montu (LHS) in the year of 20,450, in the month of Neb Ptah, in the season of Pert, the 10th day of the first week for Murry Hope, resident of the United Kingdom, England, sanctioned by the order of Her Grace (LHS) direct imperative through the offices of the Temple of Tahuti (Thoth) by the high priest thereof, Sau-Tahuti: Astrologer/Mathematician royal to the Great House: The text of the communication reads:

'The Star System also known as the Star of Auset (Isis) or Sebu-em-Auset.

'Acknowledgement in the Ammonite esoterical history:

'Known by us as the Star of the New Day (or year) and the commemorative star of the ascension of Our Lady Auset (Isis) to the Lotus Throne of the Great House (LHS) a little over 10,450 years ago. Known as the Star of Commemoration of the birth of the five great Neters (gods) upon the Mountain of Creation, Sinai Mountain in the Sinai, Egypt namely: Us-Ar (Osiris), Auset (Isis), Setekh (Set), Nebt Het (Nephthys) and Heru (Horus). The star of the added on days of the Epact, which are five days for three years and six days on the 4th year.

'Esoterically known as The Source from whence came the Neters from out of the Universe to our peoples, the Ammonites, and our cousins the Tutsi* peoples. The Tutsi people hold we the Ammonite peoples to be the Ones of the Shining Faces who left their footsteps upon the mountains of stone by the tone uttered from their mouths, the Ones who created "The Mountains" of perfection in the north

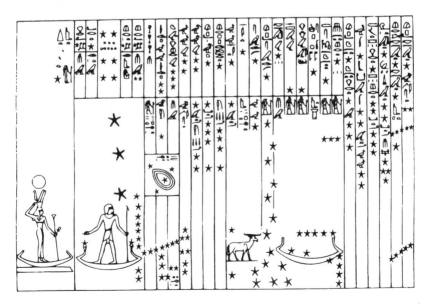

Fig. 4.2 List of the decans followed by Orion and Sirius. Ceiling of the tomb of Senmut. Deir el-Bahari, eighteenth dynasty.

and whose voice commanded the respect of God, who departed from us (the Tutsi) by moving to the east, out of the beloved land, soon to be ravaged by the savages (Arabs) of the lands to the east. The Ammonites wrote upon the rock of the mountain with fingers of fire, travelled upon the air without wings, moved rivers out of their courses by thought, and gifted us (the Tutsi) and our cousins (the Dogun) [sic] with the gift of our origins and great magic. And when they left, they caused great sorrow amongst our peoples, (the Tutsi), some going east to the land of the mountains by the sea, some going back to the Source in the heavens where they say by mathematics the spiritual history of their world took place, as it did upon their and our races of this world, and of which our cousins, the Dogun, know more of, for we achieved to the side of Hekau, "Words that Move" and they, the Doguns, to the matters of origin. And although our skins vary greatly we are one race, for we married and lived with these Shining Ones in our ancestral lands, for they prophesied the coming of the wild ones who shall cause the name of their leader the one of evil to be heard throughout the Holy Land as God Itself, but who in turn would succumb to the Shining Ones, [who] though in hiding still, shall join to our people once more and cause a new age to begin. End of edict.'

We also tell of the coming of Nebt Sekhmet Montu to the southern lands of Egypt at the time of the Star of Sirius arising but it may not be of much value to you. Should you require it, a letter of its account will be sent to you upon H.G's (LHS) approval.

(The Scribe apologises for his English grammar but, then, how many of us can speak or understand his tongue, so I feel he is to be congratulated on effecting such a clear description of the old Siriun connection.

*I have used the African spelling rather than his phonetic rendering 'Tootsie', which can have less erudite connotations!)

This missive is certainly packed with information. Let us start from the beginning. The date 10,450 obviously alludes to the Siriun calendar, and tells us that somewhere around 8000 BC – during the Age of Cancer – major changes occurred on our planet. These were accompanied by the arrival of the five Neters, each of whom I see as representing a Principle. Even Set, if viewed in the context of chaos, serves to fulfil a role as far as the prophetic content of the story is concerned. The 'writing on stone with the fingers of fire' suggests lasers, while the description of air travel, probably of the silent rather than fuel propulsion type, is indicative of a people with an extremely advanced technology who were able to draw upon gravitational forces or energies as yet untapped by modern science. The Dogons, it appears, inherited the knowledge of the stellar regions from whence these beings came, while the Ammonites were taught the *Hekau* – 'words that move' (Sonics?). The fact that these beings married and bred with the indigenous peoples of Africa suggests that they were hominids, which brings us right back to the eternal question: Atlanteans, or the hominids from Sirius, or a combination of both? For example, what if the Atlanteans did not possess aircraft, but were 'saved' from the catastrophe for genetic reasons, perhaps by some extraterrestrial agency? I have heard much talk about a similar situation arising in the event of a possible future pole shift following in the wake of, or being triggered by either the greenhouse effect or the intrusion of some external cosmic body. However, I have to confess to being somewhat sceptical as far as this kind of scenario is concerned. On the subject the Dogons, I shall have much to say in Chapter 5.

The Tutsis may well have been the enigmatic Garamantes of the Oasis of Djerma in the Fezzan, about whose exploits Herodotus wrote in 450 BC, and whom modern scholars would no doubt equate with the Tuaregs. Herodotus claimed to have it on the authority of the Egyptian priests 'that the black dove and oracular oak cults of Zeus at Ammon in the Libyan desert and of Zeus at Dodona were coeval.' '... The Ammon oak was in the care of the tribe of Garamantes' who claimed their ancestor to have been 'the first of men'. It has been suggested to me that there is a similarity between the word Tutsi (Tootsie *sic*) and Watusi, the latter being a pastoral people, distinguished by their tall stature, who also hailed from Rwanda and Burundi. One cannot help wondering whether the sporadic violence between the two main ethnic groups in Rwanda, the Tutsi and the Hutu, which started around 1959 and recently reached genocidal proportions, can have any bearing on these traditions? Interestingly, I have always viewed 1960 as the year in which the Earth's descent into chaos received its first cosmic booster!

Temple affords a lot of credence to an article entitled 'A Sudanese Sirius System' by the French anthropologists Marcel Griaule and Germaine Dieterlen, which refers to the French Sudan area and not the Republic of Sudan over 1000 miles to the east, below Egypt. Griaule and Dieterlen wrote of four tribes, the Dogon and three related ones, who held as their most sacred religious teaching a body of knowledge concerning the Sirius system and the star Sirius.[4] One of these tribes was undoubtedly the Tootsie [sic] of our Egyptian friends, while the others could conceivably be the Bambara and Bozo.

I was particularly impressed by the prophecy at the end of the Egyptian letter: that the evil ones would eventually succumb to the Shining Ones, who are in hiding, whereupon a new age will dawn. It is not surprising to find the same belief among Dogon tradition – that their Siriun visitors will one day return – a 'certain star' will once more appear in the sky and will be a testament to the Nommo's resurrection.[5] Are we talking here about the Age of Aquarius? And if so, could these 'hidden Shining Ones' refer to some Siriun time-capsule? After all, Uranus, ruler of Aquarius, entered his own sign on 12 January 1996! Naturally, I will include further information from Egypt in this book as I receive it.

So, were the five Neters extraterrestrials from Sirius, royalty from Atlantis – or simply apologues of cosmic overshadowing? Neither, it would seem, since, according to Budge, they were not all born on the same day, the order in which they arrived carrying considerable significance (see also p. 153). But more of this in Chapter 9. However, there is a specific reference in the *Hermes Trismegistus* which might serve to throw some light on this somewhat doubtful area of enquiry. In *The Virgin of the World*, in which Isis (or her representative Teacher) engages in the instruction of Horus (the student or neophyte?), the text runs as follows:

Thus spake the Elements; and God, fulfilling all things with the sound of His [most] holy Voice, spake thus:

'Depart, ye Holy Ones, ye Children worthy of a mighty Sire, nor yet in any way attempt to innovate, nor leave the whole of [this] My World without your active service.

'For now another Efflux of my Nature is among you, and he shall be a pious supervisor of all deeds – judge incorruptible of living men and monarch absolute of those beneath the earth, not only striking terror [into] them but taking vengeance on them. And by his class of birth the fate he hath deserved shall follow every man.'

And so the Elements did cease from their complaint, upon the Master's order, and they held their peace; and each of them continued in the exercise of his authority and in his rule.

And Horus thereon said:

'How was it, mother, then, that Earth received God's Efflux?'

And Isis said:

'I may not tell thee the story of [this] birth; for it is not permitted to describe the origin of thy descent, O Horus [son] of mighty power, lest afterwards the way-of-birth of the immortal Gods should be known unto men – except so far that God the Monarch, the Universal Orderer and Architect, sent for a little while thy mighty sire Osiris, and the mightiest Goddess Isis, that they might help the world, for all things needed them.

''Tis they who filled life full of life. 'Tis they who cause the savagery of mutual slaughtering of men to cease. 'Tis they who hallowed precincts to the Gods their ancestors and spots for holy rites. 'Tis they who gave to men laws, food, and shelter.

''Tis they who will, says Hermes, learn to know the secrets of my records all, and will make separation of them; and some they will keep for themselves, while those that are best suited for the benefit of mortal men, they will engrave on tablet and on obelisk.

''Tis they who were the first to set up courts of law; and filled the world with justice and fair rule. 'Tis they who were the authors of good pledges and of faith, and brought the mighty witness of an oath into men's lives.

''Tis they who taught men how to wrap up those who ceased to live, as they should be.

''Tis they who searched into the cruelty of death, and learned that though the spirit which goes out longs to return into men's bodies, yet if it ever fail to have the power of getting back again, then loss of life results.

''Tis they who learned from Hermes that surrounding space was filled with daimons, and graved on hidden stones [the hidden teaching].

''Tis they alone who, taught by Hermes in God's hidden codes, became the authors of the arts, and sciences, and all pursuits which men do practise, and givers of their laws.

''Tis they who, taught by Hermes that the things below have been disposed by God to be in sympathy with things above, established on the earth the sacred rites o'er which the mysteries in Heaven preside.

''Tis they who, knowing the destructibility of [mortal] frames, devised the grade of prophets, in all things perfected, in order that no prophet who stretched forth his hands unto the Gods should be in ignorance of anything, that magic and philosophy should feed the soul, and medicine preserve the body when it suffered pain.

'And having done all this, my son, Osiris and myself perceiving that the world was [now] quite full, were thereupon demanded back by those who dwell in Heaven, but could not go above until we had made appeal unto the Monarch, that surrounding space might with this knowledge of the soul be filled as well, and we ourselves succeed in making our ascent acceptable [to Him]...'[6]

An ascent of the body in a starship, or of a soul via the agency of death – to which does the text refer? Perhaps Thoth, the Lord of Time, in his wisdom, may one day see fit to enlighten us. The word 'daimons' refers to orders of spirits, such as those of the devic kingdoms, the Elements, and such intelligences which are the directive 'minds' behind all atomic and molecular structures, and not to the evil entities of popular world religions.

Whatever they were, or wherever they came from, Isis, Osiris and their kin certainly arrived with good intent and a teaching of Light. From Sirius or Atlantis we cannot say with certainty, but we can take a look at the fate which, according to the myths, later overtook this hapless family after they reached Egyptian soil, assuming they were Earth hominids rather than divine beings or Siriuns. Perhaps the legends may serve to apprise us further.

Queen Isis, we are told, was a great ruler in her own right. No mere consort she, but a magician of considerable skill who taught men to grow corn, make cloth and garb themselves. She instituted marriage and instructed her people in the art of healing. Those of scholarly inclination will no doubt have re-course to Plutarch for the finer details, but here is the essence of the tale:

Osiris and his sister/wife Isis, ruled over the lands later called Egypt, although no one knows for sure whether their kingdom was an earthly one or whether their story and deeds related to some more elevated realm. The myth tells us that they were divinities from heaven (Star People?) who had descended to Earth to assist in the development of mankind. Osiris had a brother named Set (Typhon) and the two brothers dwelt amicably in Abydos with their wives, Isis and Nephthys, who were also sisters. Osiris was a gentle king, much loved by the people having taught them the arts of civilisation and promoted piety, gentleness, good health and well-being amongst them.

While travelling to visit southeast Asia (India, according to some authorities) with his wife, Osiris was suddenly summoned by his brother to return. Set was, unknown to Osiris, extremely jealous of his brother's popularity and had conspired with seventy-two others (that number seventy-two again!) to arrange a banquet to celebrate the king's homecoming. As part of the entertainment a strange box was introduced, and one after the other the guests were invited to try it for size. Only Osiris was able to slide comfortably inside, however, whereupon the conspirators shut and sealed the lid. We are told that Osiris entered the box (or tomb?) on 7 Athyr (13 November), the very day and month when Noah was purported to have entered the biblical ark! The box was then thrown into the Nile, or the sea, and carried onwards by the current until it was eventually caught up in a tamarisk tree. (Could this be another version of the Flood myth?)

Isis, who had been visiting Chemnis, received news of what had happened. Accompanied by Nephthys' son, Anubis, she set out to search for her husband's body. She located the tree, but it was guarded by a magical power which prevented her from approaching it. As she anxiously watched, the King of Byblos came looking for a tree to serve as a column for his palace, and much to the dismay of Isis he chose the very one that held her husband's body. Using her magical powers, Isis changed herself into a dove and uttered plaintive cries to dissuade the men from cutting it down, but to no avail. So she resumed her mortal appearance and offered herself at the palace as a nurse to the queen's child. Once near the tree she was able to neutralise the evil magic of Set and gain possession of the box.

But her troubles were far from over, for Set heard about her deeds and artfully contrived to steal the box as she slept. To ensure that Isis should never again find her husband, Set cut the body of Osiris into fourteen pieces, which he dispersed in various places. Isis, however, was not deterred. Joined by her sister Nephthys, who had abandoned her husband as a result of his dastardly deed, her nephew Anubis, and their uncle Thoth, Isis travelled far and wide until she had located every piece of the body except the phallus, which had been irreverently devoured by an oxyrhinchid (or some say a spider). Isis, therefore, fashioned a wooden facsimile of the missing member, pieced the body together, and brought it to Abydos for burial. Together with Nephthys, Anubis and Thoth, Isis wept bitterly over her husband's remains and chanted magically. Thoth also made the full force of his magical powers available to her, and Osiris was temporarily restored to life so that Horus could be conceived. Osiris then ascended into heaven and continued to watch over Isis while she bore his son.

According to another version, Osiris remained in the box in the tamarisk tree for three days and three nights, but on the third day he rose and ascended into heaven at the time corresponding to the feast of Christmas. The lowest point of the sun at the winter solstice on 22 December was believed to coincide with the death of Osiris, his resurrection or rebirth becoming a reality three days later, on the 25 December. In this version of the tale, Isis is the virgin mother to Horus, the spirit of Osiris having effected the conception from 'on high'.

A third legend tells how Horus was conceived by Isis and Osiris while they themselves were still in the womb of their mother, Nut (the sky). When Thoth was able to arrange for their birth on the five intercalary days, the five children born to Geb and Nut were Isis, Osiris, Nephthys, Set, and Horus. Some authorities opine that the Horus referred to in this story was either an earlier deity upon whom the name was later bestowed, or one of the other gods – Sekhmet or Hathor, perhaps, or even Thoth or Anubis. No doubt 'ET' buffs will delight in this latter version, the idea of Horus being conceived while on a journey to Earth from Sirius providing them with an interesting alternative to the usual explanations of this tantalising myth.

Another point that is often raised by esotericists is, if these Neters were actual people and not beings from the stars, gods or such, how is it that their energies have persisted over the centuries? And why is it that invocations or rites offered to them actually work? We are back to the 'aspects of the self' concept. Of course, there are god-energies within us – after all, as children of the universe, we resonate to the innumerable aspects of the forces of creation, and since we are 'gods in the making' who are, at this moment in time, limited by both our somatic and spiritual development, one or two of these god-energies are likely to feature more prominently in our psychology than others. Jung called them archetypes, different archetypal energies tending to play different roles in our lives as necessity demands. However, such archetypal essences may well be individually manifested in some parallel, complementary universe, wherein they may be addressed for guidance and help. It is rather like the questionable idea that everyone who prays for help or guidance, or who claims communication with the subtle dimensions, is automatically contacting his or her own 'higher self'. Logic demands that one poses the questions: are these higher selves islands unto themselves; do they not communicate amongst each other? Isis, Osiris, Horus, Sekhmet, may well have been incarnate beings in the past, whether from Atlantis or Sirius, but *these people carried the embodiment of certain principles that are important to the evolution of mankind and all other life forms on this planet.* In invoking them we stimulate the Isis, Osiris or Horus aspects within ourselves, which serve to resonate with the original source of that archetypal energy, so both schools of belief contain more than a grain of truth.

To return to our Isian family: the saga continues that following her husband's ascent to more exalted realms, the evil Set, realising that the child Horus was to be the avenger of Osiris, resolved to destroy them both. However, being skilled in matters magical, Isis was able to use her powers to avoid her pursuers. In a lonely place where no one would find her, and assisted only by animals and nature spirits, Isis brought forth her son, who was sickly in his early years, but later grew to great strength and comeliness. Upon reaching manhood Horus went forth to settle his father's debt with Set, much as the heroes of myth and fairy-tale have done since man first mastered the art of story-telling. The legend tells us that a great battle was fought in which Set used every conceivable diabolical weapon, whereas Horus fought fairly and wisely. The contest was judged by Thoth, Lord of Time, and Horus carried off the laurels. Set was banished for a period which the gods judged to be long enough for him to repent the error of his ways. Horus offered the crown to Isis, but she declined his invitation and chose to place her son in the seat of rulership. She then ascended to heaven to join her husband.

The ancient Egyptians feared Set in spite of Horus' victory, so what is this strange tale actually telling us? Many years of research have convinced me that the Isis/Osiris story did not occur in the past, but *has been re-enacted over the centuries since the advent of the five epagomenal days.* In other words, we are part of it and will be until the return of Horus, when our planet is restored to its original position in relation to the sun! The long sojourn Isis underwent in the wilderness, trying to raise her sickly child against all odds, covers the centuries since the mythical 'Fall', when disease, suffering, ignorance and disorder have ruled our planet. Isis (the gentle feminine principle) wanders hungry and homeless, trying to raise her child who is destined to restore the order represented by her husband, Osiris, to a suffering world.

This tale is re-echoed meaningfully in the Gnostic myth of the Sophia (Wisdom), the feminine aspect or anima of the Divine Christos, who descended to the 'lower realms' (Earth) in order to help mankind, but became imprisoned therein by Ildabaoth (Chaos). But take heart, dear readers. The Aquarian Age is believed by many to be the Aeon of Horus, during which the pendulum will once again swing from chaos to order. Set's banishment, mentioned in several versions of the myth as being between 1000 and 10,000 years, therefore represents a time in the history of our planet when order will replace chaos among the nations of the world, and within the hearts of humankind. An ancient Greek legend tells of how the world changes its axial position every 10,000 years. Chaos science confirms that swings between order and disorder occur at regular intervals, and frequently take place in most unexpected ways that would appear to defy all the known laws of physics.

Horus is reminiscent of the archetypal character of the young, handsome prince in a children's story who is cheated of his inheritance by his parent's enemies and forced to regain his kingdom through his own wisdom and prowess. He is raised among ordinary folk of humble origin, has no cultural or educational advantages, and is aided in his quest through gaining an understanding of their feelings, sufferings and skills. When he is deemed ready, he sallies forth and rights the wrongs of the past, frees the oppressed, and restores peace, order and harmony to the land. In other words, he banishes chaos. Bonwick reminds us that the gentle, feminine side of Horus' character is marked in the Tentyra planisphere, as the lion with a virgin's face, which might also infer an association with the zodiacal sign of Virgo. According to the late Alan Leo, all the saviours of the world were born with the sun in this sign, and science has recently confirmed that Jeshua, known as The Christ, was born on 15th September in the year 7 BC. However, correcting the error would mean withdrawing the Roman calendar and 1996 would become 2003. One of the researchers, David Hughes, an astronomer at Sheffield University, examined contemporary astronomical records and pin-pointed the Star of Bethlehem to the rare conjunction of Jupiter and Saturn in Pisces in 7 BC. That fits the historical records. One reason that Joseph and Mary left for Nazareth was to pay the tax which was levied by the Romans in 8 BC. In Siriun terms, however, the combination of lion and virgin are highly significant, as we shall later see.

The character of Osiris appears to convey a priestly rather than a kingly quality. Dr M. Esther Harding, writing in *Woman's Mysteries*, sees him as a moon god, in keeping with the Thoth/Khonsu tradition prevalent among Egyptian male deities who appear in the company of dominant or magically gifted goddesses. The fact that he was frequently portrayed with a greenish face or skin has resulted in some scholars placing him in the fertility context. Sir James Frazer, for example, viewed Osiris in terms of a primitive corn-god or god of crop fertility, and opined that the story of his resurrection was intimately connected with the annual revival of vegetation, from which the Egyptians derived their own hope of life after death. Views have changed over the years, however, and more recently, W. B. Emery stated that the Osirian cult, 'although having characteristics of nature worship, was primarily the worship of dead kingship, and the myth of Osiris seems to be an echo of long-forgotten events which actually took place.'[7] The Element of Water, which is essentially passive, would also seem to feature strongly in the Osirian archetype, ancient illustrations frequently portraying the Neter seated on a throne surrounded by water, from which stems a sacred lotus in which the Four Sons of Horus (four Elements or points of the compass) are standing, (See *Fig 4.3* also Chapter 12.)

Many of these early-Egyptian creation-divinity myths could also be seen in the atomic context in the fusion sequence from hydrogen via helium, and finally to the carbon which constitutes the principal molecular structure of our planet. The significance of sound or sonics is also present in the Isian myth. According to one legend, Isis obtained her magical powers from Ra rather than Thoth. The old god was bitten by a venomous snake which Isis herself was supposed to have conjured up. Failing to understand the origin of his affliction, Ra sought the help of Isis, who refused to heal the old god until he revealed his secret name, thus passing his power to her, after which he went into decline. Seen in the Sirius context, this suggests that Isis, as representing Sirius A – the large, blue-white star we see in our night sky – inherited the knowledge or energies of her binary companion, Sirius B, originally a yellow star similar to our own sun before its collapse.

Nephthys is sometimes seen as the hidden aspect of her sister, Isis, whereas she is, in fact, a goddess in her own right. Her archetype is essentially concerned with the deep unconscious, the contents of which are seldom revealed to the conscious self. On such occasions as this does occur, however, the effects can be extremely traumatic. Nephthys is both the Concealer and the Revealer, indicating that for the uninitiated those things that cannot be handled are best left concealed, whereas the Initiate must invoke her powers of revelation before he or she can pass beyond a certain point along the Path of Inner Knowledge. Her purported 'marriage' to Set, Lord of Chaos, further enlightens us as to the ancient Egyptians' cognizance of the human psychological condition and its resonating cosmological principles. The hidden aspects to which her archetype relates often involve the shadow or id – that aspect of the self which must eventually be

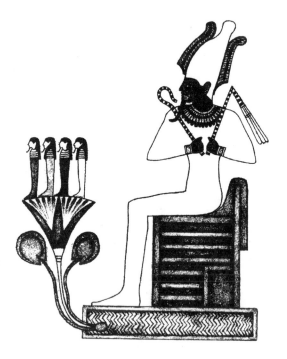

Fig. 4.3 The Throne of Osiris and the Four Sons of Horus.

faced and conquered if we are to master chaos and enjoy the fruits of the stability accorded by such a victory.

Seen in the psychological context Set is an interesting character, since many ancient philosophies and now science, it seems, deem that the universe is ever poised between the extremes of chaos and order, the manipulation or mastery of one being essential to the progress and stability afforded by the other. The fact that Set, representing the chaotic mode, was included among the five Siriun Neters is highly significant. To me it suggests that true knowledge must always accommodate freewill, and while that freedom of choice may furnish the building blocks for evolutionary progress both somatic and spiritual, it can also provide the tools of destruction. Those tools may manifest in a collective fashion via the technology, religion, psychology and politics of the age, or subjectively through the shadow, id, or lower nature of the individual.

The ancient Egyptians (and their Atlantean teachers) were well aware of these facts. To ensure the continuiy of this knowledge, they encoded it within cryptic parables for us to decipher in years to come. They were also cognisant of the fear that would overtake us when we finally resolved these enigmas, so they ensured that we were acquainted with the happy ending which will inevitably follow the initial suffering caused by the violence of the swing. One is sometimes tempted to question whether each of the five epagomenal Neters were, in truth, the conveyors of Siriun energies, since Osiris is frequently mentioned as connected with Orion while Set has ancient associations with the constellation of the Bear. Perhaps the fact that they are lumped together as a family unit should be taken more in the galactic sense and not as Siriun gospel. Then, as I explained earlier, there is also the question of their birth on different days. (See Chapter 9).

In the myths, most of Set's activities were connected with his implacable hostility towards Osiris and Horus, the spirits of fertility and order. In the legend of Set's inevitable defeat by Horus we are told that Horus employed the office of the law, whereas Set replied with trickery, subterfuge and brute force. Therein lies a wisdom teaching which implies that as humankind evolves spiritually, law and order – of the cosmic sort of course – must eventually triumph over chaos and brutality. The Horus-Set confrontation is re-echoed in the myths of many ensuing cultures:

Apollo and Python in Greece, Mikaal and Lucifer of the Bible, and St George and the Dragon in British folklore being examples, although some feminist and goddess-orientated writers have tended to see these allegories in terms of the male principle overcoming the old goddess worship that predominated during the matriarchal Silver Years.

The Neters were often associated with certain colours. Set's was bright red, a shade abhored by the ancient Egyptians on account of its association with their Evil One who, according to legend, had bright red hair! For those interested, I have supplied full details of the magical colours, attributes and spiritual hieroglyphics of the main Egyptian gods in my books *The Way of Cartouche* and *Practical Egyptian Magic*.

Sirius having featured so strongly in the teachings and beliefs of the archaic past, this seems as good a point as any to subject the binary system to more detailed scrutiny in the light of modern knowledge. And since the information to hand is nothing if not extensive, it is deserving of a chapter to itself.

Endnotes:

1 R. A. Schwaller de Lubicz, *Sacred Science*, page 27.
2 Ibid., pages 174–7.
3 R. K. G. Temple, *The Sirius Mystery*, pages 194–5.
4 Ibid., page 18. 5. Ibid., page 32
6 G. R. S. Mead, *Thrice Greatest Hermes*, Vol. 3, pages 121–3.
7 W. B. Emery, *Archaic Egypt*, page 122.

CHAPTER 5

Sirius – the Binary Star

Sirius, in the constellation of Canis Major, is one of the brightest stars in our night sky, and being only eight-and-a-half light years from the Earth also means it is one of our nearest neighbours. Around the middle of the last century the astronomer Bessel studied Sirius over a period of time and noted a perturbation in its movements, indicative of the presence of another body close enough to effect a gravitational pull of some considerable force. Yet, due to its extreme brightness, Bessel could find no trace of a mass large enough to affect a star of this size. Some years later, a very small white dwarf star was discovered circling Sirius, the orbital period of which was calculated to be around fifty Earth years. (Technically speaking, Sirius B does not orbit Sirius A, *per se*, rather both stars orbit a common centre of gravity.) This second star, lost in the glare of its companion, became known as Sirius B, sometimes called Digitaria, and has since been photographed.

Astronomers have now learned more about the nature of white dwarfs – stars that do not give out much light, but exert an enormous gravitational pull because of the extreme density of their atomic structure. A white dwarf is a star that has used up its lighter hydrogen and helium atomic fuel and has collapsed, which means that the remaining elements have become so densely packed that the nature of its substance hardly equates to matter as we know it. When atoms are compressed to such an extent the resulting mass becomes extremely heavy. Temple tells us that a cubic foot of the surface of Sirius B would weigh 2000 tons, and a matchbox filled with the star's core material would weigh approximately fifty tons!

Some astronomers believe they have detected a third star in the Sirius system. A man named Fox claimed to have seen it in 1920; and again in 1926, 1928 and 1929 it was supposedly seen by Drs van den Bos, Finsen and others at the Union Observatory. Then, suddenly, the elusive star disappeared! More recently, Irving W. Lindenblad, of the US Naval Observatory in Washington, probed the Sirius system. He failed to detect a third star, although he gleaned much additional information about Sirius B in the process.

In his controversial book, *The Sirius Mystery*, Temple postulated that beings from the Sirius system visited Earth many thousands of years ago and were partly (if not entirely) responsible for the leap from primitivity to the high standard of culture and civilisation achieved by the ancient Egyptians between the years 4500 BC and 3400 BC. His hypothesis was based in part on knowledge of the Sirius system possessed by the Dogons, an African people who live in Mali (the former French Sudan). These people he believes to be the direct descendants of those pre-dynastic Egyptians who could have witnessed the arrival here on Earth of aliens from the Sirius system, their information dating back to those early days when their ancestors received it directly from their galactic visitors. In what other way, he questions, could they have gained knowledge of the existence of the invisible Digitaria or the other astronomical details they apparently have possessed for centuries concerning this distant system? In the light of the information contained in the letter received from my Egyptian contacts, who, incidentally, had never heard of Temple or his book, his conjectures would appear to have a ring of authenticity about them. What a pity he did not come across the Tutsi data, it would certainly have helped him to tie up a few loose ends.

The whole of the Dogon religion and its accompanying rites are built around the concept of the Sirius system. The Dogons considered Digitaria to be of greater significance than its larger and brighter companion, even though it was not visible to them. They also possessed knowledge of a third luminary which they called Sorghum-Female, *emme ya* the 'sun of women', the 'little sun' (which Temple has designated as Sirius C), which is accompanied by a satellite planet they call the 'star of women'.

Sorghum-Female they believed to be larger than Digitaria and four times lighter in weight. To them it was the seat of the female souls of all living and future beings. This star of women is represented by an equidistant cross and outlined by three points, a male symbol of authority, surrounded by seven dots, or four (female) plus three (male) which are seen as the female and male soul. The Sorghum-Female system is therefore shown as in *Fig. 5.1*. The Dogon *bado* rite, a tribal ritual which honours the one-year axial rotation of the star Digitaria (Sirius B), also contains a reference to 'the pattern of the star of the master of the Shoemaker', which Temple tells us is:

> ... composed of a vertical axis supporting, two-thirds of the way up, a bulge, Sirius (S), and broken at its base to form an elongated foot jutting to the left at right angles, the course of the star of the Shoemaker (C). It is topped by a semi-oval whose arms extend quite low down; the meeting point (D) with this oval symbolizes Digitaria,

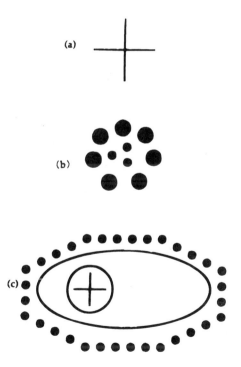

Fig. 5.1 (a) The star of women. (b) The star Sorghum-Female. (c) The Sorghum Female system.

whose course is traced by the right arm (F). But this arm is also the star of women whilst the left-arm is Sorghum-Female (E) The lower part of the axis (SC), longer than the upper part (SD) reminds one that the Shoemaker (C) is farther than Sirius is from the other stars, and revolves in the opposite direction.

I find this reference to the 'Shoemaker' somewhat confusing, since Temple fails to qualify it further and it is not referenced in his index. There would appear to be some information that is either missing, or has become lost in translation, and interested readers are therefore referred to the original work. (See *Fig. 5.2*).

Sirius, the Dogons believe, was simply a companion star to the essentially 'male' dwarf star, the orbit of which they depicted as elliptical. The fact that they had no access to the theories of Kepler struck Temple as significant. Furthermore, the Dogons reckoned the orbiting period of Sirius B around Sirius A to be fifty years, which has again been proven to be accurate by modern scientific calculations, the number 50 assuming a significant

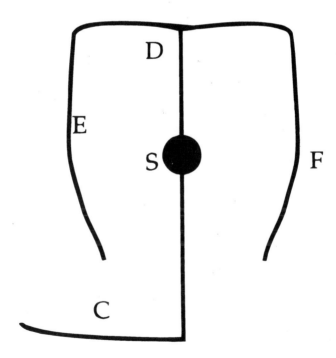

Fig. 5.2 The course of the stars of the Sirius system.

role in their sacred rites. They were also aware of the massive weight of Sirius B long before astrophysicists had postulated the nature and existence of collapsed or dwarf stars.

Another interesting factor involved in Dogon beliefs concerning Sirius is to be found in the nature and meaning of their Siriun Rite, summarised in the following Dogon statement, which re-echoes the soul's eternal search for its twin on the one hand, and man's continual quest for individuation (the uniting of the anima and animus) in the pursuit of true knowledge, wisdom and perfection on the other. The deeper, obvious alchemical inferences here speak for the wisdom of the originators of the rite and its accompanying metaphysical philosophy, while its similarity to certain teachings in the Gnostic *Pistis Sophia* cannot be ignored:

> Digitaria, as the egg of the world … was split into two twin placentas which were to give birth respectively to a pair of Nommo In-structors. What happened, however, was that a single male being emerged from one of the placentas; in order to find his twin, this being tore [*sic*] off a piece of this placenta, which became earth. This intervention upset the order of creation: he was transformed into an animal, the pale fox, *yuruga*, and communicated his own impurity to the earth, which rendered it dry and barren. But the remedy to his situation was the sacrifice, to the sky, of one of the Nommo In-structors which had issued from the other placenta, and the descent of his twin to earth with life-giving, purifying rain. The destiny of Yourougou is to pursue his twin to the end of time – the twin being his female soul at the same time. On the mythical level, Digitaria is thus considered to be Yourougou held in space by Nommo, relent-lessly revolving around Sirius, or Yasigui in other words, and never capable of reaching it.[2]

Interestingly, the number 50 also receives emphasis in many other seemingly unrelated beliefs and magical systems that follow throughout the pages of history. In the Sumero-Akkadian mythology, the fifty Anunnaki or 'great gods' being the sons of An or Anu, who were usually anonymous, the emphasis being on their number, and their influence over the lives of all living things. Temple alludes to the constellation Argo, as represented by both Jason's ship and its fifty Argonauts, as well as Noah's ark. Jason's *Argo* carried Danaos and his fifty daughters from Egypt to Rhodes, and Temple quotes Richard Hinckley Allen as stating: 'The Egyptian story said that it was the ark that bore Isis and Osiris over the Deluge, while the Hindu's thought it was the ark that performed the same office for their equivalent Isi and Iswara.'[3] Iswara is referred to in modern scholarship as 'Ishvara' which incorporates the Sanskrit word *ishu* – an arrow. Bow and arrow symbols frequently appear in connection with both Sirius and Orion in other mythologies besides the Egyptian, notably the Chinese.

Seven having ever been a sacred number, seven times seven (fortynine) therefore assumed a special significance which rendered every fiftieth day as one of great magical or esoteric import. The Essenes, for example, followed this numerological system, and their Christo-Gnostic association is one which I have taught in seminars and lectures over many years. Suffice it to say, however, that Jeshua (Jesus, later known as the Christ), who is reputed to have been steeped in the inner teachings of the Essenes and Therapeuts, must have had access to this information, and were it not for those Gnostic fragments that have survived the persecutions of the ages we might never have had an inkling that he was familiar with such knowledge. After all, the word 'Pentecost' means 'fiftieth' – the fiftieth day after the Feast of the Passover!

The Egyptians and Dogons were by no means the only races to accord special powers to Sirius. Another African tribe, the Bambara, called it 'the star of foundation' *sigo dolo*, which is the same term used by the Dogon, while like the Dogon they also referred to the companion star (Sirius B or Digitaria) as *fin dolo.* Jointly the two stars were called *fâ dolo fla* (the two stars of knowledge) because 'it represents in the sky the invisible body of Faro' conceived as a pair of twins – the implication being that the star is the seat of all learning. According to Bambara legend, Sirius was Mousso Koroni Koundye, whose twin, Pemba, maker of the earth, was a mythical woman whom he continually chased through space, but never managed to catch. This renders Mousso Koroni Koundye comparable to the Dogon Yasigui. Both of these female characters are said to have inaugurated circumcision and excision, as a result of which Sirius is known to both the Bambara and the Dogon as the 'star of circumcision'. The Bozo, were also familiar with the system. They called Sirius *sima kayne* (literally: Sitting Trouser), and its satellite *toñõ ñalema* (Eye Star). Can we possibly effect a connection here between this

Eye Star and the fabled Eye of Ra which was passed between the Egyptian deities Hathor, Bast and Sekhmet?

Among other knowledge comparable with modern astrology and astronomy, the Dogon were aware of the four major moons of Jupiter, which they named *dana tolo unum* (children of *dana tolo* – Jupiter), and the rings of Saturn, which are only visible through a telescope. Saturn, which they associated strongly with the Milky Way, they called 'the star of limiting the place': how astrologically appropriate! These are but snippets of the vast astronomical knowledge possessed by these people, which they insist they received from their Siriun visitors centuries ago. They also possessed a clear knowledge of the human circulatory system and the existence of life in other parts of the universe. According to their tradition, there were many populated 'stars' and the intelligent life-forms living thereon were not always hominids. They say that humankind (as we know it) lives on the Fourth Earth, but on the Third Earth there were 'men with horns', *inneu gammurugu* (satyrs?); on the Fifth Earth 'men with tails', *inneu dullogu* (feline people?); and on the Sixth Earth 'men with wings', *inneu bummo*. All this information, they claim, was given to them by beings of superior intelligence (gods), who arrived on Earth from the Sirius system back in the mists of time.[4]

A vestige of seemingly corresponding information found its way into the Hermes Trismegistus, probably via ancient Egyptian sources since there are slight variations in the version, appearing in Vol. 3 of the G. R. S. Mead translation, under the *The Virgin of the World* material, which takes the form of a series of instructions from Isis to her son Horus (The initiated priestess of the goddess to her pupil?). The text runs thus:

> The difference in your rebirths, accordingly, for you, shall be as I have said, a difference of bodies, and their [final] dissolution [shall be] a benefit and a [return to] the fair happiness of former days. ...
>
> But the more righteous of you, who stand upon the threshold of the change to the diviner state, shall among men be righteous kings, and genuine philosophers, founders of states, and lawgivers, and real seers, and true herb-knowers, and prophets of the Gods most excellent, skilful musicians, skilled astronomers, and augurs wise. ...
>
> Among winged tribes [they shall be] eagles, for these will neither scare away their kind nor feed on them; nay more, when they are by, no other weaker beast will be allowed by them to suffer wrong, for what will be the eagles' nature is too just [to suffer it].

> Among four-footed things [they will be] lions, – a life of strength and of a kind which in a measure needs no sleep, in mortal body practising the exercises of immortal life – for they nor weary grow nor sleep.
>
> And among creeping things [they will be] dragons, in that this animal will have great strength and live for long, will do no harm, and in a way be friends with man, and let itself be tamed; it will possess no poison and will cast its skin, as is the nature of the Gods.
>
> Among the things that swim [they will be] dolphins; for dolphins will take pity upon those who fall into the sea, and if they are still breathing bear them to the land, while if they're dead they will not even touch them, though they will be the most voracious tribe that in the water dwells.[5]

Although both this and the Nommo statement could be seen as referring to the most evolved animal species on this planet, I am inclined to think that both relate to life-forms external to Earth, which provide advanced schooling for highly evolved souls who have learned as much as they can from exposure to the hominid experience provided by this planet. The allusion to both dragons and lions could be seen to have Siriun connotations, since the former obviously refers to the lizard family rather than the dragons of popular fairy-tale myth. All the traditional archetypal *dramatis personae* are present in Nommo mythology: the god (Nommo) who will be sacrificed for the purification and reorganisation of the universe:

> He will rise in human form and descend on Earth, in an ark, with the ancestors of men ... then he will take on his original form, will rule from the waters and will give birth to many descendants. ... The Nommo divided his body among men to feed them: that is why it is said that as the universe 'had drunk of his body' the Nommo also made men drink. ... He was crucified on a *kilena* tree which [sic] also died and was resurrected.[6]

Then we have Ogo, the chaotic disrupter; as he was about to be finished (being created) he rebelled against his creator and introduced disorder into the universe. Eventually he will become 'the Pale Fox' *(le renard pâle)*, which is the image of his fall. The planet in the Sirius system from which the Nommo collectively issued was said to be 'pure', as against our own solar system which is, according to Dogon teachings, decidedly 'impure', being referred to as the placenta of the evil Ogo. Our own planet Earth is, significantly: 'the place where Ogo's umbilical cord was attached to his placenta. ...'[7]

I find it fascinating that these simple African tribes should have sustained such a profound and accurate cosmic teaching for so many centuries, and one cannot help but view them, along with those mystically erudite Egyptian souls who were generous enough to trust me with the teachings of their inner traditions, as the worthy custodians of the Light and knowledge of the stars. Needless to say orthodox astronomers tend to view all this with considerable scepticism, although they would appear to be at a loss to explain how the Dogons obtained this knowledge.

There would seem to be little difference between these accounts of Siriun landings and the information these gentle visitors bestowed upon their hosts. The fact that they left a sense of love and a yearning for their return may be taken as evidence of their kindness, generosity and cosmic maturity. The Dogon Ogo and the Egyptian Set have much in common, while Yourougou's eternal search for his anima re-echoes both the Isis-Osiris tale and that of the Gnostic Christos and Sophia.

Sirius A has always been associated with Isis, and Dogon information would seem to confirm the feminine nature of this beautiful blue-white star. Osiris could therefore be seen as Sirius B. Could the Isis/Osiris legend be describing a series of actual events that took place in the Sirius system prior to the collapse of the Osirian or Sirius B star, and how does the third star feature in this saga?

Sirius C is sometimes linked with Nephthys, the hidden one, or her son Anubis, while Temple theorises that the three Siriun stars might possibly be equated with the three Egyptian goddesses Isis, Anukis and Satis, and quotes Neugebauer as stating specifically: 'The goddess Satis who, like her companion Anukis, is hardly to be taken as a separate constellation but rather as an associate of Sothis' (Sirius).[8] Anukis and Satis, the wives of Khnum, were frequently portrayed together with Sothis sailing in the same celestial barque. There is a theory popular in Europe that when Set usurped the Osirian throne and banished Isis and her baby son, Horus, the wilderness to which they were sent refers to a planet of harsh environment *outside of the Siriun system*, Earth, for instance, during an earlier stage of its development; and since, both metaphysically speaking and as embraced by the scientific concept of non-locality, all time is one, Isis is still with us, albeit unrecognised and rejected (the feminine principle in a male-orientated world!), endeavouring to raise her son,

Horus (the knowledge, beauty and wisdom of the Aquarian Age?). It bears consideration.

General opinion tending to consider Sirius A as carrying feminine energies, Sirius B as masculine, and Sirius C or Sorghum-Female, (if indeed the latter is a star and not a large planet), also in the feminine context, the inference would be that the feminine influence predominates in this system. Following through the idea that our solar system was seeded from Sirius, this would surely be a point in favour of the Great Mother or Creatrix principle rather than the masculine father-god so beloved of certain popular religions. I was interested to note Bauval and Gilbert's accociation of Osiris with Orion or Sah, the Sahu being considered the most elevated of the subtle 'bodies' which I chose to allot to Osiris (see *The Way of Cartouche*). In metaphysical terms, to become 'Osirified', indicated that the soul had attained to some exalted position in the spiritual hierarchy. My Egyptian contacts also informed me that according to their ancient beliefs not everyone has a BA or soul – the 'subtle vehicle' necessary to the ascent to the next stage of spiritual development. This has to be earned over many lifetimes. So until this has been achieved we are bound to the confines of the Earth. This equates with information of a paraphysical nature which I have recently covered in my book *Cosmic Connections*.

As Sirius was the most important star for the ancient Egyptians, the preceding four decans, which comprise the constellation of Orion also, as Bauval and Gilbert have suggested (see *The Orion Mystery*), assumed significance in their beliefs. The final portion of Orion rises above the horizon one 'hour' before Sirius, thus giving it the appearance of a kind of advanced guard. Sirius was known as Sept, *spd* or *spdt*, the 't' ending indicating the feminine, while the old name for Orion was Sah. Another interpretation is that the Isis/Osiris episode exemplifies a cosmological drama, with Isis (the Divine Mother) representing the Earth, being miraculously impregnated by the dead Osiris (Sirius seeding this solar system and our planet in particular) and giving birth to Horus (humankind) who is obliged to fight ill-health in youth (the learning of self-healing) before he is strong enough to overcome the evil of Set (his own lower nature, and other misplaced energies) and establish his father's kingdom on Earth (the spiritual maturity of *Homo sapiens*).

The now-spent Sirius B might well represent Egypt's Osiris, hence the association of that Neter with the dead, or those who have passed on to another, more subtle dimension. When a great star collapses (dies), the guiding Essence (deva) behind its growth and development ascends to a higher plane or moves to a time-zone nearer to the Centre or Creative Force. On the other hand, the same principle could be applied to Ra, whose energies were also withdrawn, which would equate Sekhmet, or one of the lion goddesses, with Sirius A.

One aspect of the Siriun question which does concern me is the description of these stellar visitors that have come down to us. The Dogons assure us that there are, in the universe, other advanced life-forms which do not resemble hominids, and yet their Teachers appear to have had certain hominid characteristics, albeit with a difference. Their Nommo visitors, however, who are referred to as amphibians who descended from the sky in an 'ark' seem to have had much in common with the Babylonian Oannes. Temple tells us:

> They are credited with having descended in an ark which, in landing, looked like figure 5.3 which portrays 'the spinning or whirling of the descent of the ark'. The god of the universe, Amma (whose name I feel certain is a survival of that of the god Ammon of the Oasis of Siwa), sent the amphibians to earth. They are called the Nommos. But just as the the Babylonians tended to speak of Oannes, the leader, instead of always saying 'the Annedoti' collectively, the Dogon often just speak of Nommo or 'the Nommo' as an individual. The Nommos are collectively called 'the Masters of Water', and also 'the Instructors' or 'the Monitors'. They have to live in water: 'The Nommo's seat is in the water.' The latter is much like the Babylonian tradition of their god Ea (Enki to the Sumerians), whose seat was also in the water, and who is sometimes connected with Oannes.[9]

May I refer to my earlier comment concerning the throne of Osiris that it is always shown 'in water'.

But were these Siriuns really fish-people, or was it their attire which tended to give them that appearance? The answer probably lies in Berossus' account of the Chaldean Creation myth, when he says of primitive men:

> At first they led a somewhat wretched existence and lived without rule after the manner of beasts. But, in the first year, appeared a

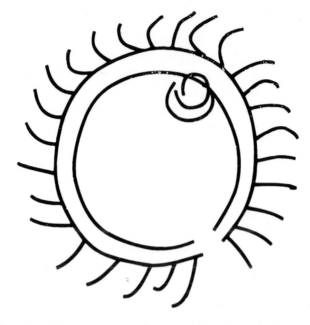

Fig. 5.3 (a) The whirling descent of the spaceship of Nommo. (Dogon drawing.)

Fig. 5.3 (b) Descent of Nommo from the sky. (Dogon drawing]

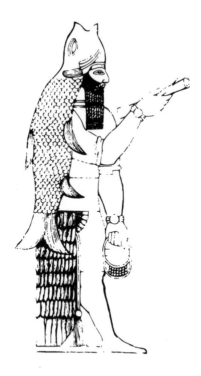

Fig. 5.4 The Babylonian water god, Oannes.

monster endowed with human reason, named Oannes, who rose from out of the Erythraean sea, at the point where it borders Babylonia. He had the whole body of a fish, but above his fish's head he had another head which was that of a man, and human feet emerged from beneath his fish's tail: he had a human voice, and his image is presened to this day.[10]

Could this not describe a person who was garbed in some form of protective suit and helmet or face mask? I am afraid the fish-man idea does little for my logic, and I am not even sure that I would consider Oannes in the extraterrestrial category. Of course, I could be wrong, but I see this being more as an Atlantean submariner, appropriately clad for his calling. The fact that his apparel was designed to appear like an aquatic creature was probably in keeping with the fashions of the day, just as we tend to design our protective clothing in accordance with the general fashions of the era in which we live. Berossus continues:

He passed the day in the midst of men without taking food; he taught them the use of letters, sciences and arts of all kinds, and rules for the founding of cities, and the construction of temples, the principles of the land and surveying; he showed them how to sow and reap; he gave them all that contributes to the comforts of life. Since that time nothing excellent has been invented.[11]

In spite of certain vague similarities between Oannes and the Dogon Nommos, the whole message is entirely different. Oannes was concerned with the kind of civilising influence that was the forerunner of today's world, whereas the Nommo teachers concentrated more on mystical and cosmological concerns – the universe *outside* of the planet Earth. These Nommo, it would seem, were not so much aquatics as people used to living in a somewhat moister atmosphere than that which existed here on Earth when they landed in those parts of Africa. The allusion to refusing food could be taken as an indication that the visitors were unaccustomed to the food they were offered by the natives.

There has been much psychic speculation as to what the people of Sirius do (or did) look like, and how many different races originally inhabited that neck of the galactic woods. I recently read an article in a popular magazine which designated two races, one hominid: 'Their colouring was, in the main, blond with lavender eyes …' and the other resembling some kind of animal. The writer suggested that Herne the Hunter may well have been their archetype.[12] Two main races I can accept, and the fair, blue or lavender-eyed people do not strain my credulity since they could easily equate with the Crystal People, the name that has been given to a very beautiful and highly advanced race of hominids, who are believed to have inhabited a planet in the Siriun system that is known to some psychics as Ishna or a similar sounding word. The name alludes to the terrain of their planet, which is said to be composed of a crystalline structure of great beauty, rather than to the people themselves. These 'Crystal People' or Ishnaans if you prefer, are seen as slight of build, with long, fair hair, slanted blue, green or yellow eyes, and golden complexions. Males and females there are, but each sex has the anima and animus so perfectly balanced that their similarity in physical appearance might well make it difficult for we earthlings to tell them apart. Their planetary neighbours, who later came to share their planet with them, are of a different species, their appearance being emphasised in the leonine statuary and art of ancient Egypt.

Ishna is presumed by some to exist in a different 'time-zone' or dimension from our own, one that could be equated with our future. However, until more concrete proof is available such 'beliefs' must be confined to the realms of conjecture, although according to a recent statement by that doyen of cosmology and theoretical physics, Professor Stephen Hawking, time travel now looms as a definite possibility so, the history of the Siriun system and its role in all of our lives, may well be substantiated during the forthcoming millennium.

After all, if we are to give any credence to our Egyptian friends, and the researches of Schwaller de Lubicz and other scholars of integrity *and sensitivity,* the Neters of the Age of Gemini, the twins Shu and Tefnut, were, as I have already mentioned, always portrayed as *a lion and a man.* In Egypt, the sun was always situated in the constellation of Leo at the date of the heliacal rising of Sirius. The Trismegistus tells us:

> And of the stars they consider Sirius to be Isis's – as being a water-bringer. And they honour the Lion, and ornament the doors of the temples with gaping lions' mouths; since Nilus overflows: *When the Sun doth with the Lion join.*[13] [Author's italics]

There is also a host more evidence, especially from Egyptian sources, to support the leonine idea, the greatest of which is possibly the Sphinx itself, whose head is human but whose body is leonine. Temple sees those 'moist regions' described in the Egyptian myths and normally associated with the Nile locale as relating to a planet in the Sirius system, a watery paradise, prolific in vegetation and containing a high moisture content both on its surface and in its atmosphere.

Until evidence of a more substantial nature is forthcoming one can only follow one's intuition in these matters, and my own tends to favour the fair people (Crystal People) and the leonids (Paschats), as the two main races of the Siriun star system, although I am given to understand that there were also some highly evolved forms of plant and amphibian life on the smaller planet believed to have orbited Sirius B which originally housed the leonids, so we may be talking about different planets and a different sun within the Siriun system (see my book *The Lion*

People). But at this point we must needs take care, as the fine line between logical speculation and fantasy can easily and sometimes unwittingly become crossed. Besides, we may well be dealing with different time references from those normally accepted by modern science as referring to the past or future. For example, since the leonid legend dates back to a time *prior to the collapse of Sirius B,* which would count in millions of years according to our concept of linear time, these beings might, now, be operating from the subtle dimensions as far as we are concerned, or existing in a universe parallel to the one we view through our telescopes. If all this strains the credulity somewhat, consider Professor Fred Hoyle's Panspermia Theory, which conceives of alien micro-organisms distributed throughout interstellar space, and penetrating the Earth's atmosphere. Hoyle's answer as to whether life originated on Earth would be a resounding 'No'![14]

As I have made an in-depth study of astrology, one of the questions I am frequently asked is: what effect does Sirius exert on a birth-chart, if any? The question of the influence of the fixed stars is adequately dealt with in several excellent books on the subject. My own reference is from Vivian Robson who says of Sirius:

> According to Ptolemy it is of the nature of Jupiter and Mars; and to Alvidas, of the Moon Jupiter and Mars. It gives honour, renown, wealth, ardour, faithfulness, devotion, passion and resentment, and makes its natives custodians, curators and guardians. ...[15]

Its magical seal is written thus   ⋈⠹⠼ , its stone is the beryl, its plants – mugwort, dragonwort, and the tongue of a snake and it ensures the goodwill of the spirits of air.

Let us return for one moment to the epagomenal Neters who are believed by some to have hailed from Sirius. Assuming the five names supplied to me from my Egyptian sources represent the complete Siriun group, Isis, Osiris, Nepthys, Set and Horus, where does Anubis fit into the picture, for he, like Thoth, features strongly in the ancient myths and appears to form an essential part of the Osirian family unit? I have read all sorts of explanations, some of which I shall enumerate.

Anubis was the son of Osiris by Nephthys, the metaphysical implications of which we have already discussed in Chapter 3, so he obviously carried the Siriun or Atlantean gene, as the case may be. Could it be that he was born after the arrival of the celebrated five, or was he simply adopted into the family at a later date as the embodiment of a principle which appeared to the priests to apply to the situation which faced them at the time? His role as psychopompus must have had some bearing on this, since Osiris had 'ascended into heaven' (moved to a more subtle dimension), and an intermediary between the halls of Osiris and our own world was obviously called for.

On the subject of Anubis, Plutarch wrote:

> By Anubis they understand the horizontal circle, which divides the invisible part of the world, which they call Nephthys, from the visible, to which they give the name of Isis; and as this circle equally touches upon the confines of both light and darkness, it may be looked upon as common to them both – and from the circumstance arose that resemblance, which they imagine between Anubis and the Dog, it being observed of this animal, that he is equally watchful as well by day as night.[16]

This and similar statements have prompted Temple and other scholars to see Anubis in the role of herald between the two stars. Temple sees Plutarch's statement as signifying why Sirius came to be called the 'Dog Star', as there is certainly nothing of the canine nature about its emanations, either exoterically or esoterically. Dog gods and goddesses have ever been associated with the Underworld, thus we have the Greek Cerberus who guarded the Gates of Hades, the dog-companion of the Eskimo goddess Sedna, who dwelt with her at the bottom of the ocean, the Sumerian Bau, the daughter of An, from whom the term 'bow-wow' is believed to have come, and Merlin's Black Dog of Celtic folklore, who accompanied him on his noctural visits to the seashore to collect the ingredients essential to his magical workings. One cannot fail to observe the similarity between the name of Bau's father, An, and Anpu, which is the Egyptian name for Anubis, which surely infers a common root at some point in the distant past.

Dr R. A. Witt, in his book *Isis in the Graeco-Roman World*, devotes an entire chapter to Anubis. He tells us that in the Pyramid Texts, Anubis, although not a member of the Ennead of Heliopolis, is important as the guardian of Osiris and guide for the dead:

> He comes to meet the dead as herald reporting from the horizon. In the picturesque language of ancient Egypt he is described as the

Counter of Hearts and First of the Westerners. When the revitalized
king arises as Anubis, the gods of the Ennead tremble before him. He
can command that death shall come as a star.[17]

The words 'First of the Westerners' caught my eye in this phrase,
and suggested Atlantean connections. Anubis, like Thoth, could
well have preceded the Siriun Neters, and been on the spot to
welcome them, having previously been schooled from stellar
sources regarding Sirius and its cosmic connection with Earth,
and therefore alerted to their arrival. Anubis and Thoth are
frequently fused into a single divinity known in later times as
Hermanubis. Both deities shared a common association with the
negotiation of the time/space continuum, and healing, which
designates them as one or more of the following:

● Scientist priests, either early Egyptian or Atlantean, who
carried the names in titular form, and who were responsible for
enlightening the natives regarding the five extra days;
● Divinities associated with certain mathematical principles, or
paths in space, such as the elliptical orbit of Sirius;
● Allegorical characters employed in parables to explain
advanced scientific principles to the unlettered.
● Time essences who have been born into human bodies for
specific purposes (see *Cosmic Connections*).

As someone who has often approached these and received positive reactions in all instances, I can attest that they do have a
definite reality, although psychologists would, no doubt, hasten
to assure me that I was merely contacting those aspects of my
own psychological economy which equate with the principles
they represent: self-healing, and the negotiation of the timeless
realms of the great unconscious. However, the same argument
could equally be applied to the Christian who prays to Jesus, his
mother or God the Father, and claims immediate help or relief.

Cosmic principles, whether they represent Sirius, Orion or any
other part of the infinite universe do have a constancy which
reaches beyond the boundaries of time and space. Whether we
contact them in their capacity as givers of light, love and
knowledge, or if, in invoking their energies, we trigger off the
darker side of our own natures, will depend very much on us,
like ever attracting like!

Endnotes:

1 R. K. G. Temple, *The Sirius Mystery*, page 45.

2 Ibid., page 48.

3 Ibid., page 66.

4 Ibid., pages 20–30.

5 G. R. S. Mead, *Thrice Greatest Hermes*, Vol. 3, pages 111–13.

6 Temple, Op. cit., page 216

7 Temple, Op. cit., page 32.

8 Temple, Op. cit., page 64.

9 Temple, Op. cit., pages 209–10.

10 G. Maspero, *The Dawn of Civilisation*, page 546.

11 Ibid., page 546.

12 *Prediction Magazine*, 'Sirius B: Cradle of the Gods' by Sue Oliver March 1990.

13 Mead, *Thrice Greatest Hermes*, Vol. 1, page 314.

14 F. Hoyle, *The Intelligent Universe*, page 158

15 V. Robson, *Fixed Stars and Constellations in Astrology*, page 208.

16 Temple, Loc. cit., page 64.

17 R. E. Witt, *Isis in the Graeco-Roman World*, page 198.

CHAPTER 6

The Book of the Dead

In order to obtain an overall view of those beliefs and cultural pursuits of ancient Egypt that are relevant to our subject matter, it is necessary to examine some of the fundamental concepts contained in their most sacred book, the origins of which are seen to predate even the archaic period.

The Book of the Dead was, to the Egyptians of old, something akin to what the Bible is to modern-day Christian fundamentalists, the inference being that it was taken too literally, especially in later dynasties when its original meanings had doubtless become obscured by the mists of time. This is understandable in the light of the fact that the Egypt of, say, the eighteenth dynasty was probably as different from dynasties one and two as mediaeval Europe is from our modern-day society, if not more so.

The very title *The Book of the Dead* is a misnomer, for its literal translation is 'Chapters of the Coming Forth by Day', the sole reason for its awesome title being the preoccupation of its contents with life after death and the preparation thereof. Only fragments of this work, in the form that it has come down to us today, are actually concerned with magical ritual or metaphysics as such, whereas whole sections refer to the state of the departed soul and its trials and existences in the more subtle dimensions. In fact, it places more importance upon what happens to us after death than on our spiritual welfare while we are incarnate. The original title – REU NU PERT EM HRU was written thus in hieroglyphics:

The ancient Egyptians, for all their inherited knowledge and priestly wisdom, were an eminently practical people. They enjoyed an ordered existence, and treated their religious beliefs as an essential part of their life's experience. Too much magical or mystical importance is frequently placed on seemingly fascinating sequences of hieroglyphics which, when translated, turn out to be nothing more than simple invoices for barrels of oil, wheat, fish or meat, plus the occasional 'red' notice indicating what justice might be served if the account was not settled before the Dog Days! It has always amazed me that people should believe that a priesthood as ancient and knowledgeable as that of ancient Egypt would leave details of its most sacred mysteries lying around in public places for the profane to muse over centuries later.

So, does this famous *Book of the Dead* really have something to tell us? The answer to this must, of course, be yes and no. Yes, because it gives us some idea as to how the Egyptian mind worked in those far off days; and no, due to the fact that, taken at face value, it presents little of interest to the layman or the vaguely curious. From a magical or metaphysical standpoint, however, it does provide some clues as to where the Egyptians obtained their original knowledge, while the discerning student of such matters will also be able to detect the various overlays which obscure the original teaching of wisdom.

According to Wallis Budge, the book is definitely *not* of Egyptian origin, for although the indigenous peoples of those parts did possess tolerably well-defined ideas about the afterlife, they could not be regarded as the authors of even the earliest recension of *The Book of the Dead*; the work presupposes the existence of ideas which the aboriginals did not possess and refers to an elaborate system of sepulture which they certainly never practised. Who, then, taught them these things? The Atlanteans, I would think, although even the earliest recension had, I feel, strayed a long, long way from the original Atlantean doctrines concerning the afterlife.

For example, during the peak of civilisation in the Old Country, which was during the zodiacal Age of Virgo, centuries before the Inundation, upon death the physical body was sonically disintegrated as it was not considered a necessary prerequisite to the journey of the spirit in other dimensions. Such things as mummification were unheard of, the 'spiritual fragment theory' was completely understood and taught from early childhood, and it was only in the latter days, when an unnatural emphasis was placed on the physical body and those pleasures associated therewith, that the idea of preserving it was considered. The one aspect of the afterlife that the Egyptians did inherit from the Atlanteans was the old Atlantean belief that, once free of its physical shell, the spirit could enter non-local dimensions or time-zones of differing frequencies. Later Egyptian priests judged these 'journeys' as necessitating special bodies, and a new concept was thus born.

Scholars have conjectured that these ideas were borrowed, sometimes voluntarily and sometimes not so, from immigrants or conquerors, but the general consensus of opinion is that they were brought to Egypt from elsewhere, the Far East perhaps, and they were definitely in existence thousands of years prior to the first dynasty.

The Book of the Dead is divided into three sections, known as recensions. These are:

1. The Heliopolitan Recension:
    (a) That which was used in the fifth and sixth dynasties and is found inscribed in hieroglyphics upon the walls and chambers of the pyramid at Sakkara.
    (b) That which was written in cursive hieroglyphics upon the coffins in the eleventh and twelfth dynasties.
2. The Theban Recension:
    (a) That which was written upon papyri and painted on coffins in hieroglyphics from the eighteenth to the twenty-second dynasties.
    (b) That which was written in the hieratic character upon papyri in the twenty-first and twenty-second dynasties.
3. The Saite Recension:
    That which was written upon papyri, coffins, etc., in the hieroglyphic, hieratic and demotic characters during the twenty-sixth and following dynasties. This was the recension which was much used during the Ptolemaic period and may be regarded as the last form of *The Book of the Dead*.

The Heliopolitan Recension can be dated back to before 3500 BC, and proof is offered by the mistakes in copying which serve to indicate that the scribes of that period were dealing with texts which were, even in such remote times, so old as to be unintelligible in many passages. These copyists reproduced them with little understanding of their meaning, inserting either their own interpretations or chancing a guess about that which they failed to comprehend. Thus the first inaccuracies crept in, although there were doubtless others as it must have been several thousand years since the originals were recorded according to the wisdom of the Atlanteans, Siriuns, or whoever.

From descriptions given, these earliest records can be dated to a period when the banks of the Nile were overrun by beasts hostile to man, while they also contain evidence which indicated that the climate was vastly different at the time when the originals were penned than that encountered in recorded Egyptian history or the annals of surrounding lands. Geological evidence of these facts is now available, and those interested are recommended to read the works of Professor Charles Hapgood, Charles Berlitz, Ignatius Donnelly and my own *Atlantis: Myth or Reality?* which provides a full bibliography of the reference material available on the subject.

As we have already noted, the Egyptian aboriginals had a stone and flint culture, while their conquerors, or those who elected to settle on their shores and effect a civilising influence, worked in bronze and other metals, and executed finely carved objects, pottery, and sophisticated architecture and building construction. These changes, however, were all suspiciously too sudden and highly radical. Later transformations or additions define clearly the varying known external influences on Egyptian life and culture, notably the Libyan, Arabian and Hyksos, and Syrian, and the points in time at which the gods or magical customs of these sub-cultures intermingled with existing Egyptian strains are easy to distinguish.

The oldest copy of *The Book of the Dead* now known to exist on papyrus is that written for Nu, the son of 'the overseer of the house or the overseer of the seal, Amen-hetep, and the lady of the house, Senseneb'. This extremely valuable document is dated to the early part of the eighteenth dynasty. Two versions of the sixty-fourth chapter are given, one much longer than the other, and to each version a note is appended assigning a date to the text which it follows. One version, it claims, was found in:

... the foundations of the shrine of Hennu by the chief mason, during
the reign of his Majesty the king of the South and North, Semti (or
Hesepti), and that the longer version was found in the city of
Khemennu (Hermopolis, the city of Thoth) upon a block of iron of
the south, which had been inlaid with letters of real lapis lazuli
under the feet of the god (Thoth) during the reign of his Majesty
Men-kau-Ra (Mycerinus).[1]

Of the two statements, one ascribes the finding of the chapter to
the time of the first dynasty, and the other to the fourth dynasty.
Both statements are correct, according to Budge, and the longer
version was doubtless the later one. Osiris and Horus are well
depicted in these versions, which speaks for their antiquity as
deities and dates their religion back to the first dynasty and
before.

Little is known about what happened to the sacred books
during the second, third and fourth dynasties. There are ideas
that have been culled from fragments and later writings, but
there is no empirical evidence to back them up. During the reign
of Men-kau-Ra (Mycerinus), a king of the fourth dynasty, we are
told that Chapters XXXV, LXIV and CXLVIII were 'found' by one
Heru-ta-ta-f, the son of Khufu, a man who was latterly considered to have been of great learning. The probability is that,
like King Semti, he revised or edited old chapters to which his
name is added in rubrics, as funeral inscriptions from that period
evidence the existence of *The Book of the Dead* as being in general
use.

During the fifth and sixth dynasties a great development took
place in funerary rites and ceremonies, and five selections of
texts from this recension have survived to the present day.
Although these earlier texts, which constitute the Heliopolitan
Recension, include the views held by the priests of Annu or
Heliopolis, there would appear to be little, if any, just grounds
for assuming that they constituted anything like the entire work.
In fact, the priests of Annu themselves effected many changes
and omissions and fully admitted doing so, probably because
they had no idea what the originals were all about and needed
more practical terms of reference through which to convey the
essence of their religious beliefs to the general populace.

Between the sixth and eleventh dynasties the sacred books
appeared to have become temporarily mislaid or abandoned,
and it was not until the eleventh dynasty that they reappeared.

However, little is really known of the events that took place in the interval between the sixth and eleventh dynasties. Although in Upper Egypt tombs of considerable size and beauty made their appearance, there were no outstanding changes in funerary procedures and no new recension of *The Book of the Dead*. The eleventh and twelfth dynasties saw the emergence of a variety of inscribed selections from the earlier Heliopolitan Recension, which differed little from the older character and contents of the fifth and sixth dynasties. In fact, there was a temporary return to the earlier ways, possibly the result of reaction against outside religious and political influences that had irked the populace in some way. Between the twelfth and eighteenth dynasties we find another break in the history of this remarkable document, and with the advent of the eighteenth dynasty the work entered a new phase in its existence, the transcriptions appearing now on papyri, whereas they had formerly been seen only on coffins, sarcophagi, pyramids and statuary.

It must be taken into account, however, that the economic climate played an important role as elaborate funeral arrangements had previously been effected only for important personages or rich people, so most of the earlier inscriptions originated in that strata of society. But with the advent of papyrus, which required less writing skill than stone and was considerably less expensive, any man or woman who could read, write, or afford the services of a scribe could have his own copies made and his personal invocations transcribed. Thus, it became the fashion for gentlemen of means to have inscriptions made for their wives or families, and this applied particularly to the members of the priesthoods. The Egyptian priesthood was not a celibate one, but neither was it given to excesses. These were essentially a family-orientated people who created their gods in their own image and likeness, as we are all wont to do if we are honest about it. They therefore tended to look after the needs of their own both materially and spiritually, and we probably have a lot to thank them for when it comes to an understanding of the lifestyle and general religious and sociological values of those times.

The seat of these transformations was Thebes, city of the god Amen-Ra, and for this reason the edition of *The Book of the Dead* which was in common use from the eighteenth to the twenty-second dynasty, is known as the Theban Recension. Although the priests of Amen did little more to start with than copy the texts of Annu, with the passing of time they slowly incorporated the name of their own god, Amen, who gradually usurped the powers accorded to many of the older deities and absorbed their attributes. As the father archetype of the Theban triad, Amen is usually partnered by the goddess Mut, and their son is the moon god Khonsu, a deity of healing, this triad appearing to re-echo the earlier Memphis gods: Ptah, the divine architect, patron of masons, his consort Sekhmet, the lion-headed one (sometimes Bast, the cat goddess) and their son Nefer-tem/Imhotep, who was also a healing divinity (See Chapter 3).

The texts of this dynasty were always written in black ink in vertical columns of hieroglyphics, which are separated from each other by black lines, but titles of chapters, and so on, were written in red. Vignettes also came into common use during these times, although there are records of their use as far back as the eleventh dynasty, so Thebes cannot lay entire claim to them. Many famous papyri, such as the *Papyrus of Hunefer* (British Museum No. 9901), belong to this period, but the general feeling among scholars would appear to be that everything was sacrificed to colour and beauty at the expense of the old truths. Scribe and artist worked together to produce a vignette of vividness and movement, rather than a text of a teaching. Long copies of the Theban Recension were apparently made in sections and then joined together, and there are indications that few of the artists employed knew what the others were doing.

One of the finest illustrated papyri in existence, the *Papyrus of Ani,* omits a large section of texts, an error which was probably made by the scribe and not influenced by doctrinal changes or priestly interventions. Vignettes do have a special value in that they sometimes depict mythological scenes and include the names of gods which do not occur elsewhere, and it is to these art forms that we owe much information concerning the judgement scenes and the Egyptian concepts of karma. Another example is the *Papyrus of Anhai* from the twenty-second dynasty (British Museum No. 10,472) showing a vignette depicting the creation which fails to relate to former texts from *The Book of the Dead*. For any interested parties visiting the British Museum, this is worth examining as it depicts the Neters arriving from 'the west' in some rather strange mode of conveyance.

In the twenty-first and twenty-second dynasties there was a gradual decline in the artistic skill employed, and both the form and content of *The Book of the Dead* showed marked changes. Inaccuracies abounded and, according to Budge, instructions copied are grossly heretical. The twenty-second to the twenty-sixth dynasties yield little regarding religious and magical Egypt, due, no doubt, to the period of upheaval and tumult through which the nation was then passing. The priests of Amen-Ra, having effected political and religious machinations to place their favoured deity above all others including Ra himself, usurped the kingdom and assumed temporal as well as religious power over their subjects. Their eventual downfall was precipitated by their inability to maintain authority in lands formerly conquered by the kings of earlier dynasties. Tributes imposed were refused, the power of rulership was slowly wrested from their hands, and the people eventually rebelled. Thus, the rule of Amen finally came to a welcome close.

With the rise of power of the kings of the twenty-sixth dynasty a general revival of the ancient religion took place. *The Book of the Dead* failed to escape this 'new broom' and strong measures were taken by the scholars of the time to re-edit the work and clear away some of the Theban debris. The exact dating of this undertaking is not known, but it is generally believed to have been carried out by an assembly or college of priests specially appointed. The result of their labours was the Saite Recension of *The Book of the Dead*, or third phase in the history of this fascinating document, which naturally also strongly reflected the religious views of the day. The Saite Recension was in use in Ptolemaic times, but the scribes were then, or so it appears, completely ignorant of the meaning of the texts they copied and also of the correct arrangements of the vignettes they added. Of special interest, among the works popular in the Ptolemaic and Graeco-Roman period, is the *Shai-en Sensen*, or *Book of Breathings*. It presents ideas and beliefs derived from the older portions of *The Book of the Dead* and it is refreshing to note that, in spite of all the external conversions and inaccuracies produced by the passage of time, the fundamental concepts of the future life were roughly the same in the minds of the people.

The Book of the Dead was regarded by many as the inspirational work of Thoth, scribe to the gods, who, according to Egyptian belief, spoke the words of creation which were then put into effect by Ptah (the slowing down of Time essential to the formation of the Singularity which was ultimately to become our Universe!). In so far as this statement is concerned, it should therefore contain some elements of Siriun wisdom although, as I have previously emphasised, the priests of old were not accustomed to making their most sacred truths too available to the profane, so any real knowledge that has managed to survive the ravages of time and the ignorance of men must needs be searched for carefully from among its pages, if, in fact, it was ever included therein in the first place.

The hieroglyphics of ancient Egypt constitutes a study in itself, and there are several books available which explain the development and evolution of the system over the centuries of Egypt's ascension. The British Museum is able to supply an excellent little booklet entitled *Egyptian Hieroglyphics* by W. V. Davies, while collectors of the cartouches of gods and kings are recommended to *The Sons of Re, Cartouches of the Kings of Egypt*, by John Rose, which includes not only the personal hieroglyphics of every historically recorded monarch, but also those of the gods. With Mr Roses's kind permission, I give, herewith, some illustrated examples which might tempt the reader to explore the author's work in more depth, (See *Fig. 6.2*).

There are, however, certain hieroglyphics which relate specifically to spiritual or transpersonal matters and these are, I believe, essential to the understanding of both the Egyptian religion and those from whom these early people originally culled their knowledge. To the early Egyptians, the spiritual economy constituted something of an entourage involving several 'vehicles' which were seen as essential to the negotiation of the subtle planes. These are:

The **Sahu,** or spiritual body – that which is abstract;

The **Khu,** or spirit – the magical essence;

The **Ba,** or soul – probably the etheric body;

The **Ka** or double – the astral body;

The **Sekhem** or 'power';

 The **Ab** or heart – the seat of the emotions;

 The **Khaibit** or shadow– the unconscious;

The **Ren** or name – the personal sonic;

The **Khat** or physical body – that which is perishable.

These may be seen to equate with similar classifications rendered by ensuing arcane traditions and systems of transpersonal

(Text continues on page 113)

| **SEKER** | **KHEPER** | **AAH** |
| A Funerary God | God of Creation | Moon God |

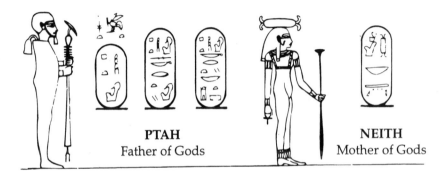

| **PTAH** | **NEITH** |
| Father of Gods | Mother of Gods |

Fig. 6.2 (a)

Fig. 6.2 (b)

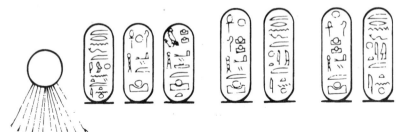

THE ATEN – SUN DISK
the god of Pharaoh Akhenaten

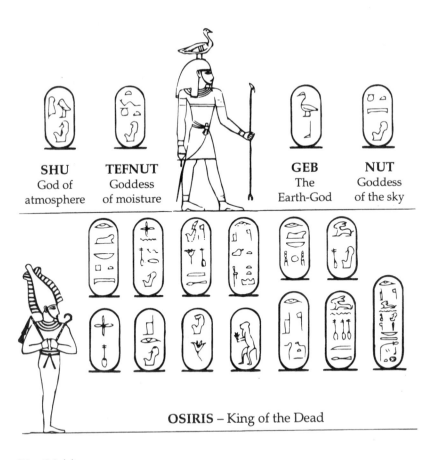

SHU	**TEFNUT**		**GEB**	**NUT**
God of	Goddess		The	Goddess
atmosphere	of moisture		Earth-God	of the sky

OSIRIS – King of the Dead

Fig. 6.2 (c)

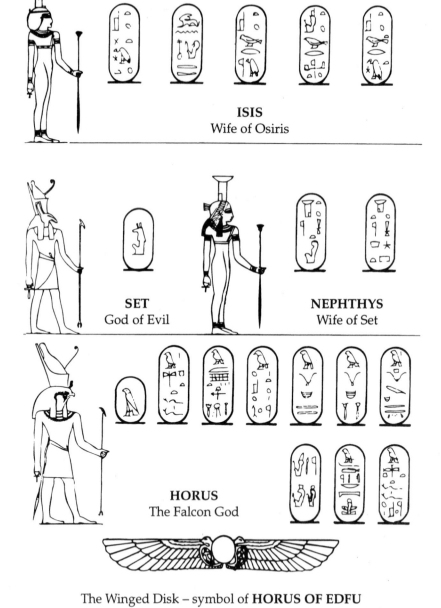

ISIS
Wife of Osiris

SET
God of Evil

NEPHTHYS
Wife of Set

HORUS
The Falcon God

The Winged Disk – symbol of **HORUS OF EDFU**

Fig. 6.2 (d)

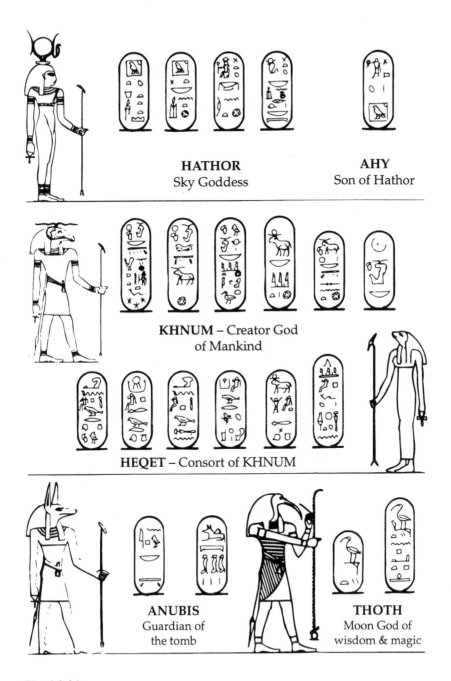

HATHOR
Sky Goddess

AHY
Son of Hathor

KHNUM – Creator God
of Mankind

HEQET – Consort of KHNUM

ANUBIS
Guardian of
the tomb

THOTH
Moon God of
wisdom & magic

Fig. 6.2 (e)

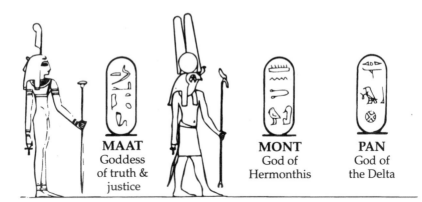

MAAT
Goddess
of truth &
justice

MONT
God of
Hermonthis

PAN
God of
the Delta

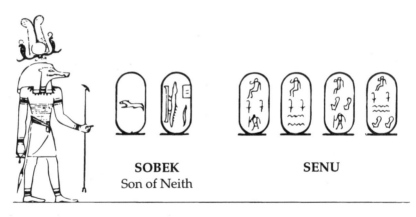

SOBEK
Son of Neith

SENU

COLLECTIVE GODS

HAPY
God of
the Nile
&
all Gods

**THE GREAT GODS
OF THE EAST
&
THE GREAT GODS
OF THE WEST**

**OSIRIS
HAROERIS
SET
ISIS
NEPHTHYS**

Fig. 6.2 (f)

psychology, which refer to either levels of consciousness or progressively accelerating frequencies, such as Etheric, Astral-Mental, Causal and Spiritual bodies; Atma, Buddha, Manas, Kama, Prana and Rupa; and a similar catalogue of nomenclatures. In my Cartouche system of self-help and divination I ascribed the various Egyptian subtle bodies to nine main divinities, including the epagomenal Neters, as follows:

1. Osiris	2. Isis	3. Horus
4. Bast	6. Hathor	7. Nephthys
8. Ptah	9. Anubis	10. Set

I also included Thoth, listing him as card number 5, but allotting the Ibis as his symbol, rather than one of the spiritual hieroglyphics or the actual hieroglyphic version of his name which may be seen in Mr Rose's illustrations. My reason for this? I cannot honestly say, other than that I was 'inspired' to so do. Logic would most certainly have demanded that I use the full hieroglyph, but somehow that was not to be. The numbers allocated to the other deities may be observed to follow accepted numerological rules.

It would seem, from a study of *The Book of the Dead* and other archaic texts, that the ancient Egyptian concept of the hereafter was somewhat complicated and highly confused. The reason for this probably lies in the fact that a series of successive infiltrations from the religions of surrounding cultures, plus the different translations and interpretations of *The Book of the Dead*, tended to produce a variety of ideas which the various priesthoods endeavoured to accommodate within their favoured doctrinal structures. Strangely enough, although the gods or Neters received considerable coverage in the ancient texts, little, if any, mention is ever made of their habitation. As Budge tells us:

> The texts of the period are silent as to the exact position of heaven, but it is certain that the Egyptians assigned to it a place above the sky, and that they called it *pet*; we must distinguish between the meanings of *pet* and *nut*, for the former means 'heaven' and the latter 'sky'. We may also note that two skies are mentioned in the texts, i.e. the day sky and the night sky.[3]

The ancient Egyptians saw the universe as divided into three portions, Heaven, Earth, and the Tuat or Underworld, each of which was populated by its own special brand of divinities. As the Egyptian religion slowly evolved, the concepts of heaven were also adjusted to suit the prevailing climate of religious opinion. Two mountains were originally seen as supporting the celestial regions, but these were eventually replaced by four pillars, each under the direction of an appropriate divinity. In time these became associated with the four cardinal points, and consequently the Four Sons of Horus who represented them. During my researches, I have encountered several different versions of the positions allocated to these godlings, the most popular being that given by Budge: Imsety to the South, Hapi to the North, Duamutef to the East and Qebhsnuf to the West, which arrangement Jung also tended to favour. However, Lucie Lamy's are different again, as shown in the following illustration. (See *Fig. 6.4*.)

My own preference, which is given in Chapter 3, is based on three factors: their imagery, those organs of the deceased over which they exercise their roles as tutelary deities, and their magical responses. In rites involving the body of Osiris, the goddesses Isis, Nephthys, Neith and Selket were also associated with the Sons of Horus: Isis with Imsety, Nephthys with Hapi, Neith with Duamutef and Selkit with Qebhsnuf. I do not doubt that the four Elements and their corresponding cardinal points featured in the old Atlantean or Siriun rites, as the case may be,

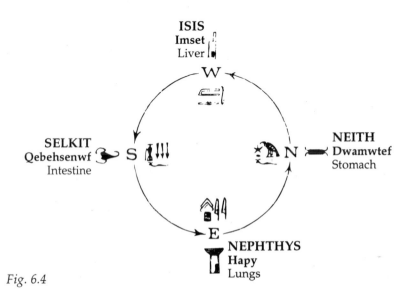

Fig. 6.4

Sirius, in the constellation of Canis Major *Courtesy of Science Photo Library*

The Temple of Hathar Dendora
Courtesy of Image Bank

The Pyramids at Giza *Courtesy of Image Bank*

Sekhmet statues
*Courtesy of The British
Museum*

Above: Tefnut (centre) *Courtesy of The British Museum*

Below: The Papyrus of Nu *Courtesy of The British Museum*

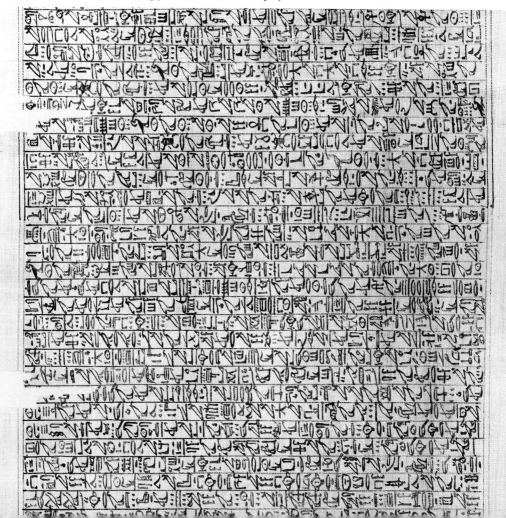

Isis leading the Queen of Nefertar
Courtesy of Werner Forman Archive

Statue of Bastet *Courtesy of The British Library*

but it is worth bearing in mind that these would naturally have adjusted when the angle of the Earth's axis changed at the time of the Flood, so perhaps I have subconsciously reverted to the old pre-Egyptian placings.

The Egyptians themselves seemed a little uncertain as to who actually inhabited 'heaven', apart from the gods that is, since several classes of beings are named as having their abode therein. These included the Shemsu-Hor, or Followers of Horus, who appear to observe the same roles as Christian angels, waiting upon the throne of Horus and, when necessary, defending him from his enemies; the Ashemu, who seem to have been some kind of etheric entities who were not necessarily connected with the human experience; and the Henmemet, a class of beings who were either destined to become human, or had already been in human incarnation. Budge. tells us that the word *ashem* is usually supposed to mean the 'form in which a god is visible', although he opines that it must have had an older meaning, long since forgotten.[4] The latter could well refer to what some metaphysicists designate as the 'plane of pre-existence' (quantum worlds of primary particles/superstring), in which the Essence is believed to dwell prior to entering one or other of the mainstreams of evolutionary experience. Since neither time nor space, as we comprehend it, would feature in such an existence, this level of pre-material consciousness could well provide a comprehensive view of the universe and the infinite variety of life-forms available for the infant Essence to make its selection. But now I am guilty of superimposing Atlantean philosophy over later Egyptian concepts, although these may well be nearer to the Siriun original that might appear at first glance.

The religious beliefs of the eighteenth dynasty, were, no doubt, as far removed from the early teachings of *The Book of the Dead* as modern-day Christianity is from the original beliefs held by Jeshua and his followers 2000 years ago – and probably before if the truth were known. The general opinion, however, seemed to be that the spirits of men could abide in heaven with the gods, provided they behaved themselves while they were on earth, and acquainted themselves with the appropriate rituals designed to ensure them a safe journey to the 'higher regions'. Ancient illustrations abound with pictures showing the weighing of the heart and other rites associated with the adventures undergone by the deceased.

One interesting piece of information, which struck me as relevant to the origins of Egyptian culture, is to be found in a description of the life led by the gods, and the kind of habitat in which they were believed to dwell. According to one myth, their food consisted of a 'wood' or life-giving plant substance which grew near the great lake in the Sekhet-hetep (the Elysian Fields), wherein dwelt the souls of the blessed. This same myth also alludes to the beautified dead living in '*a beautiful, fertile region, where white wheat and red barley grew luxuriantly to a great height, and where canals were numerous and full of water, and where material enjoyments of every kind could be found.*' (This is surely more reminiscent of Plato's Atlantis than of some sublime existence far removed from the physical plane, while the Elysian Fields concept has a decidedly Hellenistic ring about it.)

The Egyptian Tuat or Underworld was not synonymous with the Christian Hell, nor did the Egyptians believe it to be beneath the Earth or in any subterranean region. It was a place in the sky where Ra, the sun god, passed after he had set or 'died' for the day, and through which it was necessary for him to pass in order to arrive at that portion of the sky in which he would arise the following morning. It was in the Tuat that Osiris was believed to judge the dead and reign over both the gods of the region and the souls of the dead who dwelt therein. The Tuat was separated from this world by a chain of mountains, in just the way that the realms of the dead are often believed to be divided from the regions of the living by great gulfs, chasms or impenetrable barriers. In the light of modern physics these may be seen in terms of differing frequencies through which matter cannot pass, while metaphysicists refer to finer vibrations or higher (or lower) planes.

The Egyptians believed that a river ran through the valley of the Tuat, a concept which also appears in other mythologies: the Greek Hades with its river Styx, for example. The banks of this river were the homes of monstrous beasts, evil spirits and demons of every shape and size, who were decidedly hostile to strangers, which is all very reminiscent of the 'lower astral' through which the Initiate must pass before he or she can ascend to more exalted spiritual realms. The Theban priests endeavoured to incorporate some of the earlier beliefs into their doctrines, the best known of which was probably Amentet, the 'hidden place', originally designated as the kingdom of An-her, who was worshipped as Abydos as god of the dead under the title Khenti Amentet, a name later usurped by Osiris when he assumed a similar rule. As *Set-Amenti* or the 'Funeral Mountain', it represented the lower regions of the Tuat.

The Tuat itself was composed of several divisions, called Pylons, which were no more than convenient references inaugurated by the Theban priests. It would take one or more books to describe the various beliefs and rites associated with the Tuat, many of which were, no doubt, the invention of later priesthoods anxious to line their coffers with the price of a ticket in the Boat of the Sun, which was believed to carry the souls of the dead away from the regions of darkness into the light of the new day. To me, these rites and credos are no more enlightened or consequential than the medieval hocus-pocus of the Grimoires, with their subjugatory doctrine of fear and superstition. As astronomer Carl Sagan once wryly commented: 'The first priest was the first rogue who met the first fool.'

The book of the *Reu Nu Pert Em Hru* was extremely ancient. Even around 3500 BC its doctrines were either seen as antiquated or too obscure to be understood by later generations. Added to this, the views expressed therein were decidedly contrary to those held by the Theban theocracy, so while they were prepared to respect its antiquity, they compiled two works of their own which skilfully manipulated the old doctrines to such an extent as to obscure or even obliterate many of the original meanings. These were the: *Shat am Tuat* (The Book of that which is in the Tuat) and the *Book of Pylons*. Both of these books divided the Tuat into twelve parts, each of which corresponded to one of the hours of the night. The divisions were called 'Field' *(sekhet)*, 'City', *(nut)*, M 'Hall' *(arret)*, and 'Circle' *(gerert)*.[5] Full descriptions of these are to be found in Budge's book, but since they occupy almost a complete chapter and are totally irrelevant to the deeper esoteric teaching of earlier dynasties and, therefore, the Siriun connection, I see no purpose in reproducing them. In this same category, I would place other heretical doctrines and concepts that found their way into Egyptian magical and religious beliefs, such as the fifteen *Aats* (districts, literally, but also seen as states of consciousness), the *Arits*, or seven reception halls through which the spirit as believed to move after death, and the Hall of Maati where the past words and deeds of the deceased are reviewed. While I can accept the concept of some form of assessment following death, much of the aforementioned is purely symbolic and should not be taken too literally.

It is a generally accepted metaphysical belief that following our demise we effect our own judgement upon ourselves. There is no grand tribunal – either celestial or otherwise – which decides on the rightness or wrongness of our past deeds. These can only be assessed by the individual soul or psyche in accordance with its overall stage of development. I can, however, appreciate that guidelines of the kind used by the ancient Egyptians were and still are of help to younger souls who do not yet understand or have come to terms with the space-time continuum. It is for this reason, and this reason alone, that I can equate these principles with a remnant of some much earlier wisdom teaching. There is surely more of the genuine ancient Egyptian/Siriun/Atlantean philosophy to be found in works such as the Hermes Trismegistus and the Emerald Tablets that in the exaggerated and decidedly overstated doctrines and rituals of the Theban period.

In commenting on the meaning of the word 'Neter', Budge draws the reader's attention to the term *Neter-khert*, which appears in the later version of the *The Book of the Dead*. Taken literally, this must surely refer to the abode of the Neters, although some writers, notably Gerald and Betty Scheuler, designate it 'The Magical Universe', a general term for the subtle planes and sub-planes that are believed to exist above or around this Earth (the etheric, astral, mental and spiritual planes of popular metaphysics, no doubt) which although invisible to the physical senses, are deemed to be none the less real. The term also refers to the location said to be visited by the dead.[6] In a further qualification, the Scheulers refer to the Neter-khert as 'the divine subterranean region', a general term for all the invisible worlds from the highest to the lowest, but not including our Earth.[7] For my own part, I am much happier with the scientific concept of non-locality, which accommodates the whole caboodle without reserve! A few of the ancient beliefs that did survive the Theban pruning, notably the 'Double Fire' or *Khet-Khet* and 'The Abyss' or *seshet* I will deal with in the context of higher magic, since they contain complex innuendoes pertaining to the initiatory process.

One cannot help lamenting the loss of the great libraries of Sais and Alexandria. How much more knowledgeable we would be had those precious records remained intact. But knowing the perverse nature of man, fundamentalists in some later age would probably have destroyed them had not the Christian fanatics stormed the Serapeum in AD 387, and in 641, Amru, general of Omar, second in succession to the Prophet, who fed the furnaces of the 4000 baths of Alexandria for six months with the Bruchion's priceless treasures, effected the job for them.

Endnotes:
1 E.A. Wallis Budge, *The Book of the Dead*, pages xxxiii–xxxiv.
2 J. Rose, *The Sons of Re*, pages 17–22.
3 E. A. Wallis Budge, *The Gods of the Egyptians*, Vol. 1, page 156.
4 Ibid., page 159.
5 Ibid., page 176.
6 G. & B. Scheuler, *Coming Into the Light*, page 11.
7 Ibid., page 15.

CHAPTER 7

The Growth and Development
of Magic

Extensive research into early history and prehistory, coupled with my personal experiences in this field, has tended to confirm the conclusions of lawyer and Cambridge classics scholar John Ivimy, who wrote:

> Classical historians traditionally dismiss tales of magic as unworthy of scholarly attention, but to us any mention of a witch's broomstick or wizard's wand evokes the smell of the scientist's laboratory.[1]

Following through the 'single source' theory, which I tend to apply to all mythology, cannot fail to lead one to a period in the long-lost prehistoric past when science and what is commonly termed 'magic' were one and the same study. The latter side would have dealt with those subtle dimensions whose code the physicists are only just beginning to break in their study of minute particles and quantum variants.

While most people accept the validity of science, even if they fail to understand quite how it works, or their religious fundamentalism precludes them from active participation in its tenets, the term 'magic' can contain sinister connotations which are, unfortunately, exacerbated by the antics of some practitioners of the art. The idea that in order to be an expert magician one needs to appear as a cross between a medieval peasant and a punk rocker does little to enhance the image of magic in the eyes of the general public, and while it is all too easy to condemn the kind of mental collectivism that designates the standards by which we are judged, let us admit there is an awful lot of affectation about! In the early days of my pursuit of metaphysical knowledge it was pointed out to me, by those who were both better informed and wiser than myself, that one did not need to walk around with one's flag permanently at full mast in order to effect what one felt to be the appropriate social statement. In fact, this very action was the standard advertisement of the ego-tripper; those who are really powerful and knowledgeable have no need or recourse to such blatant exhibitionist behaviour!

Experts such as the late A. E. Waite have tended to describe magic as a science, while others prefer to think of it as an art. In fact, it is both, for as Einstein so wisely commented: 'Imagination is greater than knowledge', the implication being that great scientific and technological discoveries usually originate as ideas, dreams, or inspirational flashes from the unconscious which are latterly labelled 'genius'. I have always admired Waite's succinct apology for the term, which bears repetition since I could not hope to effect such an excellent job myself:

> The popular conception of Magic, even when it is not identified with the trickeries of imposture and the pranks of the mountebank, is entirely absurd and gross.
>
> 'Magic, or, more accurately, Magism,' says Christian in his *Histoire de la Magie*, 'if anyone would condescend to return to its antique origin, could be no longer confounded with the superstitions which calumniate its memory. Its name is derived to us from the Greek words MAGOS, a Magician, and MAGEIA, Magic, which are merely permutations of the terms MOG, MEGH, MAGH, which in Pehlvi and Zend, both languages of the eldest East, signify "priest", "wise" and "excellent". It was thence also that, in a period anterior to historic Greece, there originated the Chaldean name Maghdim, which is equivalent to "supreme wisdom", or sacred philosophy. Thus, mere etymology indicates that Magic was the synthesis of those sciences once possessed by the Magi or philosophers of India, of Persia, of Chaldea, and of Egypt, who were the priests of nature, the patriarchs of knowledge, and the founders of those vast civilizations whose ruins still maintain, without tottering, the burden of sixty centuries.'
>
> Ennemoser, in his *History of Magic* (as translated by Howitt), says: 'Among the Parsees, the Medes and the Egyptians, a higher knowledge of nature was understood by the term Magic, with which religion, and particularly astronomy, were associated. The initiated

and their disciples were called Magicians – that is, the Wise – which was also the case among the Greeks. ... Plato understood by Wisdom nothing less than a worship of the Divinity, and Apuleius says that Magus means, in the Persian language, a priest. ... India, Persia, Chaldea, and Egypt, were the cradles of the oldest Magic. Zoroaster, Ostanes, the Brahmins, the Chaldean sages, and the Egyptian priests, were the primitive possessors of its secrets. The priestly and sacrificial functions, the healing of the sick, and the preservation of the Secret Wisdom, were the objects of their life. They were either princes themselves, or surrounded princes as their counsellors. Justice, truth, and the power of self-sacrifice, were the great qualities with which each one of these must be endowed; and the neglect of any one of these virtues was punished in the most cruel manner.[2]

Egyptian magic is usually divided into High Magic and Low Magic, the descriptions 'black' or 'white', to use two crude and inflammatory terms, being decided by the intention of the operator. It should be borne in mind that all universal energies are of themselves totally impersonal. It is only when they are utilised that they assume a 'shade', the intensity of which is decided, albeit unconsciously in some cases, by the manipulator. And so it is in everyday life. We may use a fire to warm ourselves, heat our water, make ourselves more comfortable in chillier climes, or we can bring arson, ruin and destruction with that very same energy. The eternal dualistic conflict between love and hate, order and chaos, light and darkness, which seems to rage upon our planet, is highlighted in the following words of Carl Jung:

> Only here, in life on earth, where the opposites clash together, can the general level of consciousness be raised. That seems to be man's metaphysical task which he cannot accomplish without 'mythologising'. Myth is the natural and indispensible intermediate stage between unconsciousness and conscious cognition. True, the unconscious knows more than consciousness does; but it is knowledge of a special sort, knowledge in eternity, usually without reference to the here and now, not couched in language of the intellect.[3]

From an ethical standpoint those moral and ethnical qualities encompassed by the word 'goodness' are not the prerogative of any one metaphysical or religious persuasion – orthodox or otherwise – regardless of the numerical superiority of its adherents, any more than the other side of the coin belongs to unpopular minority groups which do not conform to the standards of popular collectives. As history will bear honest witness, all creeds have at some time spawned both saints and sinners.

The Scheulers define Low Magick [*sic*] as being concerned with more immediate benefits such as health, protection, financial gain and other matters appertaining to the needs of everyday life, and High Magick [*sic*] as aiming towards the growth, evolution and spiritual development of the practitioners. Egyptian low magic covered all forms of divination, fortune telling, talismanic magic, potions and unguents galore, and a variety of spells designed to right wrongs and bring about a more comfortable and less worrisome earthly life and a safe journey to the Elysian Fields following their demise. Under my category of terms, the latter would be defined as 'mundane occultism'. I would not, however, include protection in the mundane category, since it surely applies to all levels from difficult neighbours to the psychological fragmentation which could threaten the psyche during its exposure to the multidimensional experiences of inter-time travel undertaken while negotiating finer (non-local) frequencies. Although the journey of the soul into the afterworld is frequently viewed by metaphysicists as falling into the category of high magic, I would disagree on this score since death is not in itself an indication of the evolutionary status of the departed soul. Over the years I have been confronted by many discarnate entities, with and without the intervention of a medium, most of whom have been considerably less informed on matters of the universe than the incarnate beings whom they purport to teach or instruct!

The ultimate aim of all magical and alchemical rites and practices should be spiritual transmutation, born of the realisation of the true and full mental powers which are the natural heritage of the human psyche incarnate within this time frequency we call 'material existence'. The achievement of this realisation serves to open the universal doors through which the Initiate may pass in his or her unending quest for knowledge, enlightenment and love to be shared with all other children of the Creator/Creatrix. Should the intention behind this quest be anything less than the ideal, the practitioner will fall victim to the wiles of his or her own ego or desire nature, and become lost in the maze of personal illusion.

I am often asked how one becomes a magician or occultist. Perhaps we should see what the ancient Egyptians had to say about this. In his book, *Egyptian Magic,* Dr Christian Jacq, an authority on ancient Egyptian texts, tells us:

It is not possible to give the answer to this essential question by offering a 'List of Instructions'. The practice of magic is not licensed by a diploma nor by passing an exam. Modern learning is almost entirely codified and does not, alas, take any account of practical experience. This was not the case in a civilisation such as Egypt.

For sure, there is a method by which one becomes a magician, but it does not reveal itself to the powers of reason. The texts do not hide it entirely but they call on our intuition and our inner intelligence rather than to our deductive or analytical faculties.

Spell 261 of the *Coffin Texts* has the title 'To become a magician'. This is what is says. The adept addresses the magicians who are in the presence of the Master of the Universe. He demands respect from them because he knows them, since they guided his steps. Is he not the one whom the Sole Lord created before there came into being two meals [*sic*] on earth, the day and the night, good and evil, when the Creator opened his one eye in his solitude? The magician presents himself as the one who controls the Word. He is the son of the Great Mother, she who gave birth to the Creator on earth, who, nevertheless, has no mother. The father of the gods is the magician himself. It is he who gives them life.[4]

Jacq sees this as a strange text, a view which might well be shared by the layman. But the Initiate sees it in terms of the god or archetypal energy within, which, when stimulated by trial and initiation, evokes a resonating response in its universal equivalent. The son of the Great Mother who gave birth to the Creator on earth, but who has no mother, may sound paradoxical, but in reality it refers to a balancing of the anima and animus, or male-female aspects of the psyche, which Jung referred to as individuation, and which, in turn, resonates to the Divine Androgyne. The gods or Neters are always there. They are eternal. But their manifestation via the agency of an Essence whose psyche or fragment is *incarnate*, is limited to the bandwidth of that person's field or soul frequency on the one hand, and the general evolutionary level of the planet in question on the other. (In the 'field' theory, consciousness is related to the spirit/psyche, which is conceived of in terms of active particles – *see* Introduction.) Thus the magician gives them life at *his* or *her* level, and not at the frequency at which they would normally operate.

Jacq supplies us with considerable detail from *The Papyrus magique of Leyden* regarding priestly initiation. Candidates, it seems, were judged far more on their esoteric knowledge than their practical skills, which could be developed later, and on their ultimate ability to commune with the 'light of the very beginning' – their cosmic origins and other dimensions beyond those associated with this world, which alone was believed to contain magic in its absolute purity. It was revealed to the Novitiate at an early stage that every human problem that faces the magician has a counterpart in the divine world, an identical event having occurred on the 'cosmic ladder' before it is manifested on earth. In other words, 'As above, so below.' It was for this reason that a knowledge of the gods, theology, mythology and the creation of this and other worlds was deemed essential.

Part of the Novitiate's magical training, therefore, involved familiarisation with the Cardinal Points and the divinities associated therewith: the four Elements of Air, Fire, Water and Earth, the principles of which needed to be mastered and understood. The ego had to be stripped away, and the Novitiate faced with his or her own id, shadow or lower self, which was frequently portrayed as some kind of monster or evil genius. Once the aspirant was able to make contact with the god form in whose service he or she was to become initiated, then he or she automatically came under the tutelary guidance and protection of that deity, so that anyone wishing to engage him or her in any form of combat – mental or otherwise – was also faced with that god-force. I recall many years ago being told that when the magician or occultist was able to *control* the four Elements (I prefer to think of it in terms of winning their friendship and confidence, rather than 'control'), his or her power was increased 'to the sixth'. It is interesting to observe how these ancient Egyptian texts accord with my own early discoveries, and I feel grateful that I encountered them before I was confronted with the written confirmation. I am sure many others working in the field must feel the same way.

The main difference between the Egyptian priesthood and the modern-day magician, occultist or shaman would seem to be the fact that for many years ancient Egypt was a sacerdotal society, and its priests were therefore accorded the privileges of their rank and office. In today's world no such acknowledgements exist, so the Initiate has what may appear to be considerably greater odds stacked against him or her, although, no doubt, there is a parity, albeit unconscious, between the overshadowing energies and the demons to be faced. It should also be borne in mind that we are fast approaching a major planetary change, so the magical situation bears more resemblance to that of the latter days of Atlantis than to early Egypt.

What is broadly referred to as low magic hardly falls within the aforementioned exalted categories, however, being more concerned with the everyday needs and superstitions of ordinary folk. So how and why is it used? Is it really effective? Which branch of the Egyptian magical brotherhood dispensed it and what are the pitfalls, if any? Let us commence with some simple examples of sympathetic magic such as the amulet.

Amulets and Talismans

The word 'amulet' derives from an Arabic root meaning 'to bear' or 'to carry'. Budge tends employ the term to cover any kind or ornament, article of dress or wearing apparel to which supernatural powers have been ascribed, but I should like to be more specific. As I understand it, a talisman is a figure or sign that has been designed and made under specific occult or astrological observances for a definite purpose. Talismans have, however, become confused with charms and amulets. An amulet is usually a small object said to possess properties that can ward off evil, prevent accidents, attract good health and so forth; charms are traditionally associated with old fashioned 'good luck'. A genuine talisman is the work of a magician, priest, occultist or shaman who understands the subtle energies of the universe and knows how to encapsulate them into an object, picture, or collection of signs and symbols, according to the needs of the applicant. When a talisman is made specially for an individual, a symbol representing that person is incorporated thereon or therein: a birth sign, magical name, or significant number, for example. The ancient Egyptians used talismans, amulets and charms, although the former were dispensable only by those skilled in the more esoteric aspects of the magical arts.

Among the talismans and amulets most favoured in ancient Egypt, Budge lists the amulet of the Ab or Heart, the Scarab, the Buckle of Isis, the Tet of Osiris, the Pillow, the Vulture, the Collar of Gold, the Papyrus Sceptre, the Ladder, the Two Fingers, the Utchat or Eye of Horus, the Ankh, the Amulet of Nefer, the

Serpent's Head, the Menat, the Sam, the Shen, the Steps and the Frog. Sometimes these figures were engraved on stones, at others woven into cloth, or simply made into small trinkets or items of jewellery. Each carried a special meaning for the soul of the deceased, full details of which are to be found in Budge's *Egyptian Magic*. As regards the attainment of material goods or wealth, it should always be borne in mind that requests for those things to which one is not karmically entitled have to be paid for in some other way. Although a money spell may produce results, something of equivalent value is also likely to be taken away from one in order to balance the karmic books.

From a process of practice and elimination over the years, I came to discover which of the old symbols carried the power of the ancients, be they Atlanteans or Siriuns, some of which I incorporated in *The Way of Cartouche* and *The Book of Talimantras* (talismans with accompanying mantras). Working with Egyptian symbology is the best way of (a) finding out which symbols are most effective and (b) ascertaining which are pre-Egyptian.

Hekau, or Words of Power

Budge tells us that the gods preserved their existence by means of a magical protection they enjoyed called *meket* and also by *hekau*: the words of power. The aim of every Egyptian, therefore, was to gain knowledge of both the protection enjoyed by the deities and especially their words of power, which they believed would render them the same privileges as the divinities they worshipped. But what exactly were these fabled *hekau*? Budge tends to favour the shamanic interpretation for many of these phenomena; the man who eats the heart of the lion partakes of the strength of the beast, and likewise the character of Unas, who appears in the Pyramid Texts as a devourer of both the body and spirit of the departed, partakes of their energies. However, Unas is also referred to as a king, whose adventures in the great beyond are symbolic rather than actual. Schwaller de Lubicz draws our attention to the fact that the glyph for Unas means 'existence', and I would like to add that when removed from the primitive shamanic context the precise descriptions rendered could easily be applied to both the molecular transformations and the accompanying spiritual metamorphoses which follow death. In other words, Unas is nothing more or less than the universal consciousness which continually re-absorbs and recycles its energies, of which our bodies and souls form but one minute segment.

Belief in the 'spiritual fragment theory'[5] was obviously prevalent in the earliest dynasties, since the 'arise and return' theme appears frequently in the Pyramid Texts:

> Return! Return, Horus!
> That Unas may return,
> By the flame drawn up by the gods,
> Who make ready the way,
> That Unas may pass,
> For Unas is Horus![6]

The contents of the Pyramid Texts is a study in itself and demands more time and space than I am able to accord it in this work. Schwaller de Lubicz and John Anthony West are, in my opinion, better authorities on the subject than Budge, as their approach is more metaphysical and, let us face it, what we are trying to do is to get to the roots of the *real* knowledge that was either lost, or so shrouded in superstition in later dynasties as to render it indecipherable.

In an earlier chapter we have noted the importance of the *ren* or name, which I translate as the personal sonic of the essence or soul, and how Isis was able to obtain her magical powers by learning the secret name of Ra. In later dynasties – the Theban in particular – the concept was extended to cover the names of a variety of entities, many of which were simply figments of the imagination of some acquisitive priest, which itwas deemed essential for the departed to know in order that he or she should end up in the right place, wherever that might be! My first task will, therefore, be to strip away this superstitious facade and concentrate on the original *hekau*, that great and mysterious power which our Egyptian friends claim was bestowed upon their ancestors by the beings from Sirius.

If one looks a little further than the obvious, the whole of the early texts are littered with clues. Let us take those enigmatic stories of Thoth (Time?), the sound of whose voice, we are told, could work such miracles as raising huge stones. He was even credited with creating the universe by the sound of his voice, after which Ptah set about organising it. All this no doubt alludes to a knowledge of celestial mechanics, while the Ptah implication is blatantly obvious: Ptah is the Master Craftsman, Patron of Masons, the Builder *par excellence,* he who converts energy into matter according to the plans agreed by Tehuti, *Time Lord and Master of Sonics!* The *hekau* originally given to the pre-dynastic Egyptians by the Atlanteans or whoever it may have been, incorporated several sonic applications, one of which was oral. As a former professional singer, I can vouch for the effect the human voice can have, both upon material objects and the human mind. Everyone is familiar with the joke about the opera singer whose high note shatters the mirror or tumbler, but how many know how to use that power in other ways?

As with all natural energies, sonics can be both useful and dangerous. Nikola Tesla discovered this to his chagrin when working on a sonic project at his New York home. It took a signed petition from his neighbours to make him cease his experiments, as the adverse effect of the energies he was releasing was causing damage to people, property and even the public utilities! Sonics is not the sort of thing one could demonstrate to a scientist, especially if one could not remember the correct system for directing its energies without causing damage or hurt. However, I have the subconscious knowledge that if I was ever placed in a position where I was required to defend my person, I *would know how to pitch my voice at a frequency that could have dire effects upon my assailant.* More than that I cannot tell, it is just an inner feeling, but there is always the worry that fear might cause one to apply such knowledge immoderately, and it is against my principles to deliberately cause suffering to another.

The Significance of Knots

Closely associated with the science of sonics was the magic of knots, since the knot was one of the sacred symbols of Ptah, and therefore connected with the *ren* or personal sonic. In Egyptian hieroglyphics the knotted cord signified a person's name, and because the knot is a symbol for the individual's existence, the knot or bow appears with some frequency in the ancient texts. The ancient Egyptians went to great lengths to safeguard a person's name, for it was a widespread belief that unless the name was preserved, one would cease to exist. The sonic implications here are obvious, and I for one believe that were we to know the exact sonic frequency of another person, that knowledge could either be used to cure or kill them! There is also a corollary in psychology, for although we may not vanish into some parallel universe if we are not hailed at regular intervals by our fellow earthlings, to be continually ignored and not allowed to express our true personality can result in a host of psychological disturbances leading to severe mental illness.

The cord, like the chain, is a general symbol for binding and connecting, so it is little wonder that Ptah, the Master Mason – believed by many metaphysicists to represent the Archons (Time Lords?), a body of highly advanced Devic intelligences responsible for the creation of universes, was vested with this symbol. The depth and extent of the scientific knowledge possessed by these ancient peoples is borne out in the words of Lucie Lamy, who wrote: '… each human being writes his name, the name that is his for lifetime, in one of the knotted loops of the infinite thread of Eternity.'[7] (See *Fig. 7.1* below).

Jacq refers to the fact that the Egyptian magician spent much of his time tying knots. He tells us:

A magic knot is a point of convergence of the forces which unite the divine and the human world. Spells 406–408 of the *Coffin Texts* are spells for knowing the seven knots of the heavenly cow.

They will be useful to the magician in manoeuvring the ferry in which he crosses the spaces of heaven. They restore the body to health and vigour. Moreover the heavenly knots find their equivalents in the 'knots' of the human body,* those sensitive points where the streams of energy upon which our existence depends, meet.[8] [*Author's note: The seven chakras.]

The number seven featured more strongly in the magic of knots than any other number and cords with seven knots frequently

Fig. 7.1

made their appearance, which is to be expected, as seven obviously carried highly mystical connotations for the Egyptians of those times. Jacq cites a ritual from the Leyden Magical Papyrus in which the number seven is used throughout: seven bricks, seven loaves of bread, seven blocks of salt, incantations to be chanted seven times, and so forth. Priests specialising in knot magic were often referred to as 'the Blowers on Knots', a title which later found its way into Arabic magic, as their rite of dedication frequently involved their breathing or blowing their magical energies into the knots. Some shamanic significance could also be read into this, since wind, or the Element of Air, was believed in primitive times to carry the breath of the gods or spirits, and could be either malign or benign according to the circumstances. Sir James Frazer draws our attention to this fact in *The Golden Bough* when he refers to 'the art of tying up the wind in three knots, so that the more knots are loosed the stronger will blow the wind'.[9] In fact, wind rites involving the use of knots were common practice amongst the ancient peoples of Finland, Shetland, Greece, New Guinea, Alaska, Borneo and, in fact, most parts of the world, which rather suggests a common source.

The four winds, like the four Elements, were well represented in Egyptian magic. Their names were Qebui, the North Wind, who was always depicted with four ram's heads; Shehbui, the South Wind, shown with the head of a lion; Henkhisesui, the East Wind, who was also ram-headed; and Hutchaici, the serpent-headed West Wind.[10]

Budge tells us of certain Arabian magicians, both male and female, who weaved spells (knots) in pieces of string or cord, and not always with the best intention, it seems. According to legend, a Jew named Lubaid, and his two daughters, bewitched Muhammed by tying eleven knots in a cord which they hid in a well. In fact, the prophet might well have died as a result had not God sent the archangel Gabriel to instruct him how to break the spell! The Bible contains an interesting reference to binding and loosing in Matthew's account of Peter's appointment as head of the Church:

> Thou art Peter, and upon this rock I will build my Church ... and to thee I shall give the keys of the kingdom of heaven. And whatever thou shalt bind on earth will be bound in heaven, and whatever thou shalt loose on earth shall be loosed in heaven.   *Matthew 16:18-20.*

This reference would appear to allude to the same kind of practices engaged in by the Egyptian priesthood, the terms 'Heaven' and 'Earth' referring to states of consciousness on the one hand, and the familiar 'as above, so below' concept on the other.

Knot rites could also be used to bind a spirit or soul to a certain place. Elemental and elementary spirits were often bound in time by the Egyptian priests, and commanded to guard certain tombs, time capsules, or power centres. I am inclined to believe they acquired knowledge of this practice from the Atlanteans, who were past masters at placing guardians at sacred places to steer (or frighten) away the profane. I have come across several of these myself over the years. If the guardian spirits are willing slaves, then I leave them with my love and respect, but should I discover them to be in bondage to evil, then I will release them *according to the Law of Equalities*. This is a magical Law which designates that when two equal forces meet, one will eventually give way to the other, who rises in status as a result. Therefore, before engaging in any form of dialogue with entities that have been placed in position by a magician, especially one from the old Egyptian priesthood, one should be careful to ascertain the power and intention behind the magus and engage, or desist, accordingly. Should the two sides of the scales be evenly loaded, then it would depend very much on the suffering caused to the enslaved entity. In other words, the ethics involved and whether these should be observed with some display of strength in the cause of freedom and light. As a Time Essence I am by nature a gatherer of information and not a warrior, so I tend to avoid confrontations of any kind other than in self-defence, or the defence of some weak spirit who appeals for help against its oppressors.

Death and Departure

Rites of passage obviously differed considerably during the long span of Egyptian history; *The Book of the Dead* abounds with them. Some are no more mystically meaningful than the sprigs of heather and cheap charms pedalled by hawkers in busy markets or fairs. As far as the really ancient beliefs are concerned, however, preparation for death was of great importance, since it served to afford the psyche a comfortable passage from one dimension to the other, free from the traumas of fear that can influence its situation in the ensuing frequencies. Stories of 'lost souls' who are helped on their way by various 'rescue groups' incarnate can be read in any of a number of books on spiritualism and allied subjects. Those enlightened ones who originally instructed the pre-dynastic Egyptians obviously placed some importance on the latter hours of a person's life and what happened to their psyche or consciousness after it had vacated its physical shell. What they originally taught we may never know for sure, but we may surmise that they stressed the infinite and eternal nature of the soul (field). Later generations, unable to conceive of immortality in some Elysian Fields without a body in which to indulge what they viewed as the more pleasant aspects of earthly existence, felt that omissions must have occurred at some point in history, which they sought to amend by working out an elaborate system for preserving the physical body, in the sincere belief that one or other of the 'spiritual bodies' might germinate or develop within it.

Mummification was not practised in pre-dynastic times. In fact, the indigenous peoples of North Africa tended either to burn their dead, or dismember them in customary shamanic fashion. Those bodies that were buried whole were laid on their left side with their head to the south. No attempt was made to mummify them. The dismemberment concept is re-echoed in the story of the cutting of the body of Osiris into fourteen pieces to be duly reassembled and immortalised by Isis, via the agency of *hekau* as instructed by Thoth, Master of the Word. In the ancient shamanic initiation rites, the body of the shaman was believed to be conveyed to a secret place where it was dismembered and reassembled according to some magical formula, which duly rendered the shamanic aspirant his or her true powers. As a matter of fact, I have had some strange experiences of this nature myself, but mainly in dream state. The idea behind this has, of course, nothing whatsoever to do with the physical body as such being purely symbolic of the rearrangement of the 'self' which is deemed essential to the aspirant to the spiritual path of service. It represents, as it were, the sacrificing of the immediate persona (body or soma) or the subjugation of the desire nature to the will of the transpersonal or higher self. I see this quite clearly in the Osirian myths and in many of the practices subsequently associated with rites of passage in ancient Egyptian belief.

Shabtis are another Egyptian concept which carries shamanic overtones. The word 'shabti' means 'those who answer', and shabtis shared many things in common with those voodoo and Wiccan figurines through which the magician could make contact with the person or persons they represented. Shabtis, however, carried none of the evil connotations often associated with waxen images of enemies, or those whom the client had paid the magician to deal with in some less desirable way; they were essentially aids for constructive forces. To the Egyptians they were magical substitutes for the dead person who would handle his or her personal affairs in the Netherworld. Shabtis first appeared in the Middle Kingdom, which far removes them from the Siriun influence and clearly defines them in the shamanic context. These figurines receive particular emphasis in the sixth chapter of *The Book of the Dead*.

There are, of course, other afterlife characters who featured in ancient funerary rites, notably the Ferryman, the Guardians of the Doors, and the Divine Tribunal. Many passages in the *Coffin Texts* describe strange passageways haunted by horrendous demons, crossroads which baffle the departed, and stretches of perilous water that can only be crossed with the aid of the Ferryman. In order to negotiate these, and other less desirable phenomena, the departed needed to know the passwords, while the officiating priests, as a part of their Initiations, were required to have negotiated all these and many more hidden dangers themselves, for only in that way could they be of any assistance to the deceased. No doubt the priesthood abounded with tricksters who extorted huge fees or offerings from the families of the deceased in exchange for a lot of mumbo-jumbo, but as any occultist worthy of his or her salt is well aware, there is always a price to be paid and a karma to be met in some other time-zone.

The Opening of the Mouth

Most of the better-known rituals associated with the 'Coming Forth by Day' appear in eighteenth dynasty texts, such as the Papyrus of Ani. My views on funerary rites, especially those of the later dynasties, have already been made abundantly clear, but there is one practice which is worthy of emphasis since I am inclined to associate itwith a much older belief, the real meaning of which had been long since forgotten, even in the very early dynasties, namely the Opening ofthe Mouth. Legends regarding the origin of this rite abound throughout the ancient texts. The *Papyrus of Nu* (British Museum No. 10,477, sheet 21) mentions that Chapter lxiv of *The Book of the Dead* was found inscribed in letters of real lapis lazuli, inlaid in a block 'of iron of the south' under the feet of the god (Thoth), during the reign of Men-Kau-Ra (Mycerinus), by the prince Heru-ta-ta-f in the city of Khemennu (see page 102). The chapter, we are told, must be recited by a man 'who is ceremonially clean and pure, who hath not eaten the flesh of animals or fish, and who hath not had intercourse with women.' The text continues:

> And behold, thou shalt make a scarab of green stone, with a rim of gold, and this shall be placed on the heart of the man, and it shall perform for him the 'Opening of the Mouth'. And thou shalt anoint it with *anti* unguent, and thou shalt recite over it the following words of power.[11]

The 'words of power' that follow this direction are to be found in Chapter XXX-B of *The Book of the Dead*. However, upon consulting the rubric in the chapter in question, I find a different set of instructions taken from the *Papyrus of Amen-hetep*, followed by a series of priestly incantations involving the names and deeds of a series of divinities, elements, animals, and so forth. One is left to assume, therefore, that the power behind these incantations lies in the way they are intoned by the priests, since there are no sonics as such incorporated in the aforementioned texts. The significance of the scarab in rites of departure is obvious, since Khepera was the divinity of resurrection and rebirth, and although the resurrection aspect is viewed in later dynasties as relating to the spirit or soul, one cannot help suspecting that those 'first teachers' used the simple scarab beetle to illustrate the theory of reincarnation.

I see the same applying to the Opening of the Mouth. According to one legend, the mouths of the gods were originally opened by Set, to whom the metal iron was sacred. Involved in this proceeding was the constellation of the Bear, believed to be sacred to Set, which hints at a cosmological rather than a personal meaning. Ritual, however, is frequently the microcosmic enactment of events that have taken place at the macrocosmic level, which places this particular ceremony in the category of a folk memory of an earlier, advanced knowledge. Scholars down the centuries have been asking what meaning this obscure ceremony could possibly have. Why, for example, should the mouth of the deceased need to be opened? As the physical mouth was obviously not the organ in question, one explantation could be that the original rite referred to the ability of the deceased to communicate with the living once the physical body had been discarded; or it could been seen as a necessary prerequisite to the speaking of the Negative Confession. Sonic implications could also be read into it, of course, and the original priestly intonations may well have carried a resonance which aided the departing soul to achieve this facility. Although we often hear of communications received from those who have passed over, many loved ones (and others) fail to maintain any form of contact, much to the distress of those they have left behind in this valley of tears. Could it be that those who do manage to communicate with ease were taught the art by the original 'Openers of the Mouth'? I refer, of course, to the Atlanto-Siriun priests rather than the sacerdotal hierarchies of later dynasties, who probably had little idea of the original *hekau* used in this rite, and therefore substituted a series of impressive nomenclatures which they believed to be equally effective?

Bauval and Gilbert tackled this issue at some length in a T.V. programme, *The Orion Mystery*, asserting that the requisite Rite required the use of a meteoritic iron implement which was inserted into the mouth of the deceased. In the sequence shown on page 62 (and also on the cover of *The Sirius Connection*), the Siriun energies are passed to Orion (Sah) and thence to Earth via Jupiter, Saturn and Mars. Interestingly, the metal sacred to the latter also happens to be iron! Bearing this in mind, I suggest that the original idea behind the rite was to afford the deceased the ability to communicate with, and thus pass through Mars, Saturn and Jupiter *en route* to Orion, wherein certain energies had to be negotiated before unification with Sirius could be achieved. The role of Anubis in this episode, as Time Traveller and Opener of the Ways, then becomes obvious.

Let us take a deeper look at the Orion/Sirius connection. Sirius is a first magnitude star in the constellation of Canis Major, whereas Orion is a constellation on the celestial equator near Taurus and Gemini, containing the stars Betelgeuse and Rigel. It was named after the giant Hunter of Greek mythology, pursuer of the Pleiades (good weather) and the Hyades (the rainy season). According to the myth, Orion was accidentally shot by Artemis at the instigation of her brother, Apollo – an indication of some celestial drama, perhaps, which was played out in the skies aeons ago? It also occurs to me that, in keeping with astronomer Heather Couper's assertion that we are all children of the stars, many of those souls who sought incarnation in Earth bodies in those early times might well have had their origins in these three constellations, the Pleiades in particular being a favourite for this role among many New Age and metaphysical believers. So, are we also dealing with a folk-memory of a long lost home? (See *The Gaia Dialogues*.)

Simplified versions of the above mentioned and similar rites are to be found in Gerald and Betty Scheuler's book *Coming Into the Light*. Although the odd Atlanto-Siriun influence may have survived in a few of these, they do not carry the impact of the originals which involved multidimensional awareness, and were mainly worked via 'mind magic' rather than set ritual. These I shall be dealing with in the ensuing chapters. I appreciate, however, that this may pose problems for many people who are uncomfortable in right-brain magical work, and still require the mental discipline and left-brain security of the set rite. But since that field is already well covered by the ancient texts, and the work of many modern scholars who have seen fit to present these in a more fashionable mode, there is a gap that calls to be filled into which Siriun magic neatly fits.

Endnotes:
1 J. Ivimy, *The Sphinx and the Megaliths*, page 96.
2 A. E. Waite, *The Occult Sciences*, pages 10–11.
3 C. J. Jung, *Memories, Dreams and Reflections*, pages 288–9.
4 C. Jacq, *Egyptian Magic*, page 27.
5 M. Hope, *Time: The Ultimate Energy*, pages 148–50.
6 J.A. West, *Serpent in the Sky*, page 156.
7 L. Lamy, *Egyptian Mysteries*, page 19.
8 C. Jacq, *Egyptian Magic*, pages 57–8.
9 J. Frazer, *The Golden Bough*, page 81.
10 E. A. Wallis Budge, *The Gods of the Egyptians*, Vol. 2, page 296.
11 E. A. Wallis Budge, *The Gods of the Egyptians*, Vol. 1, page 357–8.

Part Two

Sirius – The Metaphysics

CHAPTER 8

Siriun High Magic

This is the point at which we leave behind all the impedimenta of popular Egyptiana and return to source. Very little, if anything, has been committed to paper on the subject of Siriun (sometimes referred to as Sothian) magic a more accurate (and infinitely more acceptable) description of which would be 'cosmic science'. This is probably because, like the elusive Pimpernel, it is extremely difficult to recognise, let alone encapsulate in a way that would render it easily understood by the layman, or the Novitiate for that matter.

What we are dealing with here is not a precise set of rites involving familiar magical paraphernalia associated with the systems or traditions of this planet, but an abstract mental experience which leaves the practitioner with no guidelines other than one's own conscience and the ability to balance both brain hemispheres. In fact, this balancing of the right and left brain is absolutely essential for the person who would venture into the uncharted realms of Siriun magic, since there are no familiar signposts, no ancient masters or founders of world religions upon whom to lean, and no books from which to study. The first and only piece of equipment which is an absolute necessity for the student who would tread this path is *self-identification*. In other words, a knowledge of one's cosmic roots. Enter shock number one!

In tracing one's origins via the labyrinthine path of time-lessness, one is likely to discover many things that are totally at variance with any existing Earth philosophy or magical teaching.

Does one then fly back to the safety of the known, or does one creep cautiously forward, bravely facing the fact that we earthlings might conceivably have got it all wrong? You see, one of the first lessons to be learned from Siriun magic is that we are not alone in the universe, and that being a member of the genus *Homo sapiens* does not confer upon us a status superior to other life forms, visible or invisible, that we might encounter on our cosmic quest. Indeed, this is *not* a path for the nervous, the spiritually insecure, or the person with set views or ideas as to what the universe is all about. On the other hand, it is an exhilarating challenge – albeit a disconcerting one at times.

Use of the left brain in conjunction with the right brain is absolutely essential to the Siriun experience. What happens is that the abstract phenomena of outer time are duly translated by the right brain and transmitted to the left brain which, in turn, clothes them in appropriate terms of reference. In other words, the left brain has to be programmed to accommodate the multi-dimensional aspects of time and space, which can mean *activating certain sections of the brain which have been hitherto unused but which were designed for this specific purpose.* From a psychological viewpoint the dangers in this are obvious, which is why left brain logic – reprogrammed – is absolutely essential to the exercise.

Siriun magic is basically mind magic. It employs the mind and brain as the tools of the psyche, via which consciousness can explore the universe, if only a little at a time, and thus familiarise itself with the nature and *modus operandi* of those generating energies which are the hub of its existence. How these energies are perceived and translated will depend upon three main factors:

1. The brain capacity (cerebral megabytes and software) of the seeker.
2. The cosmic age, status or field band-width of the soul fragment effecting the investigation.
3. The time capsule or ring-pass-not into which the knowledge is built, the releasing of which will relate to the group evolution of the species within which that particular soul-fragment or field particle of the seeker is encapsulated.

It is for this reason that some 'travellers' view the gods or 'Old Ones' in specific human or personalised forms, while others conceive of these intelligences in terms of abstract energies associated with the stuff of which the universe is perceived (with our limited knowledge) to have been made.

Let us clear up a few more obvious questions that are bound to arise concerning the subject of mind magic. Special effects, either personal or phenomenal, are not essential to its accurate practice. One does not, for example, need to put on a physical or shamanic show when externalising. Lighting a candle, or using an incense appropriate to one's own personal frequency can help inasmuch as it is an aid to spiritual or psychic security, while there are some known magical symbols which do resonate with the Siriun waveband, the sistrum, for example. Temple draws our attention to the fact that the Greek for Sirius, *sierios*, bears similarities to *seistron*, which in Latin became *sistrum*, a percussion instrument which dates back to Atlantis, used in the worship of Isis and Bast. Since Siriun magic shares its archetypes with some of the very early Egyptian magical references, certain symbols are valid in both systems. The Eye, itself forming part of the hieroglyph for the name of Osiris, is one example, while the actual hieroglyph for Sothis (Sept), incorporated the five-pointed star in conjuction with the column and was written thus. (See *Fig 8.1* below.)

We have therefore established three essentials to the safe performance of Siriun (inter-cosmic) magic:

1. The need for personal cosmic identity, which relieves one of the necessity to strap-hang on any existing faith, tradition or Earth-orientated philosophy. The overall climate of insecurity which prevails on Earth has promoted a tendency for

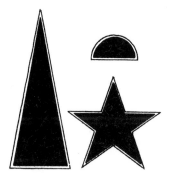

Fig. 8.1

people to become group-minded in that they feel more secure following a belief or philosophy that is espoused by a large number of people. In times of trouble, fear or emergency, they retreat to the safety of the 'group belief', rather than to the security of that aspect of the 'divine' that is present within their own psyches. The discovery of one's own personal cosmic identity helps alleviate those spiritual insecurities that are likely to prove a problem for the student wishing to pursue the Siriun magical Path.

2. The ability to externalise; to project mentally beyond the time-space barriers and therefore well away from the influence of the Earth or this solar system. According to several of the more profound schools of metaphysical belief, there is a malign influence surrounding Earth which inhibits true spiritual growth and cosmic understanding. The aim of the would-be Siriun initiate is therefore to break through this barrier, which has affected our conscious and unconscious programming for so many centuries, and thus gain a clearer, broader, and more accurate view of some of the many dimensions and life forms that abound in the universe beyond our planet. Science is already opening many doors for us in this direction, and we must be spiritually prepared for what will come to many orthodox believers as profound shocks, so that we may fulfil our roles as helpers in the days of transition that lie ahead.

3. The balanced employment of both brain hemispheres when dealing with Siriun energies is essential. All inter-cosmic experiences are integrally bound to the timelessness factor. The boundaries of inner and outer time are entirely different, the former being erected by the prevailing physical conditions and the thoughts and energies of those beings incarnate within the energy frequency of the material world in question. On the other hand, the 'ring-pass-nots' of outer time are an insubstantial phenomenon of cosmic law, the acquisition of their password being a bonus that only comes with the kind of spiritual maturity that is borne of profound inter-time knowledge, wisdom and experience.

Entering a world of timelessness automatically opens up the portals to the past and future. Can we handle such knowledge? Will it blow our mental fuses? Gurdjieff referred to what he called 'buffers', those self-erected cushions which serve to soften life's blows and render them unnoticeable and imperceptible. Psychologists believe that without these buffers many of us would be unable to handle such contingencies as sudden shock, extreme grief or great personal loss. Gurdjieff insisted that these buffers were not the creation of nature, but rather of man himself, and mostly the product of the unconscious, referring to them as 'appliances by means of which a man can always be in the right.'[1] In other words, among other things, they monitor our conscience.

To these comments I would like to add the following: we create 'buffers' as a protection against that which our minds cannot handle and our brains cannot compute. I see them as personal 'ring-pass-nots' which certainly operate in Siriun magic, provided the motivation behind our intention is the light of knowledge and the love of all. So, while they might not actually interfere with our learning process, they will help to ensure our mental equilibrium at all times. For those interesred in the practical application of Siriun energies, further information is supplied in my book *The Lion People*.

In the aforegoing we may evidence the significance of the knot as a recording symbol which binds together the experiences of inner and outer time, and as the knot symbology played an important role in Egyptian magic this seems as good a place as any to introduce the Egyptian deities into the Siriun scheme of things, and extract from the ancient texts those portions that are relative to the Atlanto-Siriun teachings.

Endnotes:

1 P. D. Ouspensky, *In Search of the Miraculous*, page 154.

CHAPTER 9

The Goddesses of the Siriun System

Both Egyptian and Dogon tradition insist that the energies of the large blue-white star in the Sirius system are predominantly feminine. The Egyptians associated it with Isis and probably not without good reason. Regarding Digitaria, or Sirius B, due to its hidden nature it has sometimes been allocated to Isis' sister, Nephthys, although more often it is designated the sphere of Osiris for reasons which have been previously explained. This leaves us with Sirius C, the Dogon's Sorghum-Female, which is truly hidden since it has not been seen by astronomers since 1929.

The feminine nature of this third luminary indicates that it belongs to one of the major goddesses of the Egyptian pantheon, and Nephthys, Hathor or Sekhmet naturally spring to mind. We should remember that Hathor was the patroness of women. In contrast, her *alter ego*, if indeed it can be described as such, was the fierce, strong and fiery Sekhmet, the lioness-headed one, also believed to be one and the same as Tefnut, twin sister of Shu, or the gentle Bast, goddess of music, dance and joy whose worship flourished in Ptolemaic times.

But what of Nephthys, the Hidden One, also designated Goddess of Sleep? She is sometimes seen as the *alter ego* or dark side of Isis, but after working with both deities for many years I am convinced that they are quite separate archetypes. In the bipolar context, Isis is seen as the extrovert – the loving mother to whose joys and tears most women can relate, while Nephthys is essentially the introvert, ruler of the deep waters of the unconscious, the dark side of the moon. I do not think that either

Isis or Nephthys have anything to do with the moon, well, not directly, anyway, and logic suggests that Nephthys might appropriately represent Sirius C.

There are some more interesting facts concerning the Nephthian archetype which bear consideration. For example, she is essentially a water goddess, the feminine aspect of Neptune, and as such she rules the emotions and relates strongly to the human condition. According to traditional elemental classifications *Homo sapiens* as a species is water-ruled. Ezekiel's vision was of the lion, eagle, ox and man – fire, air, earth and water respectively, while of the Four Sons of Horus one has a human head. Sumerian art features a lion, an eagle, and an ox upon whose back is mounted a peacock – the traditional symbol of pride which is said to represent humankind.

It is no coincidence that variants of the name Nephthys appear in renal-related diseases – Nephritis, for example. My nanny used to refer to the renal system as 'the waterworks' and I have noted from my studies of medical astrology that the position of Neptune in a birth chart does have some effect on the satisfactory (or otherwise) functioning of the kidneys. Problems of an emotional nature which feature the deep unconscious are also likely to affect the soma via the renal system, which is one reason why those among us who resonate with the Nephthian archetype should pay special heed to any deep-seated emotional traumas and endeavour to externalise them whenever possible. It can, of course, be argued that Tefnut, goddess of dew and gentle rain, also has water connotations, which simply reinforces the argument that later archetypes became superimposed over earlier versions of the same manifest principle.

Another aspect of the human psychological economy which the Nephthian archetype represents is the Shadow: that which is hidden. Although the bright rays of the spiritual sun are frequently advocated as the antidote to the Shadow, without the sun there would be no Shadow, for it is surely the buildings, people, trees, mountains and all things natural to Earth which cast the shadows we see on our bright and sunny days. This suggests that both Light and Shadow are essentially a part of the earthly experience or of any scenario which features that atomic/molecular structure we call matter. The energies of both Nephthys and Isis are therefore contingent upon each other. In other words, we need to plumb the depths of our deep unconscious in order to come to terms with our Shadow, and in so doing we learn the highways and byways of both the heights and the depths. After all if one looks down from a great height one will see not only the beautiful gardens, rivers and trees, but also less pleasant aspects assail one's vision. Rising above a town in a jet aeroplane may well afford one an excellent view of the municipal gardens, but the gasometers, corporation rubbish dumps, slum districts, and other, less salubrious areas of the overall panorama are also thrown into relief.

The Isian archetype is also far more complex than may be imagined initially. The gentle and caring Isis may well be the archetypal mother at one particular level, but unlike the Virgin Mary she was also a magician *par excellence* who, by cunning connivance, extracted from Ra the secret of his name (personal sonic). Isis has also been conceived of in the Triple Goddess context – Sothis, Satis and Anukis being her three Siriun aspects.

So what does this tell us as far as Sirius is concerned? Isis, Osiris and Nephthys were archetypes representing the solar genii of the three Siriun stars (if indeed Sirius C is or was a star and not a planet – I have my doubts), and that upon the collapse of Sirius B (the ascension of Osiris to a higher or more exalted frequency) Isis acquired his power in the form of Horus, their son. Just as many of us believe our solar system to have been seeded from Sirius, so the Siriun system itself may also have been seeded from a star in another, more central, part of the galaxy. Was that star the original Ra, from whom Isis gained her knowledge of sonics, and whose Eyes were kept 'in the family', so to speak, being passed from Ra to Osiris and thence to Horus? *The Book of the Dead* and the Pyramid Texts make frequent mention of Ra, Osiris and Horus as being one and the same entity, or reincarnations one of the other. Or perhaps they are simply alluding to a group of enlightened beings who either came from Sirius or were acquainted with the fact that the Siriun system was closely associated with the evolution and development of our own star and its satellites:

> As concerning the divine Twin-Gods they are Heru-netch-hra-tef-f and Heru-khent-an-maati; or (as others say), the divine Soul that dwelleth in the Divine Twin-Gods is the Soul of Ra and the Soul of Osiris; [or (as others say),] It is the Soul which dwelleth in Shu [and] the Soul which dwelleth in Tefnut, and these are the double divine Soul which dwelleth in Tattu.[1]

In this context, the energies of Digitaria, or Sirius B, could therefore be seen as having passed to Horus. But since we have tended to view the final episode of the Isian drama as being acted out in the present, wherein the *dramatis personae* are still working towards wresting the Throne of Righteousness from the dictatorship of Chaos, the Aeon of Horus has yet to come! Interestingly enough, the contest between Set (Chaos) and Horus (Order) was judged by Thoth (Time). As the tangled threads of myth and legend are slowly unravelled the Siriun prophecy begins to take on a new, and more comprehensible meaning.

There are, however, alternatives to the Isis-Osiris-Nephthys allocation of the Siriun stars, Sekhmet/Hathor/Ra being one, with Sekhmet for Sirius A, Ra for Sirius B, and Hathor, traditionally the Egyptian patroness of women, for Sorghum-Female (Sirius C). Does the legend perhaps not infer that following an assault by his enemies, which was foiled by the intervention of his daughter, the old god retired to some higher plane (changed frequencies to a different and more subtle waveband?). According to current scientific thinking, the process of transition from a yellow star to a white dwarf, which is what Sirius B has become, is as follows: (1) The main sequence, which is the present stage of our own sun; (2) expansion to a red giant; (3) contraction to the horizontal branch; (4) gross expansion to a red supergiant and the expulsion of the expanded shell into a planetary nebula; and (5) contraction to a white dwarf. Might not the effect of stage 4 appear as a giant serpent encircling the orb – the Apep that worried Ra and was eventually despatched by his daughter Bast or Sekhmet?

Another option would be Ra as Amon, 'the Hidden One', for Sirius B, and his children Shu and Tefnut for Sirius A and C respectively. After all, the name Amon, Amen or Amun is surely close to the Dogon 'Amma', whose Nommo (Instructor) son is believed by those people to be connected with the future salvation of our world in much the same way as Horus, son of Isis. The mystery deepens – or does it? I think not, since what we are dealing with are surely the same archetypes to whom successive post-Atlantean generations have ascribed different nomenclatures.

The ancient Egyptian texts contain references to the *Khet-Khet* or Double Fire – the Fire of Solidification and the Fire of Dispersion – represented by Isis and Nephthys respectively. I can

vouch for the efficacy of the latter as I have used it myself to
disperse a violent crowd. So although this lesson from ancient
Egypt is usually read as referring to the journey through the
Abyss, or *Seshet*, wherein the energies of the former life are
dispersed (Nephthys), to solidify in the process of rebirth (Isis),
hidden within this all too obvious allusion is a major metaphysical mystery! Those priests of the old Siriun tradition were
more than clever in the way they masked their magical secrets,
making no attempt to conceal them, but constructing them in
such a way that they could only be read and understood *at their
higher frequencies* by those who were ready to do so. They realised
that since most people are motivated either by fear or by the
desire nature, the natural tendency among the unenlightened
would be to interpret them in either of those contexts, which is
exactly what happened and has been happening ever since. The
mysteries of Isis and Nephthys are therefore seen as relating only
to death or the afterlife on the one hand, and the more mundane
interests appropriate to the desire nature on the other. Nor was
this knowledge of the human psychological condition misplaced, since only the true Initiate, who is sufficiently selfless to
seek beyond the gratifications of the flesh, the acquisitions of the
world, and the fear of what lies beyond the grave, would be
likely to spot the truth.

The Nephthian dispersement phenomenon should not be
confused with Setian energies, for although both are basically
chaotic, each operates at a different level. As for the descent into
the Abyss, or chthonic regions, this is essential to any form of
metaphysical study since the universe is by no means all
sweetness and light, and sooner or later the Novitiate is bound to
encounter energies which are not compatible with his or her
own, and which must be either negotiated or dealt with in a just
and charitable manner.

Engaging in a dialogue with the Egypto/Siriun deities, and
therefore with the archetypes (and facets of the Self) which they
represent, is an essential part of Siriun magic. Whichever aspect
of each deity is contacted will naturally depend very much on
the archetype predominating in the personality of the Novitiate.
More maternal types of either sex will be inclined to attract the
maternal Isian energies, while others may be drawn to her
queenly role, her social awareness, or her magical power.
Likewise with Nephthys, although those who would invoke the

Hidden One in her role as the Revealer should take special care to ensure that the knowledge they request will not prove too much for them to handle, Siriun magic being a noted fuse-blower! I could relate some hair-raising stories of people I have known who actually met their end through invoking the Revealer, limitations in their left brain software rendering them unable to rationalise the shock; or as Gurdjieff might remark, 'their buffers were insufficiently oiled to take the impact!'

In this chapter I have dealt only with Isis and Nephthys; Osiris, Horus, and Set are yet to come. One question which is bound to be asked is, what about the planet which is believed to orbit the third, or Nephthian star, Sirius C or Sorghum-Female? Well, there is always Anubis, Nephthys' son by Osiris, which makes sense, if you care to think about it. Although I do not think the inhabitants of that planet are or were canines! The Dogons referred to Sorghum-Female as 'The Sun of Women' and its solitary planet as 'The Star of Women'. A confusion of terms here, a sun being a star and not a planet. So, what if the 'sun' was actually a large planet like Jupiter, and the supposed satellite a moon – both carrying passive/receptive (feminine) energy patterns? It bears consideration. In fact I am inclined to the option that a very beautiful, hominid-type species inhabited what the Dogans have referred to as the 'Sun', hence the allusion to 'the planet of women', indicating people without the rough appearance usually associated with the males of our species! It is also my belief that the Osirian sun, Sirius B, once had an orbiting planet which housed a leonine race. Osiris' animal was always the lion, and a passage in the *Hermes Trismegistus* describes how Osiris:

> ... coming to him [Horus, his son] out of the Invisible, worked through him and trained him for the fight. [against Set].
>
> He then put this test question to him: 'What does he consider fairest?' And when he said: 'Helping father and mother in ill plight,' he asked a second: 'What animal does he think most useful for those who go out to fight?'
>
> And when Horus said 'Horse,' he marvelled at him, and was quite puzzled why he did not say 'Lion' rather than 'Horse'.
>
> Accordingly Horus said: '"Lion" is a needful thing to one requiring help, but "Horse" [can] scatter in pieces the foe in flight and consume him utterly.'[2]

Although little mention is made in *The Book of the Dead* and other ancient Egyptian texts concerning the horse, esoteric sources have always acknowledged it to be the animal sacred to Horus, especially the white horse, which was later venerated by the Celts, while in Atlantis the horse or unicorn was sacred to Danuih, the Earth goddess.

There are numerous references in *The Book of the Dead* to the 'Lion-god' in connection with Osiris – too many, in fact, to enumerate them all. I particularly liked the stanza in Chapter XXVIII, which concerns the guarding of the heart, and is accompanied by the vignette. (See *Fig. 9.1* below.)

> Hail, thou Lion-god! I am the Flower Bush *(Unb)*. That which is an abomination to me is the divine block. Let not this my heart *(hati)* be carried away from me. ... Hail thou who doest wind bandages around Osiris and who hath seen Set![3]

The impregnation of Isis constitutes one of the major mysteries surrounding the epagomenal Neters, since it constitutes the pivot upon which the whole Osirian drama is based. If we are to believe that Isis was actually impregnated by Osiris *after his spirit had left its body and arisen to a higher plane,* then this places the goddess in the same category as those other mothers who conceive in some miraculous way, and then give birth to a child who is destined to become a world saviour. I am inclined to dismiss the idea of a wooden phallus as something that was added later by a people who could not comprehend the idea of any women giving birth without the aid of a male member, albeit a facsimile of the original! Thoth's *hekau* and Isis' own magic makes more

Fig. 9.1

metaphysical sense, and since time was obviously involved we might well be dealing with a dynasty rather than a single incident. After all, as we have already observed, the Osiris-Nephthys episode can be easily translated in terms of principles, so why not Isis and Osiris?

As previously mentioned (see page 68), the order in which the five epagomenal Neters were born also presents something of an enigma. Budge tells us that the children of Nut (the sky), were not all brought forth in the same place or on the same day. Day one witnessed the birth of Osiris; day two saw the emergence of Horus; day three was Set's day; day four belonged to Isis while day five was Nephthys' birthday. The first, third and fifth of the epagomenal days were considered unlucky, the second is not described as either lucky nor unlucky, but the fourth is said to be a 'beautiful festival of heaven and earth'.[4] The days of Osiris, Set and Nephthys, and presumably those deities, could therefore be seen to have unfortunate connotations; Horus was obviously an unknown and consequently an unproven quantity, while Isis was much loved by all. Could we possibly be dealing with a cosmological drama, with each deity representing an era (that is, Isis: the zodiacal Age of Virgo) rather than an individual?

But what if Horus is the direct connection between our solar system and the Sirius sun, which might explain the conflicting myths regarding his birth: (a) that he arrived on the second of the epagomenal days following Osiris and (b) that he was born to Isis here on Earth, following her impregnation from 'heaven' or wherever? Could the child of Isis, seeded by Osiris (Sirius B) represent humankind? If so, that would make Set (Chaos) the testing ground for Horus (Order), which the Son of Isis has first to conquer before he is worthy to ascend the throne of his father. The myths tell us that Horus was a sickly child whose survival was doubtful at one period. Taken in the context of the Horus/hominid analogy, perhaps *Homo sapiens* is the sickly child whose survival is still debatable!

Isis, in her role as the Great Mother or Creatrix, having been seeded by her husband Osiris (Sirius B prior to its collapse), would certainly make metaphysical sense and would naturally connect any beings incarnate within the Siriun complex with their earthly 'cousins'. The legend tells us that when Horus and Set finally came to battle, Horus was limited in his weaponry by Cosmic Law, whereas Set employed every despicable means to overthrow the God of Light; and so it is with people here on Earth. Gentle, caring and decent folk (Horus people) will only choose to fight in a just cause or in defence of home and country, whereas Set's minions will stop at nothing to attain their evil ends.

New information regarding the formation of the universe, which could perhaps be seen as relevant to our subject matter, has recently been published by Professor Richard Ellis and his colleagues at Durham University. Ellis has developed a fibre-optic scanner which can measure the light emitted from several sources simultaneously, which he planned to use to construct a three-dimensional galaxy map. The information received from the first probe certainly came as a shock. Since previous studies had indicated that galaxies were found in clusters, the distribution was not expected to be smooth, or follow any precise mathematical pattern. Imagine their amazement when their new equipment revealed the fact that these clusters appear at regular intervals of around 400 million light years, and turn out to be evenly distributed along a narrow cone of the universe, suggesting the universe may be a giant honeycomb of regular repeating galactic cells! No current theory predicts such a periodic pattern.[5] This picture surely conjures up the concept of a giant brain, the implication being that the creation of all life is no haphazard affair, and that there is, after all, some 'supermind' behind it all, an idea which has recently been explored by mathematical physicist Professor Paul Davies in his book *The Mind of God*. Bearing all this in mind, the concept of Sirius, and other stars in our corner of the galaxy, exerting a precise influence upon the life-cycles and evolution of the resident energies or Essences becomes easily credible.

Let us abandon temporarily the dizzy galactic heights and descend to Earth once more. Over the centuries, many different mystical rites and mysteries have been ascribed to Isis, among the best known of which is probably that of the Veil. Since great secrecy is usually attached to what is to be found behind that Veil, and we are on the subject of the Mysteries of Isis, dare we take a peek to see if those precious secrets carry any Siriun connotations? And why not!

The first surprise is that there is no Veil as such, only that which has been created by the mind of the individual, which will vary in intensity according to the soul-age (field band-width) and stage in initiatory development. As with all the other

Egyptian 'mysteries' what lies behind Isis' Veil can be perceived at any of several levels, and there are probably other frequencies beyond those as well. The first thing of which it reminds me is that recent researches into genetics have shown that the female XX chromosome carries a much broader range of frequencies than the masculine XY, which has a limited mode of expression. I have yet to find a scientific paper which identifies these frequencies or the specific feminine talents to which they relate, but I strongly suspect that adaptability and what is popularly termed 'feminine intuition' may feature somewhere along the line. However, I could be off beam.

Esoterically, this is suggestive of the Creatrix mode – Isis, and if Isis as the main Siriun star was indeed the Creatrix of our solar system, then our sun must also carry the feminine emphasis, as I have long suspected. The ancient Egyptians always accorded the moon a male personality, and although both Ra and Horus are viewed in the solar context, Osiris, like Thoth and Khonsu, is decidedly lunar. As has already been emphasised, contrary to the traditions of many other pantheons, the Egyptians saw our own planet in the male form of Geb. Perhaps they knew something we do not?

Now I have never patronised what are generally termed Women's Mysteries on the grounds that we should be working towards a closer relationship between the two sexes, and anything which could vaguely be seen as divisive is hardly conducive to this end. People's rites, if rites we must have, is much more Siriun, especially if there is a fair distribution of the sexes, or the anima-animus balance among those participating. However, part of understanding the Isis Ray involves comprehending her magical aspects, as distinct from her archetypal maternal role, and it could well be that this Siriun talent has found its way into today's world via a specific genetic coding *which is carried exclusively by females*. In other words, the Siriun gene, if there is such a thing, is transmitted via the mother.

There are other, more obvious, interpretations of the Isian Veil, such as that which is concealed from the profane, the various subtle or inner planes, and certain truths available only to those who have been initiated into her mysteries, as exemplified in the *Metamorphoses* of Apuleius, the Roman philosopher and satirist (c. AD 125–180) whose tale of how Lucius prayed to Isis for release from his asinine disguise [an aspect of the lower self or desire nature, perhaps?] is considered by many authorities as autobio-graphical. Although the Veil of Isis can mean many things to many people, especially in the personal sense, it is a mistake to relate it purely to the mystical as I am fast learning that these Atlantean or Egypto/Siriun symbols contain a complete range of meanings from the scientific and practical to the deeply esoteric or abstract. Where Sirius is concerned, however, the connotations of Isis' Veil are somewhat more cosmological, and tend to be involved with the Creatrix aspect of the feminine principle, as applied to both the Siriun complex and our own solar system.

The worship of Isis continued long after Egypt ceased to be a major power in world affairs. Dr R. E. Witt, writing in *Isis in the Graeco-Roman World*, cites the Oxyrhynchus Litany, from the *Oxyrhynchus Papyrus* 1380, as a sort of Egyptian *Te Deum* to the glories of Isis, and emphasises its connection with the locality of Memphis. Comparing this litany with the early *Hymn to the Sun*, ascribed to the eighteenth dynasty Pharaoh Akhnaton (Amenophis IV), Witt notes great similarities and remarks:

> Isis does not identify herself with the solar disk: but she does assert that she has ordained and accompanies the course of the sun and that she exists in the sun's rays. Just as the Aton divides the races of men so that each utters its own speech, so Isis has drawn up the Greek and non-Greek 'dialects'. The rays of the Aten are in the midst of the great ocean: when He shines, the ships have the way open to sail up and down stream. So Isis presides over shipping and rivers, winds and sea.[6]

Witt offers further evidence of Isis' solar or stellar associations, as against the lunar nature so often ascribed to her, and quotes the words of Lucius, which would most certainly meet with the approval of those who have chosen to follow the worship of the feminine principle in its Isian form:

> Thou who art the holy and eternal saviour of the human race ... worshipped by the powers above and honoured by the powers beneath, thou who dost set the earth revolving in its orbit, source of the sun's light and ruler of the Universe ... art obeyed by the stars and makest the seasons return, thou joy of the gods and mistress of the elements. At thy behest the winds blow, the rains bring forth the food, and the seeds take root and turn into sprouting plants.[7]

Now this is surely more like the Siriun goddess than the pale shadow of a maternal deity that supposedly originated among the pre-dynastic nomes of the Nile Delta! To confine Isis to a lunar role is metaphysical error in the extreme. She, like her four brethren have far wider, and more cosmic connections which are all intimated within the legends and myths if we only open our eyes and look for them. The Egyptian myths strike me as being rather like verbal versions of those puzzle pictures which show an ordinary, everyday scene, but wherein are concealed figures, faces, shapes or numbers which could go totally unnoticed were it not for the 'puzzle' element that immediately sets one searching for them amongst the vases of flowers, tables, chairs, light fittings, and ordinary impedimenta of everyday life. In fact, I was looking at one just recently and it took me quite a while to locate some of the creatures and implements indicated in the instructions. I could not find them all, but then I did not really have the time, and that, surely, is the case with many of us in this day and age: we look at something and see only what we want to see; in parapsychology this is referred to as the 'experimenter effect'. Time can be both an ally and a hindrance, but then I suppose it all depends on one's soul-age or field band width as to how one employs whatever time one has for life's experiences.

Endnotes:

1 E. A. Wallis Budge, *The Book of the Dead*, Vol. 1, pages 102–3.

2 G. R. S. Mead, *Thrice Greatest Hermes*, Vol. 1, page 290.

3 E. A. Wallis Budge, *The Book of the Dead*, Vol. I, page 142.

4 E. A. Wallis Budge, *The Gods of the Egyptians*, Vol. II, page 109.

5 *The Guardian*, 23 March 1990.

6 R. E. Witt, *Isis in the Graeco-Roman World*, pages 103–4.

7 Wallis Budge, page 109.

CHAPTER 10

Osiris, Horus and Set

Dualism is the theme of this chapter: the eternal dual between darkness and light, chaos and order, good and evil, in whichever context it arises. Many Earth religions have been founded upon this notion and it would appear to be as valid in other parts of the galaxy as it is here. This does not mean, of course, that the inhabitants of planets in the star systems of Aldebaran, Orion, or wherever, share our concept of Satan, since not all living entities in the galaxy, let alone the universe, may have experienced the need to accord personal identities to the negative forces or misplaced energies they may have encountered during their evolutionary journeying.

Before embarking on our analysis of the story of Set versus Osiris and Horus, therefore, we should consider some alternative beliefs apropos the subject of evil, or what the more polite among the metaphysical fraternity might prefer to refer to as 'negative energy'. Since the question of protection inevitably arises in the study of any occult, religious or transcendental pursuit, one is naturally asked from whom or what does one need to protect oneself. The answer to this will depend, of course, on one's personal concept of good and evil, or the established dogmas on the subject to which one has elected to adhere. Many esoteric traditions accept the fact that in the subtle dimensions all is not sweetness and light, others see evil as existing only in the hearts and minds of humankind, while a third faction denies its existence completely, either as an ethical concept or an organised force, which would seem to suggest the absence of any moral guidelines.

It is not my intention to stand by any existing dogma or doctrine concerning the nature of evil, but I will offer an alternative theory based on Siriun magic, which some may accept and others may not. It matters not either way, since in the final reckoning it is entirely a matter of personal conscience and the ultimate judge of 'the self' *is* 'the self'. Those readers who are already familiar with the concepts I espouse are asked to bear with me, as there are certain to be people unfamiliar with these views who would like to know where they stand in the system of Siriun mind magic concerning the recognition and handling of misplaced or malignant energies.

According to my Siriun contacts, what is generally termed 'evil' is nothing more than displaced or disorganised energies which have come adrift from their natural time-zone (their own spot on the evolutionary time dial). Standards of ethics are relative to periods of evolutionary development. Those conditions we see as social evils in today's world were not viewed in such a light as recently as 100 years ago, just as our present ethics will no doubt be decried as barbaric by future generations.

There are a very definite set of Cosmic Laws which function regardless of how we might feel about them here on Earth in any particular period of [time] history. This may come as something of a disappointment to those who are seeking excuses to give vent to their destructive or negative tensions. Just as the effect of combining certain chemicals can be guaranteed, so it is with Cosmic Laws which are constant throughout all zones of inner and outer time. Time, in fact, is the keyword here as time-warps are usually involved in those energy misplacements which are inevitably lumped together under the devil's umbrella! Just as the Dogons claim to have heard from their Siriun contacts that Earth was an impure planet – a place where the evil Ogo's umbilical cord was attached to his placenta – certain esoteric teachings also refer to our world as a 'fallen planet'; a sphere which is out of its correct time sequence in relation to the rest of the solar system and galaxy might be a more appropriate description, which has resulted in the growth and spread of a virus. For those interested in a more detailed description of this viral manifestation, I have covered the subject in greater detail in my book *The Gaia Dialogues*.

Undesirable or disharmonious force-fields are built up by tensive energies that are set in motion by those intelligences in both inner and outer time which operate outside the wavebands of Cosmic Law. There are techniques for avoiding these which involve side-stepping, or changing to a time-zone frequency wherein they are unable to function or are negated by counter-forces. Many ancient rites were built around this premise, although the original reason and logic behind them has become lost along the corridors of linear time. A parallel to this concept would be the instances of certain diseases that existed in centuries past, which have since been conquered by science so that the evil they represented in their time no longer poses a threat, due to changes in accepted standards of hygiene which prevent their development or spread in the first place.

'Evil' is a misplaced or misdirected energy that is out of its correct time sequence, but since there are many ways in which it can or may manifest, this simplification could well convey the idea that its existence is being denied, which is far from the truth. Of course evil exists, but only as relative to time. Anything which transgresses Cosmic Law could loosely be labelled as 'evil'. Those who elect to run counter to the cosmic flow automatically set in motion a series of contra-energies that take form as they gather momentum, eventually assuming a collective identity which feeds greedily on all that is around it. This misplaced force-field can be utilised by intelligences that have chosen to abandon temporarily the ways of light and love and pursue the path of chaos. Thus, what are broadly referred to as 'evil forces' assume personalities according to the philosophical or religious inclinations prevalent in the age in which they first manifested. However, science has now established that chaos is eventually self-organising; so, for all their rebellion, stray energy fields and their accompanying intelligences eventually find their way back to the matrix. This may be evidenced in many of the tales of fallen angels, immortals and mortals who have transgressed the laws of some mythical 'heaven' and the prodigal sons of all beliefs. The Egyptians and, no doubt, those Siriuns or Atlanteans who were the source of their original information on the subject, were also well aware of the chaos versus order factor which they highlighted in their parables, personalising the former as Set and the latter as son of Horus.

Of course, there will always be those tensions which form part of the lessons offered by each time-zone, which usually result from interplay within the group or collective experience of the race or planet in question. This observation has given rise to the aforementioned concept of dualism, or the idea that the forces of good and evil are in a constant struggle for supremacy. In one sense this is a fair assessment, for each time-zone or period of history does present relative tensions against which those functioning within that circuit can push or thrust. It is only when the accumulated potential of that tension mode becomes out of control, or out of balance, that the resulting force-field lends itself for utilisation by energies incompatible with Cosmic Law. Some believe this to be the problem with out planet today.

Another point to be taken into consideration is incompatibility, with people, places or even simple artifacts of life. The fact that all energy patterns or frequencies are not necessarily compatible does not make them evil. Most of us have, at some time or other, entered premises in which we have felt decidedly uncomfortable or ill at ease, or met people who have had the same effect on us. This should not be taken as an indication that the other party or parties are evil. It is simply a basic law which operates via one's chemistry and psychology that alerts one to the fact that certain incompatibilities are present. It can even apply to chemicals and foodstuffs, in which case the soma reacts by creating an allergy!

The negotiation of chaos is the inevitable Herculean labour of the Initiate. It cannot be avoided, and it is never more accentuated than in Siriun magic. The Dogons tell us that the dwellers in the Siriun system had overcome their particular Set, but since the whole Osirian drama was then transferred to this solar system, and to Earth in particular, we are now faced with the same battle that our Siriun cousins fought and won in some other space-time continuum. Could we not read into the myth that during this battle Osiris was temporarily overcome by Set, but eventually saved by Isis? Or, translated into terms more comprehensible to us mere mortals: two Masculine Principles met, one aiming to destroy the other, but through the intervention of the Feminine Principle, the nobler of the two side-stepped (ascended to another dimension which was not accessible to his pursuer), leaving the gentle Feminine Principle to cope with the destructive and malevolent masculine energy, whose pride she had offended by her intervention.

Moving the whole scenario to another, more primitive environment – Earth – naturally gives the aggressive Set the upper hand; well, temporarily, anyway. And so it will be until Isis can persuade the young souls of the new planet, by kindness and love, to accept her benign ways by virtue of their own free will, thus freeing themselves once and for all from the evils and suffering that inevitably result from the rule of chaos. But Set's ways are much more exciting to many earthlings. The macho image, with its accentuated ego-centricity, sex, brutality and power complexes prove particularly attractive to many members of the male of the species, although there are obviously women who also fall victims to the Setian wiles. Poor Isis, does she stand a chance against such enormous odds? I believe she does, since she has the magic of Thoth, the Lord of Time on her side, while her son Horus, the destined enemy of Set, slowly grows to maturity and finds his strength and purpose. She also possesses knowledge that Set does not – the magic of names or sonics, which means that with the passage of time she can effect changes on Earth which will *preclude souls of Setian inclination from incarnating here in future years.*

Remember that we have said that certain energies can only function within given frequencies; alter those and the problem is solved. But Isis, or Sophia, as many might prefer to call her, being in harmony with Cosmic Law, is obliged to abide by its precepts. She must wait until a sufficient number of people here on Earth become aware of the true nature of their planet and awaken to what is being done to ruin it (become cognisant of Cosmic Law), which is precisely what is happening in our present day and age.

Another point to be taken into consideration, when comparing Set's play for the minds of earthlings with a similar battle in the Siriun system in which he was unsuccessful, is the elemental emphasis which differs considerably between the species concerned. The two main races of the Siriun system, the Crystal People, who are/were hominids, and the leonid Paschats, were predominantly air and fire respectively, while we of Earth come under the influence of the element water. The strong watery emotional nature exhibited by *Homo sapiens* renders us considerably more malleable than the cool and detached intellect of air, or the ardent individualism of fire. As any psychologist knows, disciplined emotion can be creative or constructive, whereas chaotic emotion is decidedly destructive. Set has certainly made full use of the latter, and one does not need to be a paraphysicist to see how!

So where, then, does Horus fit into this picture? As the son of Isis, which could broadly be translated as a highly evolved being from the Siriun system, he is her Nemesis. *The Book of the Dead,* Pyramid Texts, and other archaic sources of arcane information are generous with their descriptions of the final battle between Horus and Set which was (or will be) judged by Thoth himself. Some of these accounts are highly coloured by the personal views of the writers, or so embellished as to render the originals almost completely obscure. But there are threads of truth to be found from among their tattered and faded tapestries. Budge tells us:

> A very early Egyptian tradition made a great fight to take place between the god of light and the god of darkness, and in later days Ra himself, or some form of him, generally one of the Horus gods, was identified with the god of light, and Set, in one form or other, was identified with the god of darkness. Thus the fights of Ra and Apep, and Heru-Behutet and Set, and Horus, son of Isis, and Set, are in reality only different versions of one and the same story, though belonging to different periods. In all these fights Thoth played a prominent part, for when the Eye of Ra, i.e., the Sun, was doing battle with Set, this evil power managed to cast clouds over it, and it was Thoth who swept them away, and 'brought the Eye alive, and whole, and sound, and without defect' to its lord. (*The Book of the Dead,* xvii, 71 ff.)[1]

From this we may learn that the battle described was an eternal one, enacted out by different *dramatis personae* in each age. The implications are inevitably stellar and solar, and therefore relate to the struggle between chaos and order which is seen to occur initially on the subtle planes before being transmitted to the lower frequencies of matter. But since, in outer time (non-locality), all time is one, the story told to the early Egyptians by their Teachers of Wisdom has, in fact, already taken place. All that now remains is for its enactment, which is already being projected onto the screen of inner time to be brought to a satisfactory close. We can then all return to our homes, wherever in the universe they may be, in safety, and in the secure knowledge that like some masked Greek chorus we have played our infinitesimal role in a major evolutionary cosmic drama. Mead also makes a point of emphasising both the elements of chaos and order and the influence of time in his comment: 'Thoth is indeed, as we have seen, the Balancer – "Judge of the two

Combatant Gods", Horus and Set; he it is who stands at the meeting of the Two Ways, at the junction of Order and Chaos. ...'[2]

It is interesting how the Eye always seems to feature in these ancient affrays. In an earlier reference, the reader's attention was drawn to the fact that the Eye of Horus is always shown with a blue pupil. *The Book of the Dead* specifically refers to this, one particular passage stating: 'Horus of the blue eyes cometh unto you', and there are also references in the early texts which affirm that Horus was golden-haired.[3] I would suggest that the answer to this probably lies in the fact that those Enlightened Ones who originally took this advanced cosmogony to the shores of the African continent, be they from Atlantis or wherever, were obviously fair-haired and blue-eyed, as I have previously suggested. It is believed in certain metaphysical circles that Horus son of Isis and his feline consort Bast (or Hathor?) are destined to be the future ruling Devic influence on this planet following the dismissal of Set. Add to this the picture of a feminine Sun, and the promise of the future could be a milder, gentler period for all who survive the much prophesied changes.

The nature of Osiris has been explored in some detail by Bauval and Gilbert, who arrived at the conclusion that the Osiris connection was with Orion, as previously discussed. However, Osiris has strong associations with the element of Water (see illustration on page 76). In my living room I have a papyrus copy of Osiris in this position with Isis and Nephthys standing behind him, which shows a funnel of energy, depicted as a silvery-white stream from 'on high' entering *the symbol of the throne on the head of Isis* who, in turn, transmits an energy-beam into the body of her husband. This conveys to me in no uncertain terms the idea that Isis (Sirius) is the major source of power which she passes to Osiris. Both Osiris and Nephthys being water divinities designates their energies as akin to the Weak Nuclear Force (radioactivity), whereas those of Isis relate to the binding qualities of the Strong Force while Sirius, as a Timegate, also accomodates Time energies in the forms of Thoth/Tehuti and Anubis (Ta-Khu and Akhantui in the old Atlantean pantheon). Set, on the other hand, in keeping with Loki, Lucifer, and similar archetypes of chaos, equates with the more chaotic aspects of Electromagnetism, (as proposed by Steiner), which would leave Horus with Gravity, all of which serves to reinforce my comments in the Introduction that Egyptian magic is nothing more than scientific facts encoded in myth and allegory for the benefit of those lacking the technology and cerebral program to effect experimental proof. The symbology of the Sirius star as related to the known energy sources and their elemental associations, with Time – without which the others would be incapable of functioning – at the helm, is shown in figure 10.1. (For full details see my book *Cosmic Connections*.)

But to return to Egypt, closely allied to the battle between darkness and light or chaos and order is the personal initiation undertaken by the Novitiate in his or her quest for universal knowledge and spiritual enlightenment. In archaic times, as with today, the descent to the chthonic regions was *sine qua non* to the initiatory experience, as was a coming to terms with the lower, chaotic nature, or 'the Set within'. These and other processes connected with the path of the Initiate inevitably involved a degree of symbology, the original meaning of which had, no doubt, been long since forgotten even in the early dynasties. However, since it was observed that the Underworld and subtle planes were in some way involved, the translators and priests of the time assumed that the whole process related to the journey of the departed soul. Included in this category would be the Boat, the Ferryman and the Net.

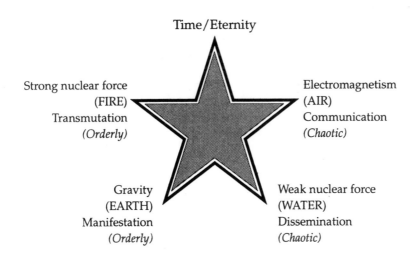

Time/Eternity

Strong nuclear force
(FIRE)
Transmutation
(*Orderly*)

Electromagnetism
(AIR)
Communication
(*Chaotic*)

Gravity
(EARTH)
Manifestation
(*Orderly*)

Weak nuclear force
(WATER)
Dissemination
(*Chaotic*)

Fig. 10.1

The Boat or Barque

There were several of these, the best known of which was the barque of Ra, in which the sun god took his daily journey across his domains. All water was seen as coming from Nun, or the primaeval ocean, which was believed to surround the world. Each evening, the sun entered Nun wherein it regenerated itself to emerge in the morning with renewed strength. Jacq tells us:

> 'To enter into the solar disk' is a special theme with the Initiates. The magician has proved his competence by establishing a cosmic order to the glory of Re and opening the mysterious eye which gives light to humanity. An odd passage in the *Coffin Texts* shows a divine being, seated on a throne and surrounded by ovals. This is the secret symbol of Re, enthroned in a serpent called Mehen. He evokes many cycles and years. Paths of fire protect the secret sun. The magician knows the dark ways by which Hu and Sha, the Word and Intuition, circulate. He knows 'the circuit of Re', the curve of the universe.[4]

An interesting passage this! The references to the 'secret sun', and 'the curve of the universe' (the space-time curve) carry highly Siriun connotations. The initiatory inferences are also obvious, but one can equally see how these could become

Fig. 10.2 The barque of the sun with its divine crew. Day and night it sails through the universe and guarantees the regulation of creative energy everywhere it goes. If the barque stops, life ceases to circulate and the universe perishes. That is why the astronomer-magician observes the heavens ceaselessly, so that he may intervene if the barque encounters any difficulty.

confused with the state of death. After all, it has been observed since the time of primitive shamanism that a kind of death, followed by a spiritual rebirth, was essential to correct magical functioning. The Novitiate was required to descend to some lower region, the domicile of hostile entities of all kinds, wherein his body would be cut into several pieces and reassembled as befitting his calling.

Jacq comments at length on ancient Egyptian healing procedures and their accompanying rites, and refers to the particular emphasis placed on the head, which was seen as essential to the survival of the spirit in the afterlife. 'In the head are hidden mysterious abilities which only the magician can awaken and bring to maturity', writes Jacq, and offers the comment: 'This ancient knowledge has been preserved in the West, notably in the masonic rituals. Let us refer to the fact that the Apprentice who perjures himself and betrays the secrets has his throat cut symbolically – he loses his head and the sense of living in spirit.'[5] I consider this to be highly relevant to the point I am trying to make.

Do we not detect in the aforegoing a hint of a direct programming into the brain, through hypnosis, perhaps, or maybe some other, more technological method that was used by the Atlanteans of this planet or their teachers from Sirius or elsewhere? I do not doubt that it is possible to program the spirit of a dying person to assume a certain spiritual stance upon shedding its earthly body; after all, the major religions have been doing it for years! I recall hearing a talk given by a well-known spiritualist medium who had visited the ruins of an ancient monastery in Italy. 'The place was full of the spirits of deceased monks,' she informed her audience. 'There they were, playing upon harps and singing their *Te Deums* to their hearts' content. When I asked them why they were performing in this manner, their spokesman promptly informed me that "things had happened just as the Church taught, and there they were, happily serenading the Divinity as *they knew they would.*"' I expect the Egyptian priests were careful to inform their dying that Anubis would lead them to the halls of Osiris, where the Weighing of the Heart, the Negative Confession, and other accepted rites of passage would take place. So, for that departing soul, take place they did!

This, naturally, gives rise to the question: can some other aspect of our spiritual economy be programmed in the same way as the physical brain? The answer must obviously be 'yes', since each of what are referred to as the subtle bodies is believed to be equipped as deemed necessary for the dimension upon which it will find itself following the demise of its physical body or *khat*. The priests of ancient Egypt, like the skilled hypnotist of the present day, could penetrate the consciousness behind the brain and reach deep down into the unconscious, at which point the said subtle vehicles are believed to be connected. However, we could go on debating this and similar metaphysical observations for pages, so a return to our subject matter is in order at this point.

Besides the barque of Ra, many other boats featured in the beliefs of these ancient people. Budge tells us that in connection with the ceremonies at the great sanctuaries, such as that of Hathor at Denderah, thirty-four papyrus boats were involved and these were lit with 365 lamps or lights. The gods of Mendes and Anubis occupied one boat, while Isis, Nephthys, Horus and Thoth each had a boat of their own. The remaining twenty-nine boats were allotted to subsidiary divinities and godlings, including the Four Sons of Horus. The 'Boat of Millions of Years', alias Ra or the sun, receives mention in several different contexts. Isis, for example, prayed that the sailors of Ra should cease rowing when she despaired of the life of her son, Horus, who had been stung by a scorpion; the priests of Ra declared that the souls of the blessed made their way after death to the boat or barque of Ra, and if they succeeded in alighting upon it their eternal happiness was assured. 'No fiends could vex and no foes assail them successfully, so long as they had their seat in the "Boat of Millions of Years"; they lived upon the food on which the gods lived, and that food was light. They were apparelled in light, and they were embraced by the god of light. They passed with Ra in his boat through all the dangers of the Tuat. ...'[6]

The allusion to the age of our star, (or Sirius as the case may be) is itself indicative of an advanced scientific and cosmological knowledge which had degenerated into a kind of magical folklore. There is also a high degree of metaphysical know-how contained in the various barque and boat allegories, which hints at a sublimity of belief which is hardly in keeping with the ethos of pre-dynastic times.

What must surely rank as my own most profound and sublime metaphysical experience occurred some years ago during a hypnogogic state. It involved a vision of a small boat that was making its way across a calm sea towards where I stood on some unfamiliar shoreline. In it were two figures, clothed in white, standing side by side: a mature man, tall, slim and fair-haired, one of his hands was on the high prow and the other on the shoulder of a youth of similar colouring, whom I would judge to have been around ten years of age. Their approach was slow, and the whole sequence was played out against a background of various shades of blue. The emotion I experienced was deeply moving and touched me at more levels than I could then comprehend. It has taken me all these years to understand that when they finally reach the shore the time will have come for me to join them on the journey 'home'.

The Ferryman and the Guardians of the Doors

Again we are dealing with initiatory rites that have become confused with the after-death experience. The adept on his or her way to the next dimension must pass through the 'four frontiers of the sky', which required the departed spirit to convince the guardians to afford free passage. This necessitated a knowledge of secret words and names which, when repeated, were guaranteed to ward off any aggressor or unsavoury spook. Magical skills of the highest order were likewise demanded of the person who would venture through the Underworld and, since the services of the Ferryman were essential to any such trip, the magician needed to know the correct way of answering the questions which the Ferryman would be likely to ask before allowing the use of his vessel, and would also have to prove to the Ferryman's satisfaction that the adept was, in fact, a genuine magician. Proof of knowledge involved not only the mythology, god names and magic of Egypt, but also mathematical and other more practical scientific skills.[7] Here we have yet another indication that the pred-ynastic priesthoods from which the Egyptians obtained their original knowledge were scientists, and possibly technologists, as well as metaphysicists. As the picture unfolds, the interweaving pattern of the original teaching and its ensuing overlays becomes increasingly apparent.

The Net

I think this is one of the most interesting of these 'afterlife' challenges, which had its origins in some totally different doctrine. Egyptian magic is not the only system which carries the net symbol. In the Greek tradition it is represented by the Net of Hephaestus, with which the vengeful Olympian smith-god ensnared his beautiful wife Aphrodite and her lover Ares, and kept them trapped therein for all the other Olympians to see. But does the Egyptian net bear any resemblance to the Olympian symbol, which is usually seen as a 'holding for display' magical tool; or does that, like its Egyptian counterpart, have 'ring-pass-not' connotations?

Let us first see what the ancient texts have to say about it. Two deities seem to feature strongly in net symbology, these being Neith, who is also called Net, and Thoth. Budge tells us that in a group of titles Thoth is called 'Great god in Het-Abtit' or the Temple of Abtit, one of the chief sanctuaries of the god at Hermopolis. According to Budge, the hieroglyphics with which the name 'Het-Abtit' are written prove that they mean the 'House of the Net' or a temple wherein a net was preserved and venerated.[8] What, then, was this net, and why should it merit a temple of its own?

According to *The Book of the Dead*, a dreaded net was believed to exist in the Underworld which was greatly feared by the dead and dying. In fact, the departed was required to know the name for every single part of it, including ropes, weights, cords, hooks and so forth, if he wished to make use of it rather than become ensnared by it after his demise. Budge opines that this was probably a folk memory of some ancient ritual combat in which one party was armed with a net, much after the style of the Roman gladiators. Ra apparently possessed a net, which he saw fit to employ in his battle against the fiends of darkness, while the Babylonian sun-god, Marduk also 'made a net to enclose the inward parts of Tiamat, the Four Winds he set forth so that nothing of her might escape; the South Wind, and the North Wind and the East Wind, and the West Wind, he brought near to the net which his father Anu had given him.'[9] These nets are surely one and the same, which indicates that the legend originated from a single, pre-Egyptian, source.

Since Thoth was somehow connected with Ra's net, it seems logical to suppose that his temple, the Temple of the Net, and the emblem represented therein, had something to do with time. Marry this concept to the 'holding' idea of the Greeks, the 'ring-pass-not' of Siriun magic, and the net in whose ropes the Egyptian soul feared to become enmeshed, and we are beginning to get somewhere. In other words, time-warps were not something in which one should become entangled. On the other hand, if one were to learn the appropriate names of the various parts of the net (originally *hekau* for controlling or moving through time, no doubt), one could, in fact, utilise the net for 'fishing' in the afterlife (gaining sustenance through time travel, knowing how and where, in time, to draw the power necessary for the next stage of spiritual ascension, or even familiarising oneself with the knowledge of universal energies free for the tapping *at the material level*?).

But let us move on to Neith, who was also called Net, 'the Lady of the West', which latter title could also hint at an Atlantean connection. Like Temple, I have never doubted Neith's association with Siriun magic. Her attributes, the bow and arrow, give her away for a start, while she also appeared in cow form in a boat. According to Wallis Budge, some authorities, notably Dr. H. Brugsch, were of the opinion that Net was just another form of Nut, but Budge insists that the root *netet*, to knit or weave, accords with another of her attributes, the weaver's shuttle. Neith's most ancient sanctuary was at Sais, the capital of the fifth nome of Lower Egypt, which was also associated with 'the House of the Net' and 'the Seat of the Net'. For those interested, I have translated the role of Hephaestus/Vulcan including the Net symbology into the scientific context in *Cosmic Connections*.

My own feeling regarding Egyptian net symbology is that it refers to some kind of time-warp in which Earth has become ensnared, which has tended to divide humankind from the rest of the universe, halt its evolutionary progress and suspend it in a kind of spiritual limbo. The need to break through this net, both within the context of the initiatory process, and following the transition we call death, has been known to true Initiates down the ages who, like the priests of old Egypt and their Atlantean predecessors, endeavoured to achieve that breakthrough and help their dying charges do likewise, thus avoiding the continual earthly cycle of death and rebirth. Time is obviously one of the keys here since most people tend to function consciously only in inner time, being totally unaware of the existence, or non-local nature of outer time other than as some weird, sci-fi concept with which a few normally rational scientists like to amuse themselves from time to time. Sooner or later, Earth scientists will crack the time code; in fact, there are researchers working on this very project as I write this book. It is well worth considering that nets have a two-fold use, the entrapment of fishes, or whatever one is hoping to catch when casting one's net, and the exclusion of that which is unwanted (shark nets, submarine nets, and so forth). So, once the net is pierced at the physical level and the uncharted territories of time and space are opened up to our cosmically innocent species, will we be prepared for the sharks in that great, timeless ocean on the other side?

The 14 Pieces of Osiris

As we have already discussed, there are several theories regarding the significance of the dismemberment of Osiris, ranging from the shamanic initiatory process, to the Freudian phallocentric idea that the loss of the male member relates to mankind's inability to come to terms with the libido. Here, now, is the Siriun version:

Just prior to the pole shift which contributed to the sinking of Atlantis, under the direction of Siriun entities the High Priests of the Old Country gathered together the great magical powers and scientific knowledge they had accumulated over the preceding centuries, and enclosed them in time capsules which were programmed to reactivate at given points in the future history of our planet. The final key, exemplified by the phallus for obvious reasons as we shall see, will only be discovered when humankind has reached a sufficiently high stage of evolution to overcome or control the desire nature and the chakra associated therewith. This is represented by the impregnation of Isis from 'heaven' with the aid of a facsimile, and in scientific terms also refers to humankind's ultimate ability to produce a perfect species via a controlled programme of genetics. The subject of a Siriun gene will be explored in depth in Chapter 14.

It will not be within the Novitate's or anyone else's power to release any of these time capsules until the destined hour, so let us dispense with that notion to start with. What he or she can do, however, is to allocate them, either in the finer dimensions of here on Earth, and piece together a picture of the future of our planet from the information to be gleaned therefrom. I did not say they could not be looked into, but they may not necessarily be understood, and they cannot be manipulated. In fact, they are very easily found but, as with all the magical symbology of Atlantis, Egypt and Sirius, each person will read them at the level of their own spiritual development or degree of occult attainment. Major mysteries are, strangely enough, never concealed as such, but simply 'occulted' or obscured from the eyes of the ignorant or profane by a process which the ancient Egyptians saw in terms of a ladder: we can only view so much from each rung, and a 'ring-pass-not' prevents us from ascending a rung or level that is not commensurate with our own Soul age, or personal stage on the evolutionary scale.

Endnotes:

1 E. A. Wallis Budge, *The Gods of the Egyptians*, Vol. 1, page 405.
2 G. R. S. Mead, *Thrice Greatest Hermes*, Vol. 1, page 56.
3 E. A. Wallis Budge, *The Book of the Dead*, Vol. III, page 602.
4 C. Jacq, *Egyptian Magic*, page 71.
5 Ibid.,page 117.
6 E. A. Wallis Budge, *The Gods of the Egyptians*, Vol . 1, page 333–4.
7 Jacq, Op. cit. page 39.
8 E. A. Wallis Budge *The Gods of the Egyptians*, Vol. 1, page 406.
9 Ibid., page 407.

CHAPTER 11

Science, Symbology and Healing

As with every other occult system, Siriun magic has its symbology, some of which has found its way into the arcane tradition of ancient Egypt via either the Atlantean missionaries or direct Siriun contact of the mental or 'close encounter' variety, depending on your beliefs. It must be understood, however, that these emblems, numbers, and so forth, are only relevant to the Siriun ray as it strikes this planet, and do not necessarily relate to any images or tokens, magical or otherwise, that might be, or have been, in usage among the inhabitants of the Siriun system itself.

Numerology

We have already considered the significance of the number fifty, in so far as Sirius is concerned, as it relates to the fifty-year orbit of Sirius B. This number features in so many myths it would take a book to record them all. Temple has effected a fair assessment of most of them, however, drawing attention to the Greek *Argo* with its fifty oarsmen, the fifty daughters of Danaos, Plutarch's account of a Persian description of the Dog Star Sirius, which is said to be surrounded by fifty gods forming the shape of an egg (elliptical orbit) in which the light god faces the dark god, and the fifty Sumerian Anunnaki, to name but four.[1]

The number seven also featured strongly in ancient Egyptian magic, and as seven times seven, or forty-nine, therefore represented a cycle, the following or fiftieth day was believed to be of special significance. Temple draws our attention to the fact that in the biblical book of Leviticus, Moses commands the Hebrews to observe a jubilee every fifty years, and Temple wryly comments that as he has never heard of their doing so, the Hebrews clearly did not understand the fifty-year orbit of Sirius B, whereas Moses, who was an Initiate of Egypt and raised by Pharaoh, obviously did.[2]

The third number of importance in the Siriun scheme of things is the eight, signifying completion, the double stars of Sirius and the transmutatory nature of the Siriun energies. Five is also seen to have Siriun connections, since the ancient Egyptians used the five-pointed star in conjunction with the cone-pointed obelisk as their main hieroglyph for Sothis. (See Chapter 8, page 143.)

Colours and Stones

The magical colour of Sirius A is sky-blue, which is also sacred to Isis, and many other archetypal mothers and virgins who have followed in her wake, and the corresponding metal is gold. Sirius B (Digitaria) responds to the colours white and green. Osiris is frequently shown in Egyptian art as a man with a greenish complexion, clothed in white. In Atlantean times its metal would have been orichalcum. The third star (or large planet), which I have associated with Nephthys, the Hidden One, also has green for its colour, but more of the silvery or sage-toned than the malachite used in portrayals of Osiris, and its metal is silver. The combination of these colours produces that lovely shade of turquoise so evident in early Egyptian art.

Table of Siriun Correspondences

	Sirius A	Sirius B	Sirius C
Number.	8	5 & 50	7
Colour:	Sky-blue	White & malachite	Sage/soft green
Metal:	Gold	Orichalcum (red gold)	Silver
Stones:	Aquamarine, all crystals	Chrysoberyl (Alexandrite) Cats-eyes	Emerald
Animals:	Serpents & dragons	Lions, cats, all felines	Jackal, Unicorn
Time Symbol:	The double pyramid	Sistrum, Boat or barque	Net

In an earlier chapter I mentioned the beryl as being the precious stone traditionally associated with Sirius. Beryl is a silicate of aluminium and beryllium, and the variety of colours it displays is probably due to very small included quantities of different metallic oxides. The best-known and most expensive of these stones is the green beryl, better known as the emerald. The next most popular beryl is the aquamarine, which in its purest form is a subtle shade of blue, sometimes with a hint of turquoise. The third stone in this group is the comparatively uncommon chrysoberyl, of which there are two varieties: the green and brownish-green transparent stones called alexandrites, and the greyish-yellow, cabochon cut stones which show a chatoyant effect, and which are named after oriental cat's eyes, or cymophanes.

There is actually something highly relevant about the latter, which establishes without doubt the connection between the energies of the beryl group and Sirius. The dark green alexandrites are the most sought after, and clear, unmarked stones exhibit the unique quality of changing colour by artificial light, the leaf-green changing to a raspberry red. This is due to the greater absorption of the red part of the spectrum by artificial light. In ordinary light the violet and yellow rays are mostly absorbed, the transmitted light being mainly composed of the red and green portions of the spectrum.[3]

My reason for drawing particular attention to this fact is that Sirius, as a system, aside from its function as a stargate or 'wormhole' has a specific function that is related to what are referred to in currently popular metaphysical parlance as 'evolutionary quantum leaps'. It acts as a sort of spiritual cosmic springboard from which the evolving soul, having arrived at a certain cosmic age, can gather together its energies and make ready to step into the next stage of its evolutionary development. This naturally allies its influence with such issues as 'missing links', particularly in relation to the utilisation of somatically evolving strains as suitable vehicles for those souls who are ready to take on the task of adding a new dimension of intelligence to primitive beings. So, just as the alexandrite shows a different colour according to the quality of light to which it is exposed, so the psyche or soul resonates to the energies of Sirius, emphasising either the red or green (agitatory or peaceful) aspects of our natures. The blue beryl or aquamarine, and the green beryl, or emerald, would therefore be the stones of the Siriun Initiate, depending on his or her affinity with one or other of the stars in that system.

Alexandrites are believed in metaphysics to resonate to the zodiacal sign of Gemini for obvious reasons. Sirius, like Gemini, also has 'twin' energies, and according to Siriun esoteric teachings Gemini is the sun-sign into which souls incarnate at a point in their evolution when they are poised between either progression to a state of new spiritual awareness/maturity or retrogression to the self-centredness of spiritual childhood. Hence, the duality so frequently found in those born under this sign, which would appear to bear some resemblance to the nature and purpose of the Siriun energies, albeit at a more personal level.

Astrology

Do the planetary influences associated with the Sirius system by astrological tradition match up with what the practitioners of Siriun magic have discovered from their workings to date? For example, do the Siriun energies really bear comparison to those of Jupiter, Mars and the moon? Vivian Robson's book was first published in 1928, and since then there must surely have been some revised ideas regarding the fixed stars and the approximation of the natures of their emissions to those of the planets in our own solar system. Having worked closely with Siriun energies for sometime, however, I fail to find anything Jupiterian, Martian or lunar about the three Siriun suns (or two suns and one large planet, as the case may be), so I am rather unhappy about including planetary references under my list of correspondences. For example, Sirius A is magical, feminine, but positive. Sirius B, although masculine, also carries strong anima energies, indicative of a state of balanced individuation, while Sirius C is decidedly feminine, and representative of the more hidden or unconscious aspects of the psyche, so it is easy to see how the moon may have become confused with its energies.

Symbols and Animals

I would list the following symbols and animals as resonating with Siriun energies:

Symbols	*Animals*
Infinity ∞	
Bow and arrow	Serpent
Double pyramid	Cat, lion – all felines, in fact
Boat or barque	Lizard
Net	Jackal
Sistrum	

Crystals of all kind are believed to resonate to Siriun energies. These played a very important part in both the development of the Siriun system itself, and were later re-echoed in the magic, science and technology of the Atlantean priesthood, although the latter was but a pale copy of the Siriun original.

There will, no doubt, be many readers who will ask, since Sirius is called the Dog Star, why I have not mentioned the dog as being a Siriun animal. This is because I do not believe that the original teachings alluded to Anubis either as a dog or a jackal. In fact, the popular Anubian figure as shown in the tomb of Tutankhamun is believed to have derived from the wolf-headed nome god Wepwawet, who also carried the title 'the Opener of the Ways', while in Atlantis, the Anubian archetype was represented by the black panther-god Akhantuih. As with all Siriun energies, those of the Anubian ray were totally abstract. The dog aspect only emerged when it became necessary to translate its meaning into terms that could be easily understood by simple folk. The idea of the dog that leads the blind, is the guardian of the home, or the companion of the hunter – he who flushes out the prey and fetches it to his master after it has been slaughtered – was eminently acceptable to a people who required similar functions from their guardian in the afterworld. Budge comments that the dog, although a favourite animal of the Egyptians, was never regarded as a divinity. He stresses that although Herodotus and Diodorus mention dogs as being part of Egyptian family life and in some instances guardians of Isis and Osiris:

> Diodorus, like many modern writers, confounded the dog with the jackal. The dog, like the jackal, may have been sacred to Anubis, but

the mythological and religious texts of all periods prove that it was the jackal-god who ministered to Osiris, and who acted as guide not only to him but to every other Osiris in the Underworld.[4]

As far as *Homo sapiens* is concerned, the real guardian against the unseen forces is the cat, a fact of which the Egyptians, Tibetans, Thais, and other archaic peoples of knowledge and wisdom were only too aware. As for the lion, one does not have to look any farther than *The Book of the Dead* for evidence of this. Allusions to the gods in leonine form abound within its pages. Here are a few examples:

> Hail, thou god Tem, who comest forth from the Great Deep, and who shinest with glory under the form of the double Lion-god, send out with might thy words unto those who are in thy presence.[5]
>
> Thou art beautiful, O Ra, in thy western horizon of Amentet ... thou openest up the path of the double Lion-god. ...[6]

The second of these two quotes is accompanied by a vignette which shows Isis and Nephthys adoring the two lion-gods:

> Tem hath built thy house, and the double Lion-god hath founded thy habitation. ...[7]

There are also similar references, some of which contain considerably more detail, on pages 142, 165, 169, 173, 195, 207, 213, 215, 220, 243, 253, 367, 393, 399 and 646 of my edition of Budge, which was published in 1901.

Some readers may resent my continual allusion to Siriun extraterrestrials. Since the Dogons and the ancient Egyptians subscribed to this theory, I think it only fair to accord it some credulity. After all, we are examining early Egyptian beliefs in relation to Sirius, which naturally merits the credos of these ancient sages a degree of respect. Besides, I tend to share their conviction that Sirius does play an important role in the evolution of our own planet and all life-forms thereon, and whether one decides to accord any credence to their story of visitors from outer space, or view the manifestation as the arrival of Atlantean priests who could have received their knowledge from any of several proposed sources, matters little in the final analysis. What we are concerned with is Sirius, the energies emitted by this binary system, how these affect us, and how they can be put to positive spiritual use.

Allocation of Gods and Goddesses to Siriun Suns

SiriusA	SiriusB	Sirius C
Isis (Aset)	Osiris (Auset)	Nephthys
Sekhmet	Ra/Atum(Ammon)	Hathor
Satis	Knum	Anukis
Bast	Ptah	Nefer-tem
Neith	Thoth/Tehuti	Seshat/Maat
Nut	Shu	Tefnut

Bast, rather than Sekhmet, is sometimes seen as the consort of Ptah and daughter of Isis, and although Nefer-tem is a male deity, his symbol, the Lotus, was also sacred to Nephthys in her role as Goddess of Tranquillity. Anubis has also been associated with Sirius C, and although he is referred to in the masculine context, as a Time Essence he is capable of switching polarities should the occasion require, which may not be seen to accord with the Dogon concept of Sorghum-Female.

The Healing Arts in Ancient Egypt

Since the ancient Egyptians did not view magic and medicine as constituting opposing factors, the practice of medicine was the task of a specific branch of their priesthood. All forms of sickness were seen as areas of imbalance between the patient and the cosmos and consequently treated at other levels as well as the physical. Healer priests were taught to treat the cause rather than the effect, which makes sound sense in the light of more recent holistic attitudes towards illness. In fact, healing was viewed as an art as much as a science or, as we might say, the Egyptian healer priest used both his right and left brain when treating his patients. Preventive medicine was also favoured, so that the illness could not enter the body in the first place. To become a doctor or healer priest required a long and arduous period of initiation, and candidates were usually required to present themselves before the Masters of the Guild at Heliopolis for their final examination. Jacq places particular emphasis on the fact that the *London Medical Papyrus* is not a secular document. He tells us:

It was found, one night, in a temple room. A moonbeam, illuminated it and it was then taken to the king. This great event occurred whilst the Ennead were conferring. Every medical document really belongs to the domain of sacred things.

This marvellous art, which is of divine origin, necessitates close co-operation between the doctor and his patient. Expertise is not enough. The effect of the medicine is given full play if the will to exorcise the evil also comes from the heart and body of the sick man. The magic spell helps to put the joint action of the sick man and his healer into concrete form.[8]

Healing a patient was often seen in terms of Horus fighting Set, or Order fighting Chaos, which makes good sense in the para-physics of today. Part of the initiation undergone by the Egyptian healer priest involved self-healing, which was seen as an essential prerequisite to the healing of others. His guide in the subtle planes was Thoth, but he would also work with one or more other divinities, according to his specialisation. Not even the simplest medical act was ever viewed as relating purely to the material world or physical body; there was always a magical link in which it had its divine parallel. Knowledge of the subtle bodies, and the necessity for the physician to adjust these in order to render the patient to a state of full health and vigour, is to be found in the *Ebers Papyrus*, although some of the medical statements contained therein have for many years been seen by Egyptologists as referring purely to elementary physiology. The increasing interest in alternative therapies has rendered their interpretation in a new light, however.

Jacq gives a series of fascinating accounts of ancient Egyptian healing techniques, many of which are decidedly shamanic and bristling with sympathetic magic overtones. In contrast, he shows us a picture of a star-goddess 'receiving energy from the sun which enters her mouth. She passes it on to a serpent, the symbol of the earthly powers, who are thus brought to life by a celestial energy. That which above is as that which is below.'[9]

It was this small illustration which gave me the Sirius clue I had been looking for amongst the scant information to be had concerning ancient Egyptian methods of healing. Although this goddess is drawing her energies from the sun, over the top of her head is the sign for Sirius!

One of the most potent symbols used in the ancient Egyptian arts of healing, magic and protection was the Eye of Horus. It was everywhere in evidence, carved on sarcophagi, on stelae, on boats. The Uraeus or female serpent, worn on the brow of the king as the 'burning Eye of Ra' was believed to scatter his adversaries. However, there were, as we know, two eyes outlined in the *Stela of Metternich* as: 'the divine Eye of the right and the divine Eye of the left', each of which carried its own special significance. The left, or lunar Eye, was essentially the Eye of Horus or the Eye of Healing, while the right Eye, or Uraeus, was more concerned with magical and protective functions.

Thoth was the principal god of healing, although Imhotep, who is believed to be one and the same as Nefer-Tem, son of Ptah and Sekhmet, was considered the master physician and later deified. Imhotep was probably a great physician who lived in very early times, who wrought miracles with his knowledge and medical expertise. I believe there has been some speculation regarding what some Egyptologists believed to be the tomb of of Imhotep, due to the fact that an unusual amount of Ibis relics were found near the entrance, the Ibis being sacred to Thoth and

Fig. 11.1 A star-goddess receives energy from the sun which enters her mouth. She passes it on to a serpent, the symbol of the earthly powers who are thus brought to life by a celestial energy. That which is above is as that which is below.

subsequent priests engaged in the discipline of healing. Since no more has been heard of this of late, one can only assume that the archaeologists were either pursuing a false trail or simply have not been able to make further progress in their search. Horus was believed to be the giver of healing to the physical body, while mental health came under the jurisdiction of Bast and the feline deities, although Jacq draws our attention to the fact that the priests of the Lion Goddess, Sekhmet, who were magicians, were also specialists in medicine and surgery. In the Theban period, Khonsu was seen as the bestower of healing, and the following very beautiful prayer came to me via my kindly Egyptian source:

O Khonsu, Of bright appearances,
Mighty One of healing,
Thee do I invoke to be with me now,
Thee who banishes all ills,
Thee who conquers sickness and afflictions,
Thee who banishes strife and woe,
O Khonsu, Traverser of Centuries,
Beloved by millions,
Bright One in Thy shrine,
Cast open Thy doors before me,
Illumine my soul with Thy Light, reach deep into my spirit
　　and heal all my afflictions.
O Khonsu, only You can banish into eternity the ills that are
　　upon my soul, make me sound of body, clear of mind,
　　pure of soul and bright in my spirit's appearance.
O Khonsu, who comes at the call of those who are sincere, as
　　I am now.
I am humble before thee and acknowledge Thy Majesty and
　　seek to be with Thee and a part of Thee.
O Khonsu, bless me with thy gift of healing so I too, may
　　heal the sick of body, of soul, of spirit.
Lift me up, O God of Light, smile upon my countenance and
　　kiss me with Thy breath of Health that I too, may know
　　Thee, know Thy grace, know Thy ways.
O Khonsu, hear me, I beseech Thee, for I come to Thee and
　　make supplication at Thy feet, Thy shrine, and I praise
　　Thee in my heart forever.
Hail to Thee, O Glorious Healer.
Anetch Hra-ku Khonsu Heh!

I find the Siriun overtones in this prayer exciting. The reference to time, in particular, is exactly in keeping with Siriun magic self-healing formulae which are based upon *moving out of the present time and depositing the misplaced energy that is causing the illness in the time-zone approriate to its origin.*

Siriun Healing

Aside from the examples I have already selected from ancient Egyptian healing methods, which tend to confirm the Atlanto-Siriun connection, the *hekau* of healing must obviously feature in this section of our study, as its Atlantean and Siriun connotations are obvious to the practitioner of either of these systems.

We have previously discussed how every living entity, at every level, possesses a personal keynote or sonic. To know this is to have the power to heal (make whole) or destroy (fragment) the entity in question. In fact, there is also a specific sonic note for every combination of molecules or molecular structure of matter. Familiarity with the sonic keynote of a certain type of stone, for example, plus a knowledge of the *modus operandi* of the sonic system, would enable one to reduce its specific gravity, disassemble its molecular structure and reassemble it in some other location. If this sounds too much like Star Trek's transporter room technique then it is meant to, since I am convinced that this kind of technology originated in the civilisations of the Sirius star system, and was later employed by the Atlanteans, albeit in a more primitive or less refined mode. It could also account for why the monolith builders sought out special stones, which they went to great lengths to move from one place to another. A folk memory of a time when the sonic of a specific type of rock used in building, perhaps, was known but long since forgotten.

Let us take a hypothetical sonic healing scenario: a kind of geometrical paradigm of the personal genetic code relating to the individual's perfect state of health is thrown into relief on a visual display unit. An appropriate apparatus is then connected to the sick person and a parallel image displayed, which highlights those imbalances that are causing the illness. The two images are then merged together and the personal sonic slowly and carefully applied until the second impression matches perfectly with the first, thus removing the affliction *by sound*. Sci-fi? Perhaps, but let us just call it 'far memory' and leave it at that! If the proposed Genome Project ever gets under way, it may well be possible for medical scientists to effect this kind of healing. After all, today's science fiction will probably be tomorrow's science fact!

Healing with sound is no new thing however. Shaman Jill Purce, who is married to scientist/author Dr. Rupert Sheldrake, practises and teaches it all the time, using the sound of the human voice. Her flyer tells us: 'Interested in the magical properties of the voice, she learnt Mongolian and Tibetan overtone chanting (producing chords of simultaneous notes octaves apart). The latter she studied in the Himalayas with the Chant-master of the Gyuto Tibetan Monastery and Tantric College. ...' Her published articles include *Time and the Music of Form, The Harmonics of Mind and Body, Healing Resonance and The Healing Voice*, among others. 'It is the healing and transformative power of sound that we need to explore. ... To maintain a person in tune is to maintain them in a state of health.' All very Siriun, Ms Purce!

All sonics are not harmonious, however, and that also goes for rhythms. Some people find certain rhythms or combinations of sounds highly disturbing. I myself cannot cope with the currently favoured 'pop' or beat music, for example, or with some modern classical compositions which effect certain dissonants. A high decibel output also disturbs me considerably. This is because both of these things clash with my personal sonic, causing a 'juddering' or jarring note which is re-echoed at all levels. There is an explanation for this which can be found in both *The Lion People* and *Cosmic Connections*.

People often ask me whether magical names, of the kind adopted in occult lodges, Wiccan covens or even solitary rites, are in any way related to the personal sonic. There are, of course, no hard and fast rules about this. Some people may accidentally stumble on a name which bears some resemblance to their cosmic keynote; others may not. As the Egyptians were well aware, however, names do carry a significance, so if you feel more at ease using an assumed nomenclature when undertaking your esoteric work, the choice is purely a personal one. But since there is no such thing as a coincidence, the chances of your inadvertently accessing your personal keynote is, I am assured, somewhat remote, unless you are an adept in the true sense of the word, and that does *not* mean taking a series of conveniently devised tests and being awarded a piece of paper at the end of it all which says you are an Ipsissimus, or whatever. One can learn so much from others, or from books, but in Siriun, or Egyptian magic for that matter, most of the lessons are learned on the subtle planes (I dislike the term 'inner planes' as it implies a restriction), or in non-locality.

The other important aid to Sirium healing is the use of crystals, which I understand had its origin in the Sirius system. I have heard crystals described as the brain cells of Gaia and in view of our planet's presumed relationship with Sirius, the connection is obviously a genetic one. Crystal healing is fast catching on as an alternative therapy, with practitioners claiming excellent results although I am inclined to question the ethics of continually 'taking' from crystal sources without effecting the requisite exchange of energies essential to correct occult functioning. As I have covered the subject in some detail in my book *The Psychology of Healing* I shall refrain from indulging in detail at this juncture, but suffice it to say that crystals featured in both the healing and science of the Siriuns themselves, as well as their Atlantean protégés. However, the latter never reached the stage of refinement attained to on the Old Planet, having fallen prey to the wiles of Set through the use of crystal power, sonics, and related energies for wrong and selfish ends. The ultimate aim of Siriun healing is self-healing, but until certain changes take place on our planet it is extremely doubtful whether those untutored in some form of mind control would be able to effect this without the assistance of a healing intermediary.

Science

Egyptologists have been unable to agree among themselves as to whether the ancient Egyptians did or did not possess a knowledge of mathematics comparable to our present-day systems. Although some fragments which appear to relate to this have survived, they have suffered so severely in translation as to make them incomprehensible to the modern Western mathematician, and yet the evidence is there in the form of the pyramids, the mathematical exactitude of which we have already discussed. What I rather suspect the Egyptians did inherit from their teachers was a knowledge of the subatomic world and the principles that dominate the cycles of both matter and evolution. Unlike mathematical formulae, which are believed to be precise, accurate and immune to subjective interpretations, in the context of quantum physics there can be no 'objective' truths – only processes and patterns of probability.

The reality of the discrete particle suddenly gives way to the world of the abstract or 'fuzzy' wave, in which time as we know and measure it ceases to respond to our particular brand of logic. One of the measurement problems in quantum physics is this: how does a fuzzy system become a discrete measurement when observed? Numerous explanations have been given by physicists for this strange phenomenon to which parapsychologists have paid particular attention, as the transition from the discrete to the fuzzy state also features in the human mental condition when the right brain is exposed to non-locality. These, and similarly related phenomena are well documented and open-mindedly researched in *Explaining the Unexplained* by Professor Hans Eysenck and Dr. Carl Sargent.

But how does all this relate to ancient Egypt, you may ask? Those enigmatic Sons of Horus, and their tall, fair-haired ancestors who brought their knowledge to the shores of the African continent, may well have been acquainted with such knowledge, and although the reality behind their 'magic' was eventually lost along the corridors of time, tiny specks of light found their way through the minute crevices for the sharp of eye and sensitive of mind to seize upon and interpret. Just such a glimmer could possibly be seen in the fabled Emerald Tablets of Hermes! Several of the statements contained within these texts carry scientific and cosmological connotations. The opening sentence of the Tables, for example, runs thus:

> What is above is like what is below, and what is below is like what is above to effect the wonders of one and the same work.

The microcosmic-macrocosmic allusion here is obvious, while this simple statement can also be read at the level of particle physics and honeycomb universes! In another passage we have:

All things owe their existence to the Only One, so all things owe their origin to the Only One Thing.

Separate the earth from the fire, the subtile from the gross, carefully and skilfully. This substance ascends from the earth to the sky, and descends again on the earth – and thus the superior and inferior are increased in power.

This is the potent power of all forces for it will overcome all that is fine and penetrate all that is coarse because in this manner was the world created.[10]

Minute particles moving at incalculable speeds, interpenetrating denser particles – the ancients seemed aware of these facts, content to comprehend their principles without the need of physical confirmation. We, in contrast, struggle with our particle accelerators and the ever-expanding range of technological impedimenta to reproduce measurable manifestations of the materially immeasurable. The thought that all these things were once known, here on Earth, makes one wonder how and where we went wrong?

In addition to their healing role, crystals were also believed to have featured in the ancient sciences which were bequeathed to the denizens of Earth from Siriun or Atlantean sources. Many reliable psychics and time-travellers have witnessed their use for the storage of energy, and as agents of or aids to nuclear fusion. A single crystal, we are told, could contain sufficient of a certain kind of energy to supply power for a country the size of Britain for several years. When their 'batteries' ran out, these crystals were also rechargeable, and the power source was solar or stellar and therefore free! Pie in the sky? Those that had the use of these conveniences in the past obviously did not think so. What a pity that they chose to abuse their knowledge and land us in the dark ages of the ensuing centuries! I am afraid I cannot offer proof of these matters, aside from the fact that they appear to be so deeply embedded in the collective unconscious as to cast the coincidence factor into doubt, if not actual dismissal.

Endnotes:

1 R. K. G. Temple, *The Sirius Mystery*, page 199.
2 Ibid., page 199.

3 M. Weinstein, *The World of Jewel Stones*, page 62 and page 108.
4 E. A. Wallis Budge, *The Gods of the Egyptians*, Vol. 2, page 366.
5 E. A. Wallis Budge, *The Book of the Dead*, page 50.
6 Ibid. page 82.
7 Ibid. page 108.
8 Jacq, C. *Egyptian Magic*, pages 108–9.
9 Ibid., page 113.
10 A. Tomas, *We are Not the First*, pages 71–2.

CHAPTER 12

Lion Power

The connection between Sirius and the feline genus may seem a strange one at first glance, and yet, if one looks into the history and customs of ancient Egypt, even at the purely surface level, the emphasis placed upon the cat and the lion families is blatantly obvious. It was not until I became directly involved with Siriun magic that I discovered the reason for this, and any further proof I needed was there for me to read in *The Book of the Dead*, the Pyramid Texts and other ancient messages that have filtered down to us from antiquity. Nor is the lion theme limited to the Egyptian ethos; as mentioned earlier, the fourth incarnation of the Hindu god Vishnu was as the Man Lion or Tawny One, while lions also featured in the religion and beliefs of other long-lost cultures as far back as 35,000 BC (see Chapter 1). All these references carry Siriun overtones, for it was not only the strength or courage of the lion that caused the ancients to pay so much attention to the leonine archetype, especially at its more esoteric level.

The importance of this archetype, as far as we earthlings are concerned, does not depend upon whether or not we subscribe to the idea that a race of leonids exists or existed in the Siriun complex in some other time frame. There are deeper implications which resonate with the genes we have inherited from our Siriun forebears who were responsible for the growth and development of the solar system in which we live. If there is anything in Professor Hoyle's panspermia theory, there are probably other stellar influences on Earth which manifest via the personal, group or racial genetic codes, but for those of us who carry the Siriun gene, the cat-lion-crystal call will be the strongest.

The Egypt of old gives us a few potent clues regarding the significance of the leonine archetype and the specific ways in which it influences our planet, and nowhere is this more obvious than in the personality and functions of the goddess Sekhmet. The fact that the Sekhmet archetype is slowly perco-lating through to the collective unconscious may be evidenced in the way that people hitherto unconnected with symbology or studies of this nature are becoming aware of her mysteries. Dr Robert Masters, the famous American psychologist, known mainly for his pioneering work as a sexologist, contributed sub-stantially to the Sekhmet ethos with his book *The Goddess Sekhmet*, published in 1988. In his introduction Masters writes:

> Over the last fifteen years I have enabled a great many persons to have, in varying degrees, experiences of what they apprehended as the Goddess Sekhmet. The Goddess has taught, and healed and protected and otherwise rewarded and punished. Some of the phenomena associated with and arising out of this work have been discussed with, and often been taken quite seriously by, Egypto-logists, archaeologists, anthropologists, parapsychologists, open-minded psychiatrists and psychologists, philosophers, authorities on magic, myth and religion, and persons of many other back-grounds. Many lives have been changed – sometimes drastically transformed – by the contemporary manifestations of Sekhmet. I acknowledge, without including a roster of names, all of those persons just referred to, but especially the ones who have actively and immediately shared with me the more intense and prolonged experiences of the Goddess Sekhmet's worlds.
>
> I might add that I summarised one such collaboration in the book *Psychic Exploration*, published in 1974 and edited by former astronaut Edgar Mitchell, explorer of both outer and inner space – and the sixth man on the moon. That particular shared experience of Sekhmet, as well as others that occurred over the years, was of great interest to another friend, the late anthropologist Margaret Mead, who developed her own strong affinity for Sekhmet.[1]

Masters' further Sekhmetian (or Siriun) association may be evidenced in his opening paragraph:

> ... I believe, as Rameses II believed it of himself, that I was 'born out of Sekhmet'. That, for an ancient Egyptian, was a quite different

statement from the one often routinely made about being 'born of' this or that Deity. To be 'born out of' in this case asserts a literal fact and reality existing in spiritual dimensions. It would require a spiritual autobiography to make my case – and one day I may write one, detailing adequately (at least for me) just why I hold to such a belief.[2]

No, Dr Masters, you and your friends in the goddess are by no means alone. There are others amongst us who also carry the Siriun gene, and are 'born out of Sekhmet'. When I first saw the set of four statues of Sekhmet at the British Museum they had been moved to a stairwell landing while their normal place of residence was being refurbished. I recall ascending the wide staircase and there they were, standing before me in all their glory. An ancient memory stirred and I was deeply moved.

Like everything else Egyptian, however, Sekhmet's energies may be translated or used at many levels. As the Warrior Goddess of Destruction and Regeneration, she is seen as an element essential to the continual cosmic cycle of birth and rebirth – the dissolution of energies into chaos for reforming at a different frequency whereas her refining fires may also be applied to subjective spiritual development. Her transformative powers would appear to carry some rather interesting connotations, especially when applied to nuclear energy. The nuclear process taking place on our sun, which provides the light and warmth we so gladly welcome, is caused by fusion rather than fission, the nuclei of the light hydrogen atoms being fused together by unimaginable pressure and temperature to make helium, thus commencing the chain which eventually produces the carbon and other elements, of which the cells of all living things are made. This process applies to all stars throughout the universe, which also pass through a series of transformations in much the same way that we do as individuals. Mythology offers no evidence to the effect that Sekhmet, the fiery one, belongs exclusively to our sun, in fact she could be seen to represent a cosmic principle which is valid at many more levels than we with our present limited understanding could comprehend. Strangely enough, this connection between Sekhmet and nuclear energy has other connotations at the more personal level. Some people appear to exhibit a greater tolerance to radioactivity than others, which would seem to be in some way connected with: (a) their particular molecular structure; (b) their personal sonic; or (c) the extent to which they are able to speed up their personal frequencies or, as Masters would probably say, negotiate their subtle bodies.

During my many years as a metaphysicist I have noticed that people either respond enthusiastically to my personal energies or the wavebands upon which I tend to work, or are greatly distressed by them, likewise when one accelerates a frequency, moving it into another, perhaps less familiar waveband, a practice which in my youth was referred to as 'taking the vibrations up'. Mind you, I am not sure where 'up' was meant to be, and assumed the term to relate to more subtle levels. I have since learned from bitter experience that one can move away from the comfort of more familiar wavebands *in many directions*, not all of which are 'up' in the spiritually accepted sense of the word. Some frequencies, especially those related to the elemental kingdoms, are decidedly more radioactive than others, and it was these, in particular, which I found affected some seekers. Two people with whom I was once obliged to work experienced considerable distress when exposed to Siriun energies.

As is the case with all of us insecure mortals, instead of acknowledging and accepting our own limitations when things fail to respond to our wishes, we seek someone upon whom to lay the blame. In matters magical the tendency is to point the accusing finger at another member of the group, or even some innocent party who is in no way connected with the situation, the usual magical rocks of derision being haphazardly fired from the slings of fear, and the unfortunate scapegoat despatched to the 'wilderness'!

As with all feline or leonine energies, the Sekhmet frequency has a fiery quality about it which can either prove disconcerting, or exert a fragmentary effect on certain people. This does not, or should not, evoke from the individual a sense of being either right or wrong, but simply different. There are several qualities of energy that I find extremely difficult to handle; perhaps 'unfamiliar with' would be a better way of describing it. None of us is perfect and none of us knows it all. It is simply a matter of self-discovery and finding the particular cosmic slot into which one can slide with spiritual ease.

Not all the leonine deities of Egypt were of such a fiery character, however, Tefnut, twin of the sky-god Shu, was a gentle divinity associated with the dew, soft rain and the rainbow, while the cat goddess, Bast, originally believed to have been a leonine entity, was a joyful deity of healing, music, and joy and happiness. The oldest known lion god was Aker, who was seen as guarding the gate of the dawn through which the sun-god passed each morning. From the Pyramid Texts it is clear that this deity's role and attributes were clearly defined in the Early Empire. In later dynasties it was believed that during the night the sun passed through a kind of tunnel (wormhole?) which existed in some nether region, each end of which was guarded by a lion-god, the two deities being called Akeru (or Akerui). These same leonine divinities later emerged in Theban times as the Twin Lion gods, seated back to back, with the sun's disc supported between them. Their names were Sef and Tuau – 'yesterday' and 'today' respectively. Ra was often referred to as 'Ra of the Two Horizons', the term 'horizon' being seen by some scholars in this context as a mathematical term denoting a system of dimensions or frame of reference. These were the Light Horizon and the Life Horizon, representing the material and spiritual worlds respectively. Ra of the Life Horizon was betokened by a flattened circle or solar disc mounted on the hindquarters of the Twin Lion gods.

There are several interpretations of the meaning of this picture. Some see the two lions as exemplifying the two primordial forces of life – desire and fear, while to others they are simply the past and the present united by the sun of the Eternal Now; in other words, the power of time. Their back-to-back position can therefore be interpreted as: (a) the masculine 'desire' force, and the feminine 'fear' force pulling in different directions (chaos?), while the weight of the Ra disc (reason and self-control) holds them in check; or (b) in the 'time' context, where the disc can be seen as the solar force that holds our planet in its orbital path and thus creates night and day – the time on our clocks – inner time. Should one or both of those lions move their position, even slightly, then the orb of Ra would adjust accordingly and we would see the sun *from a different angle* than we do today. The irony of this philosophy, however, lies in the idea that if desire and fear do get the better of us, the energies emitted world-wide could cause Shu and Tefnut to rise and dislodge the disc of Ra. To think of it another way, it is the thoughts and deeds of the denizens of Earth that decide whether the poles will shift, the axis will tilt and calamity will befall us all, as was the case in the latter days of Atlantis.

The universality of this symbology may also be evidenced in the fact that the Hopi Indians also had a similar legend of twin gods, named Poqanghoya and Palongawhoya, guardians of the north and south axes of the Earth respectively, whose task it was to keep the planet rotating properly. They were, however, ordered by Sotuknang, nephew of the Creator, to leave their posts so that the 'second world' could be destroyed because its people had become evil. Then the world, with no one to control it, teetered off balance, spun around crazily, then rolled over twice. Mountains plunged into the sea with a great splash, seas and lakes sloshed over the land; and as the world spun through cold and lifeless space it froze into solid ice.[4] The Hopi also insist that their 'first world' was destroyed by fire and their 'third world' by water.

While on the subject of the Hopi Indians, it bears mentioning they share with the ancient Egyptians a knowledge of Sirius, which they know as 'Blue Star Kachina'. An age-old belief that exists in their tribe tells of how beings from the Siriun system came to earth 250,000 years ago and deposited time capsules, some of which are due to be triggered off prior to or immediately following the advent of the next millennium.

The 'twin' principle is decidedly Siriun and, as we have already discussed, the Law of Polarity operating strongly throughout all things carrying the Siriun influence. Lion power is active, fiery and extrovert; its colours are any of those flame shades that contain a sufficient element of gold to cool the overactivating hues of the red spectrum (strong reds being essentially Set's colours) with the yellow of reason. Its energies, which are of a transmutatory nature, function by effecting *external* change. Crystal power is passive, airy and introvert; its colours are blue and green and combinations thereof, and it refines energies via the process of absorption and crystalisation, through which it effects *internal* change. Together, these comprise those aspects of the Siriun energy output which directly concern our solar system, manifesting within a broad spectrum of frequencies, the nature of which are essential to cosmic evolution and quantum leaps in particular, since the objectivity of one accommodates the external aspects, while the other is more concerned with the the inner or subjective mode. In other cosmic time-zones, although the principles are constant the rules and applications are somewhat different, since the path taken by different evolutionary streams varies from galaxy to galaxy.

Confirmation of the dual nature of these energies may be seen
in the following stanza from one of two hymns quoted by
Brugsch and cited by Budge:

> O Amen-Ra, the gods have gone forth from thee. What flowed forth
> from thee became Shu, and that which was emitted by thee became
> Tefnut; thou didst create the nine gods at the beginning of all things,
> and thou wast the Lion-god of the Twin lion-gods. ...[5]

The goddess Sekhmet is always portrayed wearing the solar
disk, surmounted by the Uraeus, or right Eye of Ra, on her head,
which symbols immediately connect her with both the Twin
Lion gods and their disc, and therefore the balance and evolution
of this planet. In her role as Divine Warrior, she wages war
against the enemies of Ra, just as her feline brothers and sisters
did against the evil of Apep. Masters writes of *the war in Heaven*
[*sic*] which is 'intruding ever more fully and terribly upon this
earth'.[6] It is this intrusion, he tells us:

> ... which has given rise to the re-entry into human time and space of
> the Great Mother, in these Mysteries manifesting as Sekhmet. To
> Chaos She brings terror and a swathe of destruction. By means of
> Love She comes to re-establish those conditions which alone can
> preserve the human race and provide for the harmonious develop-
> ment and fulfilment of human beings as individuals, but also as
> parts of the Great Cosmic Whole *that The War in Heaven is about* – the
> eventual outcome: *either Being or Nothingness.*[7]

A sobering thought, but then that is surely what the Siriun message
is all about – giving Geb or Gaia, as the case may be, a hand to
control those of his or her errant brood who are holding back the
others, or alternatively packing them all off to a remand planet in
some distant galaxy where they can cool their heels among souls of
their own spiritual age and kind, and work out their violence,
greed, hatred and other chaotic characteristics together.

Notice that Masters says 'to Chaos She brings terror'. In other
words, she is the enemy of Set, since Set is nothing more than
chaos personalised! Sekhmet's transformatory powers, harsh as
the myths would have us believe them to be, should not therefore be seen in the same destructive context as those of Set, since
the initiation of the refiner's fire is essential to rid us of the dross
of our baser natures or the destructive element of chaos that
lurks within us all. Initiation by fire also serves to purify our

non-local components, thus bringing us into closer contact with the Divine Spark within us, and cementing our bond with the Infinite. Chaotic energies, on the other hand, are by nature fragmenting and dispersive.

From the aforegoing, it may be seen that the leonine archetype assumed great significance in all Egyptian thinking, from the cosmological to the everyday. Lion gods and spirits were therefore looked upon as the guardians of all places and property, and the heads were often carved to represent members of the family, priests, priestesses, or Pharaohs and their wives. The Greeks called these 'sphinxes'. One of the names of the Egyptian Sphinx was Hu, 'the protector'; another was Hor-em-akhet or 'Horus of the Horizon' which immediately connects its erection with those enigmatical 'Sons (or Followers) of Horus' the Shemsu-Hor. Curiously enough, the name 'Hu' also occurs in the Celtic myth of Hu Gadarn, an Atlantean person from the sea who guided a band of settlers to the prehistoric shores of Wales. There is also an uncanny similarity of sound between the names Hu Gadarn and the Tuatha de Danaans (pronounced Tuar-de-Danans), those strange fairy people with magical powers who, according to legend, landed on the shores of prehistoric Ireland.

One question that is bound to arise concerning the employment of these twin lion and crystal powers is, does Siriun magic involve the same occult distinctions between medium and magus as certain schools of the Western tradition? The answer must be 'No'. Siriun mind magic can be worked in a group or solitarily. As it combines essentially the employment of the two brain hemispheres, both the rationale and intuitive aspects of the personality are brought into play, or should be, in *equal proportions*, neither dominating, but each complementing the other. Thus, the practitioner must supply his or her own protection and assume responsibility for his or her actions in both inner time and non-locality. The aspirant's psychic faculties, therefore, need to be well-trained and tested, thus avoiding the downward spiral of self-delusion. As Jung wrote:

> We are that pair of Dioscuri, one of whom is mortal and the other immortal, and who, though always together, can never be made completely one. The transformation processes strive to approximate them to one another, but our consciousness is aware of resistances, because the other person seems strange and uncanny, and because

we cannot get accustomed to the idea that we are not absolute master in our own house.[8]

If you cast your mind back to the Dogon's Siriun philosophy, as outlined in Chapter 5, you will find it easy to relate the twin complex of Sirius A and Sirius B to this aspect of human psychology that Jung has outlined so clearly, the twinning implications relating at a higher octave to the process of individuation or balancing of the anima and animus, which is a *sine qua non* to the spiritual advancement of the soul.

He or she must therefore have the courage of the lion when faced with strange or unfamiliar adversaries or unrecognisable abstract energies, and the mental clarity of the crystal so that that which is learned is duly assimilated, refined, and translated into the parlance of today's world. For what use knowledge if it cannot be communicated to those who need it?

Endnotes:

1 R. Masters, *The Goddess Sekhmet,* page vii.

2 Ibid. page vii.

3 W.A. Budge, *Egyptian Theological Systems and Dogmas,* pages 28–9.

4 Goodman, J. *The Earthquake Generation,* pages 160–1.

5 E.A. Wallis, Budge, *The Gods of the Egyptians,* Vol. 2, page 88.

6 R. Masters, *The Goddess Sekhmet,* page 204.

7 Ibid., page 204.

8 C. G. Jung, *The Archetypes and the Collective Unconscious,* page 131.

CHAPTER 13

Siriun Heritage

It is to G. R. S. Mead that we owe much of the information that has filtered through from ancient Egyptian times concerning the more exalted mysteries of Egyptian and Siriun magic. His *Thrice Greatest Hermes* is culled from fragments of writings spanning a wide period of time, which he meticulously catalogued and incorporated in three volumes. Much of this ancient Egyptian philosophy was also to influence both Judaism and early Christianity, although the more potent factors were conveniently dismissed during those power struggles that inevitably scarred the infanthood of the Christian Church. Many of the old truths, however, found their way into the teachings of the Gnostics and post-resurrection gospels, such as the *Pistis Sophia*, which have also been made available to us through the scholarship of Mead.

Another work which serves to fortify the Hermes literature is *The Egyptian Mysteries,* a superlative work by Iamblichos, translated from the Greek by Alexander Wilder, MD, FAS, and first published in 1911. It consists of a series of dialogues between Porphyry, distinguished scholar and foremost writer in the later Platonic period, and one Anebo. Porphyry, (c. AD 232–304) was a native of Tyre and his name Molech, or King, was rendered by Longinus into 'Porphurios', denoting the royal purple as a proper equivalent. He was a disciple of Plotinus who later broadened his philosophical interests to include other beliefs. In his personal life he followed the Pythagorean discipline, and was a severe critic of the Gnostic beliefs then current, including with them the newly popularised Christian faith. Being essentially a mystic, Porphyry regarded the ceremonial rites of the Egyptian theurgy with mistrust, favouring Mithraism, while Iamblichos followed the cult of Serapis, which was then the state religion in Egypt. The scribe, Iamblichos, is said to have lived c. AD 255–330, although these dates are unverifiable. Of Anebo we know little; he is referred to as an Egyptian priest, his name indicating that he was probably in the service of Anubis. Porphyry addressed him as 'prophet' or servant of divinity and expounder of the sacred oracles, and it is in this capacity that the philosopher sought his explanations regarding the Egyptian theological doctrines, religions beliefs and sacred rites. These dialogues display the outwardly marked differences between logical Greek thinking and the more mystical approach of the Egyptians, although the irony lies in the fact that beneath the ethotic facade there is basically little difference, if any.

But let us first cast our attention to the *Hermes Trismegistus,* which could be seen to constitute the Bible or main book of reference for the modern student of Egyptian philosophy, being considered as a more accurate assessment of the inner teachings of ancient Egypt than *The Book of the Dead* and other early texts directly related to the Egyptian ethos. This reasoning is based on the belief in an oral tradition which, like that of Celtic Druidism, cloaked its deeper mysteries in a language recognisable only to the Initiate or Adept. Its writings, like the fabled Emerald Tables, are believed to have been inspired by Thoth/Tehuti himself.

The title 'Thrice Greatest' often evokes questions. According to some authorities the term is of late use, although the fact that it was known in Roman times may be evidenced in the famous epigrammatist Martial (AD 40–104?) who in singing the praises of one Hermes, a famous gladiator, brings his paean to a climax with the line: *Hermes omnia solus et ter unus!*[1] Mead opines, however, that the term was in evidence long before Roman times and cites the trilingual inscription on the Rosetta Stone, extolling the virtues of Ptolemy Epiphanes (210–181 BC), which refers to Hermes as the 'Great-and-Great'.[2]

Using Manetho (see Chapter 1, Endnote 2) as his reference, Mead concludes that the first Hermes mentioned therein alludes to the first priesthood among the Egyptians, who used a sacred language, the knowledge of which was long since forgotten by the time of the second Hermes, which we may presume to be a much later priesthood, the members of which were probably a cross between the Shemsu Hor and the indigenous population of those parts. He tells us:

> The two successions of priests and prophets were separated by a 'flood'. This 'flood' was presumably connected with, if not the origin of, the flood of which Solon heard from the priests of Sais ... of which we have considerable information given us in the *Timaeus* and *Critias* of Plato. The Good Angel is the same as the Mind, as we learn from the Trismegistic literature, and was regarded as the father of Hermes Trismegistus. This seems to be a figurative way of saying that the archaic civilisation of Egypt before the flood, which presumably swept over the country when the Atlantic Island went down, was regarded as one of great excellence. It was the time of the Gods or Divine Kings or Demi-Gods, whose wisdom was handed on in mystic tradition, or revived into some semblance of its former greatness, by the lesser descendants of that race who returned from exile, or reincarnated on earth, to take charge of the new populations who had gradually returned to the lower Nile planes after the flood had subsided.
>
> Thus we have three epochs of tradition of the Egyptian mystery-cults: (i) The first Thoth or Agathodaimon, the original tradition preserved in the sacred language and character in the stone monuments of the Seriadic land, presumably the Egypt prior to the Atlantic flood; (ii) the second Thoth, the Thrice-Greatest, the mystery-school after the period of the great inundation, whose records and doctrines were preserved not only in transcriptions but also in MSS, still written in the sacred character, but in the Egyptian tongue as it was spoken after the people reoccupied the country; and (iii) Tat, the priesthood of Manetho's day, and presumably of some centuries prior to his time, who spoke a yet later form of Egyptian, and from whose demotic translations further translations or paraphrases were made in Greek.[3]

In more recent times the 'Thrice Greatest' appellation has been ascribed a number of more metaphysical meanings, such as the Law of Three Requests (see Glossary), body, mind and spirit, instinctive, rational, intuitive, conscious, unconscious and super-conscious and so forth. The numerological associations of the number three have also been read into the title and I do not doubt that there is something in this. Siriun enthusiasts would doubt-less add the three stars of the Siriun system, but since there is some doubt concerning one of these which could possibly be a large planet and not a star at all, I would rather reserve judgement until more proof is forthcoming.

The *Trismegistus* represents part of a collection of ancient Egyptian occult teachings which are distinguished from the 'Hermes Prayers' of Egyptian magic and the Hermetic alchemical literature. In fact, they stand alone. They comprise:

(a)   The Corpus Hermiticum (body of the teachings), which includes the Poimandres, a collection of fourteen sermons, and the Definitions of Asclepius involving instructions from Hermes to Apollo's son, later deified as the Greek god of medicine.

(b)   The Perfect Sermon, also known as the Asclepius, as it is addressed to a character of that name. This exists only in the old Latin version, the Greek now being extinct.

(c)   The Excerpts from Stobaeus. There are twenty-seven of these excerpts from otherwise lost sermons that were 'discovered' and translated by one John Stobaeus, a pagan scholar from the end of the fifth and beginning of the sixth centuries. Stobaeus collected extracts, some of which are very long, notably the collection entitled *The Virgin of the World*, from the Greek authors and occult schools of his day. This appears in the form of a series of instructions and accompanying dialogues between Isis and her son Horus, which are concerned with the magical and mystical teachings of ancient Egypt, and is considered by many magical authorities to be the most interesting by far.

(d)   References and fragments from the early Christian fathers. The early Christian scholars and Church doctors frequently saw fit to comment on the *Hermes Trismegistus* and there are twenty-five short fragments of note that have come down to us. Because of the heretical nature of the Hermetic doctrine, these writers tended to speak out against it, which very act has, in fact, helped to keep it alive. It is interesting to observe that in spite of their opposition on dogmatic grounds, they convey an underlying acknowledgement of, if not an actual respect for, the Trismegistic power and philosophy.

(e)   References and fragments from the early philosophers, not necessarily of Christian persuasion. From Zosimus, Fulgentius and Iamblichos we have three fragments, and from Julian, the emperor-philosopher (irreverently labelled 'the apostate' by his Christian contemporaries), there are a number of valuable references and acknowledgements.[4]

The testimony afforded by these historical passages accords with much of what has come down to us via oral tradition, mystical inspiration and those Egyptological scholarly studies which have endeavoured to concentrate more on the spiritual or hidden mystery aspects of that discipline. Errors have obviously crept in, with translators tending to reinterpret the texts in the light of their own experiences, particular magical leanings, or the current trends of occultism fashionable at the time. These fragments are but scant remains of what must once have been a fountain of information, largely reserved for the dedicated student or Initiate, much of which would have been entirely lost were it not for the diligent efforts of one Hermetic apologist selecting some of the sermons to exemplify the loyal nature of the *Hermes Trismegistus* with respect to the position of kings!

The fact that these fragmentary odds and ends have somehow managed to straddle the centuries, in spite of severe mutilation suffered during the process of translation and retranslation, is truly a miracle. At times, when persecution was rife, they existed purely as secret works, carefully concealed by those faithful adherents to the old wisdom; at other periods they remained safely in the possession of private collectors, those sons and daughters of Thoth who are the 'guardians' of the word. But, in spite of all the opposition from the minions of Chaos, both incarnate and discarnate, a few gems of the old truths have managed to filter through to us.

An index of full references would occupy too much space and is not really relevant to our subject matter at this point. However, for the benefit of the dedicated researcher who prefers to check his or her facts, here are a few verifiable sources. Embodying the Hellenic and Orphic tradition as related to *Hermes Trismegistus,* there is the *Bibliotheca Graeca* of Joannes Albertus Fabricius (fourth and last edition, Leipzig, 1790). From alchemical and medieval literature we have the works of M. P. E. Berthelot, namely, *Collection des Anciens Alchimistes Grecs* (Paris, 1888) and *La Chimie au Moyen Age* (Paris, 1893). Arabic writings include Beausobre's *Histoire Critique de Manichée et du Manichéisme* (Amsterdam, 1734) (i.) 326; also H. L. Fleischer, *Hermes*

Trismegistus an die menschliche Seele, Arabisch und Deutsch (Leipzig, 1870); O. Bardenhewer, *Hermetis Trismegisti qui apud Arabes fertur de Castigatione Animae Liber* (Bonn, 1873); and R. Pietschmann, the pupil of Georg Ebers, who devoted the fourth part of his treatise, entitled *Hermes Trismegistus nach ägyptischen und orientalischen Überlieferungen* (Leipzig, 1875), to a consideration of the Hermes tradition, *'Bei Syrern und Araben'*.[5]

Another single manuscript was found in the eleventh century in sad condition. Whole quires and single leaves were missing when it came into the hands of Michael Psellus, a gentleman greatly involved in the revival of Platonic studies at Byzantium. Sadly, though, large chunks of the Psellus translation were torn out because they sought directly to justify polytheism or 'heathendom', so once again the serious student was cheated. Reitzenstein, the Theosophical scholar did as much as he could to piece together the fragments of truth, and Mead highly applauds his efforts.

Much of the trismegistic literature is taken from the original Greek texts, although three influences were later superimposed on the early Greek, Hebrew and Egyptian originals. The Jewish influence was Essenic or Therapeutic (the word Essene is, Mead tells us, Greek and not Hebrew). The *Trismegistus* then came under the influence of the early Christian Gnostics, many of whom adopted large chunks of it in defence of their beliefs which were subsequently labelled 'heresies'. The most notable of these was Basilides, whom Carl Jung believed to be either a fragment of his own group soul, who guided him through the *Seven Sermons of the Dead,* or himself in a former life. The Valentinian Gnosis was also strongly Hermetical. The trismegistic literature therefore carries a distinctly Gnostic flavour in places, so the student is advised to strip away these Christo-Gnostic overleaves in order to effect a closer contact with the Egyptian original.

The whole series which comprises the *Trismegistus* is attributed to the direct inspiration of Thoth/Tehuti, who is referred to therein as 'the master of wisdom and teacher of mankind'. Thoth, the texts inform us, 'ordained measure, number and order in the universe'; was master architect, and his consort was Nehemaut, known to the Gnostics as Sophia, and as Maat to the Egyptians. Maat's symbol was a white feather (sometimes also associated with Thoth himself in his judicial capacity).

According to the *Hermes Trismegistus* there were three grades in the Egyptian Mysteries of Thoth:

> *Mortals* – those who were instructed but who had not yet gained inner vision.
> *Intelligences* – those whose vision enabled them to tune into other life-forms within the universe.
> *Beings of Light* – those who had become one with the Light.

The Gnostics later labelled these as *hyle, psyche* and *pneuma,* and added the following distinctions which are outlined by Mead: '(a) the lowest, or *hylics*, were those who were so entirely dead to spiritual things that they were as the *hyle* or unperceptive matter of the world; (b) the intermediate class were called *psychics*, for though believers in things spiritual, they were believers simply, and required miracles and signs to strengthen their faith; (c) whereas the *pneumatics* or spiritual, the highest class, were those capable of knowledge of spiritual matters, those who could receive the Gnosis.' Mead also adds a further commentary which serves to qualify the question of equality:

> It is somewhat the custom in our days in extreme circles to claim that all men are 'equal'. The modern theologian wisely qualifies this claim by the adverb 'morally'. Thus stated the idea is by no means a peculiarly Christian view for the doctrine is common to all great religions, seeing that it simply asserts the great principle of justice as one of the manifestations of the Deity. The Gnostic view, however, is far clearer, and more in accord with the facts of evolution; it admits the 'morally equal', but it further asserts difference of degree, not only in body and soul, but also in spirit, in order to make the morality proportional, and so to carry out the inner meaning of the parable of the talents.[6]

In Gnostic literature, Thoth is the tutor to both Isis and Osiris and is one of the sacred eight, four pairs of divinities, each a syzygy or male and female power, active and passive, which is the oldest example of the Gnostic Ogdoad. Thoth's job, the *Trismegistus* informs us, is to keep perfect equipoise; hence his main symbol, the Caduceus. Note the emphasis on the number eight, which is but one pointer in the Siriun direction in this exciting work. There are others, as we shall see.

Amongst the wealth of knowledge contained in the trismegistic writings there are certain salient points that are relevant to both ancient Egyptian and Siriun studies. References to a land of enlightened people that existed before the Flood, and to the fact that Thoth/Hermes and the other 'gods' came from such a country, are numerous and leave little doubt in any open mind as to where the Egyptians obtained their occult knowledge. It is interesting to note that the old truths were translated from the tongue of the mother country into the native Egyptian and doubtless suffered not only in translation in those early times, but in subsequent analysis by later generations of scholars to whom the whole pre-Flood story was little more than a fable.

Regarding the Manetho quote concerning the Seriadic land (see Chapter 1, Endnote 2), Mead answers those who claim there is no historical record of any such land or country, with the following statement:

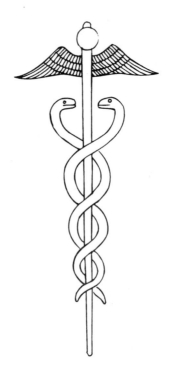

Fig. 13.1 Thoth's main symbol, the Caduceus.

In the astronomical science of the Egyptians, the most conspicuous solar system near to our own, represented in the heavens by the brilliant Sirius, was of supreme interest. Cycles of immense importance were determined by it, and it entered into the highest mysticism of Egyptian initiation.[7]

It is surely logical to assume that Egypt was Manetho's Seriadic land (from Seirios – Sothis, according to the Greek translation).

Mead refers to Nile records in ancient times being self-registered by pyramids, obelisks, and temples, while in later times nearly all monuments were built according to the type of the masonic instruments of the Egyptian astrogeological science. This science, he continues, was studied in more recent times by an Egyptian, and the results of his researches printed for 'private circulation' and a copy of them is to be found in the British Museum. Mead states that in the preface the author writes:

> The astrogeological science gave birth to a monumental system, by means of which the fruits of the accumulated observations and experiences of the human race have been preserved, outliving writings, inscriptions, traditions, and nationalities. The principal monuments had imparted to them the essential property of being autochronous landmarks of a geochronological nature. Many of them recorded, hydromathematically, the knowledge in astronomy, in geography, and in the dimension and figure of the earth obtained in their respective epochs. They were Siriadic monuments, because their magistral lines were projected to the scale of the revolutions of the star Surious [*sic*] in terms of the standard astrogeological cubit.[8]

Here we may read of an Egyptian scholar confirming the strong Siriun influence on the evolution and development of his land in archaic times. I have so far been unable to obtain further information regarding this document, but anyone with more time to spare, and a greater aptitude for persistence, might well meet with success.

In antiquity there were constant references to the 'pillars of Hermes' or 'Mercurii columnae', from which many of the ancient writers claim to have gleaned their information concerning prehistoric times, several of which I have already cited in Chapter 1, Endnote 8, notably the quote from Ammianus Marcellinus, friend of the Emperor Julian.

A highly significant passage from the Hermetic texts appears in the writings of Sanchuniathon, who is described by Philo as 'a man of great learning and a busy searcher (after knowledge) who especially desired to know the first principles from which all things are derived.' Philo continues to inform us that Sanchuniathon:

> most carefully examined the books of Taaut, for he knew that Taaut was the first of all under the sun who discovered the use of letters and the writing of records. So he started from him, making him as it were his foundation – from the Logos whom the Egyptians called Thouth, the Alexandrians Thoth, but whom the Greeks have turned into Hermes.[9]

The paragraphs relating to the creation are of particular interest and far removed from the primitive thinking normally associated with other indigenous peoples of the African continent. I feel they are worthy of detailed quotation:

> He (Thoth) supposes the beginning of all things to consist of a Dark Mist of a spiritual nature, or as it were a Breath of dark mist, and of a turbid Chaos black as Erebus; that these were boundless, and for many an age remained without a bound. 'But when,' he says, 'the Spirit fell in love with his own principles, and they were inter-blended, that interweaving was called Love; and this Love was the origin of the creation of all things. But [Chaos] did not know its own creation. From its embrace with Spirit Mot was born. From her [Mot, the Great Mother] it was that every seed of the creation came, the birth of all the cosmic bodies.
>
> ' [First of all] there were [Great] Lives devoid of sensation, and out of these came subsequently [Great] Lives possessed of intelligence. The latter were called Zophasemin (that is to say, "Overseers of the Heavens"). The latter were fashioned in the form of eggs, and shone forth as Mot, the Sun and Moon, the Stars and the great Planetary Spheres.
>
> 'Now as the [original] nebula began to lighten, through its heat mists and clouds of sea and earth were produced, and gigantic downpours and torrents of the waters in the firmaments. Even after they were separated, they were still carried from their proper places by the heat of the sun, and all the [watery and earthy elements] met together again in the nebula one with the other, and dashed together, amid thunder and lightning; and over the crash of the thunderings the [Great] Rational Lives before-mentioned watched, while on the land and sea male and female cowered at their echo and were dismayed.'[10]

Strip this statement of its obvious overlays and we find a knowledge of cosmology which is more in keeping with modern
scientific thought than what is commonly accepted as 'magic'.
We have, in fact, the 'opposition' to thank for some of the
information that has managed to side-step the branding irons of
persecution and make its tortuous way to our present age,
Hippolytus' *Philosophumena; or Refutation of all Heresies* being a
classic example. In 1842, Minoides Mynas, a learned Greek who
was sent on a mission by the French Government, discovered in
one of the monasteries on Mount Athos the only surviving
manuscript of this very valuable document, which has been
ascribed to the fourteenth century. It originally consisted of ten
books, but, unfortunately, the first three and the beginning of the
fourth are missing. The first book had been previously ascribed to
Origen and was already known, and the missing volumes dealt
respectively with the doctrines and mysteries of the Egyptians
and Chaldeans.[11] Hippolytus claimed to have divulged all these
so-called mysteries, as well as those beliefs adhered to by the
Christian mystics of his time, whom he labelled 'heretics'.

One cannot help wondering why the Egyptian and Chaldean
mysteries were obliterated, and we can only surmise that the
information they contained was too powerful for this early
Church father to handle. Either that, or he was afraid they might
set his flock a-thinking! Those people who had a hand in the
suppression of cosmic knowledge that has produced such a
devastating affect on our planet must, one would think, have a
lot to answer for, plus a karmic debt beyond our conception.

The trismegistic literature is a study in itself and to cover all
the points salient to the Egyptian or Siriun theme would prove
too lengthy a process. However, there are some interesting
contributions from such classical stalwarts as Philo, Plutarch and
Plato. Philo of Alexandria (born sometime between 30 and 20 BC
and died about AD 45), a Jewish Hellenistic scholar, was an
apologist for the Therapeuts, a healing branch of the Essenes,
and it is to him that we owe much of the information available
concerning the mystical activities of that order. His comments
include the concepts of an active and a passive causation
principle at the god-source, the logos being the son of this
father/mother god responsible for our solar system and all
movements therein, via the agency of the physical sun: the
Isis/Osiris/Horus story, in other words.

Plutarch the Greek, who lived in the second half of the first century AD chose the Egyptian theme of Isis and Osiris as his subject. As a priest of the order of Apollo and Dionysus, he was well versed in the magical procedures of both systems and their attendant mysteries, as well as possessing a deep knowledge of the Egyptian tradition, which he no doubt culled from fragments now extinct. The Greeks endeavoured to equate their own deities with those of the Egyptian pantheon and Plutarch, writing on the Eleusinia and Orphic rites, effects some interesting correspondences: Dionysus with Osiris, Horus and Bast with Apollo and Artemis being examples. His Siriun connection comes via the sistrum, about which he wrote:

> The sistrum (σειστρον) also shows that existent things must be shaken up (σειεσθαι) and never have cessation from impulse, but as it were be wakened up and agitated when they fall asleep and die away.
>
> For they say they turn aside and beat off Typhon [Set] with sistra, signifying that when corruption binds nature fast and brings her to a stand, [then] generation frees her and raises her from death by means of motion.
>
> Now the sistrum has a curved top, and its arch contains the four [things] that are shaken. For the part of the cosmos which is subject to generation and corruption, is circumscribed to the sphere of the moon, and all [things] in it are moved and changed by the four elements – fire and earth and water and air.
>
> And on the arch of the sistrum, at the top, they put the metal figure of a cat with a human face, and at the bottom, below the shaken things, the face sometimes of Isis and sometimes of Nephthys, – symbolising by the faces generation and consummation (for these are the changes and motions of the elements). ...[12] (See *Fig. 13.2* overleaf).

Personally, I find this comment of Plutarch's exciting for several reasons. Note the allusion to the Double Fire of Isis and Nephthys, also the evolutionary role played by the four Elements: 'when corruption binds nature fast and brings her to a stand'. In other words, when one evolutionary epoch has reached a standstill, and a quantum leap becomes necessary, the leonine or feline energies of Sirius are brought into force for, as we have already discussed, Sekhmet is the enemy of Chaos, and Chaos can manifest just as strongly through inertia as through ill-judged movement. Stagnant water, for example, provides a

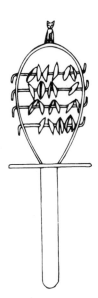

*Fig. 13.2 The sistrum which contains
four things which are shaken,
representing the four Elements.*

breeding ground for impurities, and as Heracles (Hercules) judged during the execution of his sixth labour, the power of *fast-flowing* water was needed to cleanse the accumulated filth of the Augean stables! Taking these things alone into consideration, it is little wonder that the sistrum is one of the most important pieces of impedimenta in the magical arsenal of the Siriun practitioner, as there are inevitably times when we, like the Egyptian priests of old, will need to conquer Set.

If we strive to illuminate those dark corners of cosmic ignorance that have not been visited by the broom of knowledge for centuries, the odds are that we will also disturb the 'creepy-crawlies' that have made their nest in the stygian gloom and, as a wise old occultist once said to me in my youth: 'If you pull the devil's tail he will squeak.' Not that he believed in a personalised Satan, but being a psychologist he realised that ignorance seldom likes its comfort shaken by the appearance of knowledge. I think it was Emerson who made a statement to the effect that God offers to every man the choice between Truth and Repose – take which you will, you may never have both! So speaketh the sistrum!

The final section in Book 1 of the *Trismegistus* is entitled *The Shepherd of Hermas*. Purportedly an ancient Egyptian script, it was circulated among the Gnostics and Essenes who espoused many of its teachings. There is a little too much vague Gnosticism in it to render it of interest to the Siriun student, however, although the Aeon doctrine presents some interesting ideas on evolution.

Book 2 of the *Hermes Trismegistus* is entitled the *Corpus Hermeticum*, or body of the literature, and it features the works of one Poimandres, whose origin and existence are suspect, since in Egyptian the name simply means 'a witness'. Poimandres, it is explained, underwent an altered state of consciousness, or psychic experience, during which he received his instruction directly from Hermes (Thoth), which suggests either a channelling situation or Samyama. For all this, there is some interesting information to be found under the title *The Shepherd of Men*. The masculine-feminine nature of the Godhead or Creator, for example: the Sophia or Wisdom, and the Christos or Will, which carry strong Gnostic overtones, but are nevertheless compatible with the Isis-Osiris teachings. From the observations recorded, it would seem that whoever received this instruction was as convinced about the divine source of his or her revelations as Christians are about the holy spirit hovering perfunctorily over them when they translate or endeavour to interpret the scriptures.

Some of these so-termed Egyptian teachings, which are reminiscent of the writings of the late Rudolf Steiner, did not strike me as being at all compatible with the old Egypto-Siriun teachings, especially those referring to the pattern of evolution. The authenticity of this particular fragment is highly questionable, however, as it would appear to carry strong Christo-Gnostic overtones, in addition to the influence of the times in which it was purportedly written. Any conjectures are therefore purely academic, and only hidden meanings should be sought for and extracted.

Our next incursion into the trismegistic literature introduces us to Stobaeus, his first contribution taking the form of a dialogue between Hermes and Asclepius, in which the master instructs the pupil in the mysteries of the cosmos and the spiritual development and progression of the soul. This section contains some interesting information concerning the Egyptian priesthood and its attitude towards celibacy, and is certainly worth perusal. Throughout this work we have the continuing theme of the Flood, the master race that existed before it occurred, and hints of a knowledge of science and astronomy comparable to a standard only attainable via the aid of an advanced technology.

Titillating pieces of information in the *Corpus Hermeticum* include the stellar nature of the Deity; the imperishability of the psyche or spirit, the etheric body, the reincarnation process, the fact that animals and people are of separate evolutionary streams, overcoming karma by will, energy and matter; the race of logos or devas and, probably the most interesting of all from the Siriun standpoint, the dual nature of the soul. Hermes tells us that only one fragment of our spirit actually enters the earthly time circuits, while the other part remains in timelessness (non-locality/shades of the particle/wave packet of modern quantum theory, no?). This concept could possibly be seen as giving birth to the doctrine of the higher or transpersonal self, which seems to have misled many people into thinking that theirs is the only 'higher self' in the universe, the idea that it might possibly engage in dialogue with the 'higher selves' of others never having occurred to them.

By far the most interesting of the three Trismegistic volumes is undoubtedly number three, which includes *The Virgin of the World* and *The Sermon of Isis to Horus*. The philosophical and magical concepts rendered here are highly advanced and decidedly prophetic. Here are some examples:

1. The complete equality of the sexes, the teaching indicating that the spirit may select a body of either sex according to its evolutionary needs.

2. Certain branches of the animal kingdom, notably lions and dolphins, being of a higher evolutionary grade than others (or of some members of *Homo sapiens,* for that matter). Although the specific references could be seen to relate to life on Earth, reading between the lines serves to open the concept to a more cosmic interpretation, and it is my opinion that this was how it was originally presented to the Egyptians.

3. Man's pollution of this planet, resulting in a revolt by the four Elements.

4. The 'Old ones' whose origins were not of this world and from whom, according to his mother Isis, Horus and his divine family sprang (remember the ancient Pyramid Text – *Horus who is in Sirius?*).

5. How wise spirits were originally ordained to occupy places of power and responsibility, but their power was usurped by younger and less experienced souls who gained their position by the employment of force (the Osiris-Set drama enacted at the material level by mankind?)

6. The nature of males and females; the elements predominant in each sex and how these should rightly manifest according to Cosmic Law.

7. The chakras of the planet Earth.

8. Our planet as a body, subject to imbalances and disease but also curable (the Gaia Hypothesis).

9. The connection between illness and the elemental balance within the human system.

10. The etheric world that precedes and is mirrored by its physical counterpart.

11. The 'gods' who descended from 'heaven' to teach mankind and then returned to their original home in the stars.

12. Books translated from some 'sacred language' into the tongue in use prior to the first Egyptian dynasty (the old Atlantean language).

13. Evidence that the mathematical nature of the universe was well understood by the ancient Egyptians and those who taught them.

14. The wheel of karma.

15. The folly of intellectual nit-picking.

16. The nature of Cosmic Law.

17. The zodiac.

18. The family of devic spirits or archangels from 'another solar' system.

19. The nature of disease.

These are but a few of the exciting and spiritually stimulating teachings to be found in this extraordinary work. It would seem logical to suppose that in accordance with normal Egyptian magical procedures the instructress (Isis) assumes the role of the goddess in addressing her son, Horus, (the student), so we are, in fact, dealing with the remnants of an extremely ancient and sound metaphysical tradition. The final references in the Hermes literature, Volume 3, are concerned with comments offered by various classical writers and merit mention if only to confirm just how much of the truth we have been deprived of over the ensuing centuries.

Clement of Alexandria (AD 150–220) tells us that the gods Hermes, Ptah and Imhotep once lived amongst men in Egypt, to which they came from a land before the Flood. Hermes, the learned father informs us, brought from those lands certain books of a medical nature that were absolutely indispensable. These numbered forty-two, thirty-six of which contained the whole wisdom discipline of the Egyptians which the priests were required to learn by heart, the remaining six applying to the healing arts of the 'shrine-bearers' (physicians).

Tertullian (AD 160–230) states that Hermes taught Plato and that the doctrine of reincarnation dated back to a civilisation that existed before the flood.

Lactantius (fourth century AD) says of Hermes that the month of September was sacred to him, and that he ruled the sign of Virgo jointly with Isis. References are also made in this fragment to the elemental kingdoms and the dual nature of good and evil.

Zosimus (third/fourth century AD) refers to Hermes as being of the kingdom of devas or archangels, a being who instructed men in all matters medical far in advance of primitive understanding. Reference is also made here of a 'counterfeit daimon' who leads men astray, but who Hermes or Thoth knew how to combat.

Julian, the Emperor, (reigned AD 360–363) claimed that Hermes was a guide from the higher planes of spirit and not a man at all. He also opined that Hermes may teach at any age in the history of man through the inspiration of a medium or channeller.

From the aforegoing it must be obvious to the student that a wealth of ancient wisdom lies hidden beneath the Trismegistic cloak, knowledge that is essentially cosmic and transcendental, and minus those tribal or parochial limitations so often imposed by certain currently favoured metaphysical traditions. It has been postulated that no knowledge is ever lost; but rather forgotten, to be relearned at some time appropriate to its replacement in and relevancy to the history and evolution of this planet.

Let us now leave the *Hermes Trismegistus* and refer to the *Egyptian Mysteries* according to Iamblichos, as translated by Wilder. This enlightening and fascinating dialogue commences with the words of Porphyry:

> I will begin this friendly correspondence with thee with a view to learning what is believed in respect to the gods and good daimons and likewise the various philosophic speculations in regard to them.

Many things have been set forth concerning these subjects by the (Grecian) philosophers, but they for the most part have derived the substance of their belief from conjecture.[13]

The learned man then proceeded to list his queries which, as one might imagine, contained a goodly share of Greek logic, and in essence questioned the wisdom and efficacy of a system that was magically based and orientated. The reply to Porphyry's letter to Anebo was handled by Abammon, the teacher, who was obviously charged with the apology and who opens his answering epistle with the following words:

Hermes, the patron of literature, was rightly considered of old to be a god common to all the priests and the one presiding over the genuine learning relating to the gods, one and the same among all. Hence, our predecessors were wont to ascribe to him their discoveries in wisdom and to name all their respective works *Books of Hermes*.[14]

The priests referred to in these dialogues consisted of many orders, including the performers of rites, prophets (seers?), the learned professions, philosophers, poets, authors, physicians, master mechanics and so forth. In fact the Egyptian priesthood, like its Atlantean predecessor, embraced all forms of learning and was by no means limited to the performance of matters religious or magical.

It would be impossible to do justice to even a section of this work, so I shall endeavour to extract briefly some of those teachings that I feel to be most relevant to our enquiry. Leaving aside the Hellenistic semantics, the information compares with that of the earliest recension of *The Book of the Dead*. There are descriptions of the gods, devas, spirits of the elements, heroes, and a host of other invisible forces that occupy the universal space between mankind and the Infinite, so often seen by orthodox religion in terms of a void or vacuum. Nor did they conceive of the human body *containing* the soul or spirit, but rather the other way round, which confirms the relationship between the spirit and the subtle, non-local force fields which surround and encase the physical body.

Egyptian astrology, we are told, was more of a philosophic than a predictive nature, although its overall affect on the evolution of the planet was fully understood and observed in rite and prayer. Nor were any of the planets considered to be malignant in the accepted astrological meaning of the word, one appropriate example being that a man suffering from scurvy who sits in the heat of the sun will increase his sufferings, but it is the scurvy (imbalance) in the man, and not the sun, that causes his discomfort. Likewise with Saturn, the Teacher; should we feel distressed by his influences, it is because we, like the slack pupil, have neglected to heed his lessons and therefore need to be brought firmly into line. It is also the nature of all things that until they attain to the Ultimate or Creative Centre, they are partial or incomplete as far as their evolutionary development is concerned and therefore need to undergo constant refining and change. As this process inevitably involves decomposition, the intelligences or energies involved therewith are frequently viewed as negative, which should not be since they are simply the servants of natural law, each doing its duty without fear or favour, and not the agents of some personalised evil force.

Our one connecting link with God, and the universe as a whole is, we are told, the *mind*. There exists within each individual the potential to reach forth and link with the universal consciousness and, through channels thus opened, draw upon the forces of life and light. How such energies are employed, however, will rest according to the soul-age (field band-width) of the seeker, and his or her basic *intention*, the objective behind their manipulation determining their 'colour'. In other words, this ancient philosophy, as outlined by the Egyptian priests, accords with much of what is known and understood concerning the ethics of magic generally.

Divination, channelling, and other such popularly accepted manifestations of the psi factor are also dealt with in this work. It seems the ancient Egyptians were none too happy about employing mediumship in their magical practices, however, being rather particular about whom they allowed to be channels for their god-forces. They were also well aware of the fact that there are just as many imposters in other dimensions as there are here on Earth, the chaotic factor manifesting throughout all wavebands or frequencies short of the Ultimate or Creative Source. Intelligences from the 'higher spheres', they tell us, are not given to producing phenomena; mirrors, crystals and other such psychic aids are, according to these ancient priesthoods, a constant source of error and deception. Emblems (symbols), however, are safe since they are often used as vehicles of divine power.

Perhaps those who complain that they do not obtain the answers they wish from psychic sources should take note of the comments made by Anebo when he was questioned by Porphyry regarding the oft-times unco-operative nature of the oracles. It is sometimes necessary for us to live our lives for ourselves and refrain from leaning too heavily on external sources who, after all, have other things to do as well as acting the parent to our spiritual immaturity. Should the gods in their wisdom see fit to deny us access to outer time, then it is usually because of some decision made by our own free will or psyche, prior to entering our body.

A clear line of demarcation is effected between what the Egyptian priest refers to as 'other parts of the soul' such as the 'higher self', and those who guard, guide or watch over us. Too many people seem only too happy to ascribe all forms of inspiration to some exalted aspect of their own spiritual or psychological economy, so care should be taken to identify these differences and observe them.

Sacred rites are dealt with in some detail and Porphyry, who was obviously not impressed by a surfeit of occult paraphernalia, questions Anebo as to why all that kind of thing was essential. Surely, he postulates, if the gods are what they claim to be, they do not need to disturb water in bowls, project bizarre objects onto magical mirrors, or appear as insubstantial phantasms guaranteed to frighten the life out of the average person. Of course, the old Egyptian magi knew that the 'bumps in the night', or what they referred to as the 'instability of spectral figures' was not the real thing, and therefore took appropriate precautions to avoid it. Since physical phenomena of this kind usually manifest in the lower wavebands, this is effected by the simple action of speeding up the frequencies, as any occultist worthy of his or her salt knows.

Perhaps a quick reference to the *hyle, psyche* and *pneuma* of the trismegistic literature will serve to show us which level of spiritual comprehension is catered for by manifestations of the 'bumps in the night' variety! The Egyptians were also against ritually-induced overt states of ecstasy (or frenzy, as the case may be). While the necessity for some to imbibe the atmosphere of overt devotionalism was accepted, any outward display or resulting abreaction was considered purely in the therapeutic context and not truly relevant to magic proper in its 'controlled' form. The validity of the Egyptian approach may be evidenced in modern studies of the clinical and psychological effects of certain rites and psychic practices, which subject I have dealt with in some detail in my book *The Psychology of Ritual*.

Free will and how it operates is commented upon in the Porphyry-Anebo dialogues, as well as the fact that the choice of the earthly condition is effected by the soul itself, the divinity being without blame in the issue. After the choice has been made, the 'daimon' or guardian angel is allotted. Our tendency to judge higher powers in terms of human emotion is faulty in the extreme. Earthly emotions do not necessarily bear any relationship to Cosmic Laws or the way things are in the universe beyond the confines of our early environs. Anebo was also generous in his comments concerning the power of healing, which he considered to be an individual gift and not attributable to powers transmitted via a medium from some guide or discarnate entity.

Blood sacrifices were not favoured at certain levels within the Egyptian priesthood, and those who followed the Inner Path conceived of the animal soul being able to ascend the evolutionary ladder *within its own kind* on other planets, if not on Earth. Therefore, in keeping with the shamans, they had no difficulty in accepting the idea of animal spirit communicators.

There is so much more one could relate from this interesting and enlightening book, but space is at a premium so this is as good a point as any to take our leave of these erudite scholars and priests, and hope that those who have found some solace and wisdom in their teachings will see fit to pursue the matter further, and study the work in its entirety.

A word of warning – playing around with Egypto/Siriun energies such as those experiments involving abstract shape-shifting and multidimensional awareness and time travel can prove highly perilous to all but the advanced student, the dangers involved proving both physically and psychologically harmful.

What kind of harm, you may ask? Well, let us look at it this way: many of today's illnesses are blamed on the holes in the Earth's ozone layer caused by the misuse of chemicals and other destructive influences wrought against Gaia, resulting in corresponding breaks in her aura. This has allowed access to entities alien to our earth bodies, which our immune systems have not, so far, been programmed to deal with. Therefore, at the purely physical level, if you choose to go wandering about in outer time you may well bring back with you entities which, having attached themselves to your aura, will naturally seek an avenue of manifestation once submitted to the frequencies of matter. And what better one than your physical body, or that of someone near and dear to you? Science fiction? Hardly! One needs only to take a look around – the evidence is there already. After all, Professor Fred Hoyle's panspermia carriers (believed to be comets) might not necessarily be selective in the passengers to whom they choose to offer a lift. It is now known that many diseases, as well as the chemicals in our bodies, are affected by such things as sunspots and lunations, so why not other parts of the universe? As to the mental hazards, aside from returning 'in one piece', the dangers of psychological fragmentation cannot be sufficiently emphasised. Of course, it could be argued that a combination of the limitations of the seeker's own 'field band-width' or soul-age plus the 'ring-pass-not' will prevent him or her from overstepping the mark which is as maybe in some cases, but not in all, as those involved in the healing arts will be only too well aware.

Endnotes:
 1 G. R. S. Mead, *Thrice Greatest Hermes*, Vol. 1, page 116.
 2 Ibid.,page 117.
 3 Ibid., pages 106–7.
 4 Ibid., pages 3–4.
 5 Ibid., page 5.
 6 G. R. S. Mead, *Fragments of a Faith Forgotten*, page 139–40.
 7 Mead, *Thrice Greatest Hermes*, Vol. 1, page 110.
 8 Mead, Op. cit., pages 111–12.
 9 Mead, Op. cit., page 124.
10 Mead, Op. cit., pages 125–6.
11 Mead, Op. cit., page 140.
12 Mead, Op. cit., page 344.
13 Iamblichos, *The Egyptian Mysteries*, page 10.
14 Ibid., page 25.

Chapter 14

As Above, So Below

The late Carl Gustav Jung observed, as no doubt had many sages who preceded him, that myth bore a striking resemblance to reality and could be interpreted validly at several levels. The ancient legends could therefore be read in any of the following contexts:

(a) Cosmological and evolutionary changes involving our own and other star systems;
(b) Aspects of human psychology;
(c) Actual events that took place in prehistoric times;
(d) Cosmic energies or archetypes directly related to both the individual and the collective unconscious;
(e) Prophecies concerning the future.

It would appear that in some non-local or timeless state, a kind of sacred drama was created which is enacted subconsciously at all levels, although at rare times a sage, artist, philosopher, time-traveller or magus is permitted to catch an occasional fleeting glimpse of its reality. Nowhere is this more emphasised than in the myths and rites of ancient Egypt, wherein one truth is concealed within another. In the process of studying these for over forty years I have watched the outer layers slowly strip away to reveal other, more exciting intimations. An analogy might be an interesting old painting in a somewhat dilapidated condition which, when submitted to the art of the professional restorer, reveals a considerably more valuable and beautiful work of art concealed beneath it.

Prior to effecting a summary of the previous chapters, I would like to share with my readers the contents of a letter I received, as I was about to start writing this final chapter in April 1990, from those kindly Egyptian followers of the Old Ways, whose helpful letter concerning their own Siriun traditions was reproduced in an earlier chapter. The opening paragraph reads:

Fig. 14.1

Written on the second day of the spring festival of Our Lord Us-Ar (Osiris), Lord of Abtu and the King of Resurrection, and written in the name of Ammun-Ra, God of Gods on this day of festivity from whom we say, as written above in our script, Anetch Hra-ku Ammun Ra Heh, and written by the permission and direct command of Her Grace Sekhmet Montu (LHS), Pillar of Millions in this our year of 12,451 AU (after Us-Ar), may She bless our writings with Her (LHS) spiritual presence. I write also at the direction of our Sage Sau Tahuti thusly:

May you have a long life and a truer communion with Our God, (both yours and ours), and may They guide your hand and all your works which come forth therefrom. Note please: Hra-ku is used in greeting as hello in English and Baraka is used in farewell as sincerely in English, although it means 'Blessings Upon Thee' in English.

The Scribe then confirms that he used the phonetic spelling of 'tootsie' rather than the African 'tutsi' as this was the way in which the information had been passed down to him and those he serves. He cites the date 12,451 AU as 'the number of years from when Our Lord Us-Ar became Lord of the Other World and departed from us.' This would indicate that Osiris, the King, must have left incarnation around 10,461 BC. Interesting! He continues: 'We do not know the name "Atlanteans" here, perhaps they are the people of the Green Sea? We know them to have become extinct shortly after Us-Ar's arrival on the earth in the Sinai but that was about 20,000 years ago. ...' (That is, around 17–18,000 BC, during the zodiacal Age of Scorpio, when Mu is reputed to have been destroyed and the Atlantean civilisation was founded, but I think we are dealing here with two different sequences of epochs, as we shall shortly see.)

This is followed by an approximate list of the astrological ages in which my Egyptian friend refers to the reign of Nebt Sekhmet Montu as corresponding to the Age of Leo, which is logical, and questions whether the Geminian Age might not relate to Us-Ar and Auset (Osiris and Isis). He tells us, 'Our faith began in the Age of Us-Ar and Auset. ...' and asserts that '... a little over 12,450 years ago Us-Ar and Auset arrived as the first pharaohs of Egypt to bring civilisation to the peoples of that land. ...' (the second manifestation?). Apologising for his translations, he gives the ages as follows:

> The void of Ammun. (Capricorn?)
> The Aeon of Nut or Division. (Aquarius?)
> The Age of Life in the Sea. (Pisces?)
> The Age of Ra. (Aries?)
> The Manifested Ra. (Taurus?)
> The reign of Us-Ar and Auset. (Gemini?)
> The Age of Retraction. (Cancer?)
> The Age of Nebt Sekhmet Montu and the destruction or Sea of Blood. (Leo?)
> The Age of Balance. (Libra?)
> The Age of Builders. (Sagittarius?)

My readers will note the absence of Virgo and Scorpio from the scribe's list, which leaves me with the impression that he is attempting to accommodate modern Western astrology when, in fact, his own traditions may relate a much broader history of the Earth. He further informs us that:

The Book of Faith was *not* revealed or found by Heru-ta-ta-fu, Bringer of His Own Hope, until the Age of the Builders [pyramids]. ... Tahuti was upon the earth from the time of the Age of Ra and Nebt Sekhmet Montu was upon the earth from the Age of the Manifested Ra. The following story is from the Age of Nebt Sekhmet Montu's first appearance on the earth and is repeated again in the Age of the Builders as well. [The sinking of Atlantis?] It goes: Nebt Sekhmet Montu as the Eye of Ra was the fiercest and cruellest of all forms, for it is She who protects The Divinity and Will of God. As Het-Heru, however, she was the happiest and most gracious of all, and her works are told in the Book of the Divine Cow, when she nearly destroyed all civilization and people. There is a sad story of how, when She left Egypt to dwell in Nubia in the south, being jealous of the excessive creations of Her Father, Ra, whom She adored, she left

Egypt to live in Nubia and changing her forms she slaughtered all creatures in Her path. Egypt became desolate, for without Het-Heru life was devoid of joy and happiness. Even Ra hid his face in sorrow at Her departure and none could console His heart over the loss of His daughter in whom His power rested. Darkness and Chaos tightened around Him and threatened Order and Systems very existence! Ra wondered: 'Who will bring My Daughter back home?' All the Gods were silent, for all feared to approach Her. So the task was given to Tahuti, wisest of all the Gods. Taking upon Himself the form of a Humble Baboon, He searched out the Daughter of Ra and approached Her carefully saying, 'Hail, Daughter of the Sun, may I speak before I die? Given permission, Tahuti told the story of the Mother Wildcat and the Mother Vulture who both mistrusted each other but had a truce, the truce being not to harm each other in any way. One day a baby vulture fell from the nest and was struck by a baby of the wildcat. Seeing the dead body on her return the vulture killed all the wildcat's babies and the wildcat in return saw all the vulture chicks killed by a burning coal in a piece of meat she brought back from the hunter's camp and placed in her nest. This was arranged by Ra as retribution for having taken revenge herself instead of asking Ra to do it! Give praise to Ra, O His Daughter, who sees and avenges all. Whose face brings all joy.

Then Tahuti, by guile, coerced Het-Heru into eating some herbs from the House of Ra, which melted away all Her anger and Her mood changed. Tahuti then told her another story as he walked Her back towards Egypt which showed Her that Ra notices even the death of a fly and that nothing has more power than the justice of Ra. This caused Het-Heru's heart to beat with great joy and pride at the fact that Her Father repays all good with good and evil with evil and, as Tahuti had pointed out, She was the Avenger of Her Father in all things! Slowly Het-Heru returned to Egypt with Tahuti and Tahuti even saved the life of Het-Heru from a serpent of evil as She slept beneath a tree. Upon arrival in Egypt there were great festivals given in Her honour and in On (Heliopolis) Ra was once again reunited with His Daughter. In Per-Ka-Ptah (Memphis) in the House of the Sycamore a great party was given in which Tahuti assumed His original form and Het-Heru finally recognized Him.

If you look at this story you will see not only moral values but also an exact account of the visitation of the *Lion Beings here and their subsequent return to their original home.* In the last story Tahuti told Het-Heru on their journey back He showed Her the cleverness of humans and their gullibilities and subsequent danger to all life forms around themselves except by the controls given by Ra. There are other Lion Gods in our files. ...

The last few lines of the missive are personal, but the scribe ends with the words: 'May I say from all here Shai-en-Renput, Happy New Year! May your spirit and heart be enlargd.'

I was deeply moved by this letter for several reasons. Firstly, the dates given coincide with those I had arrived at independently as a result of my own research and the kindly assistance of those leonine intelligences who see fit to allow a smidgin of wisdom to fall on my eager ears from time to time. Secondly, both the Mu-an and Atlantean cataclysms appear to be laid neatly at the feet of Sekhmet, that is Sirius – the House of the Leonine One! Both catastrophes were obviously linked to evolutionary quantum leaps, and many genuinely inspired people have been given to understand that we are due for another of these in the not too distant future; hence, the sudden appearance on the psychic scene of the Paschats, the Lion People of Sirius. The myths have always made it abundantly clear that Thoth was of an older generation of gods than the five epagomenal Neters, and from the aforegoing and other legends one is almost tempted to think of him in terms of a Siriun hominid. After all, his assigned wife, Seshat, was essentially a star goddess and, according to the ancient texts, 'a measurer of Time'. (A time traveller?)

The aforegoing story of the Sekhmet episode certainly differs considerably from that which normally appears in books on Egyptian mythology, in which the goddess is said to have been made drunk by imbibing a large amount of beer, after which she fell asleep, thereby ceasing her destruction (see Chapter 3). The allusion to Ra hiding his face in sorrow obviously refers to a period when the sunlight was blocked out and the Earth went to waste as a result – a period of nuclear winter? The Eye of Ra, which was the exclusive weapon of Sekhmet, is described as a bright and burning object (a planetessimal or comet, perhaps?) which fell upon the Earth, causing untold damage. If we are seeing Ra in terms of the Siriun system, and Sekhmet as his daughter, this would also explain the astrological allocation of Mars-Jupiter energies to Sirius, Sekhmet being a kind of warrior goddess or avenging angel, as it were, and Ra the expansive, kindly, paternal, Jupiterian being. From the myth, however, it appears that one could not function without the co-operation of the other and therein lies another mystery, the answer to which might conceivably be found within the beliefs of the Dogons.

Another point that caught my eye was the reference to 'The Book of the Divine Cow' (presumably Hathor?). Irish mythology also carries a similar title, 'The Book of the Dun Cow', which relates the history of Ireland prior to and following the Flood, and undoubted survived through the agency of archaic oral transmissions. One cannot help feeling that all this is no coincidence!

What we can glean from it, however, is that the epagomenal Neters *first* exerted their influence on the Earth around the time of the sinking of Mu and the subsequent founding of the Atlantean civilisation, their input being somehow connected with the quantum leap which the Siriun forces deemed essential to the evolutionary progress of the planet. This 'Transmutation', which was effected by Siriun Lion Power, was 'crystalised' in a mutation which took place in the genes of a certain family. (Isis, Osiris and their kin?) So, was it Atlantis and not Egypt that was the initial recipient of this myth that was subsequently carried through that civilisation until the Age of Cancer when first Thoth and then the Isis/Osiris clan, being the direct descendants of the original 'family' (and probably reincarnations of the same), made their appearance in what we now know as Egypt? Was this same drama, therefore, being re-enacted or repeated in a subsequent era? Surely we are back to our allegory, which could be likened to a picture that some later artist has painted over an ancient masterpiece because he or she could not afford a canvas? In other words, because the canvas of knowledge was not available at the time, the myth or sacred drama had to be perpetuated by whatever means was at the recorder's disposal.

The epagomenal days could, therefore, be seen to coincide with the arrival of the Isian family in Egypt, which infers that they need not necessarily have been added to the length of the year at that precise period, but could have originated during the sinking of Mu when, according to our Egyptian friends, *the five Neters first arrived*. Another explanation could be that it was the Atlantean scientist/priests (the scribes of Thoth?) who explained the 365-day year to the Egyptians. But there is something here that does not ring true, since it was the Sothic calendar that was important to the peoples of Egypt from the earliest times, and there would appear to be a strong connection between the Sirius doctrine and the 'People from the Green Sea', as our friend calls them.

As regards the aforementioned 'ages', since these do not con-cur with with those of the Great Year as we understand it, and in the light of Schwaller de Lubicz' observations as recorded in Chapter 1, (ref: Endnote 15), one wonders if they refer to some aspect of the ancient Siriun calendar rather than the zodiacal signs as accepted by modern astrology? The Age of The Builders, for example, designated as Sagittarius, could be connected with Neith or Satis, both of whom shared the bow and arrow as their attribute and are seen by Temple as having Siriun significance. Viewed in the broader context, however, these Egyptian 'ages' do give us a fairly comprehensive picture of the birth of our solar system and possibly one particular phase of the universe itself. The Age of Nut or Division, for instance, could be either inter-preted in the Earth-sky context as the Shu-Tefnut saga, or as relating to a specific astrological age. Schwaller de Lubicz sees it as Gemini, while our Egyptian friends suggest Aquarius (the Leo-Aquarius axis epitomised by the Sphinx?). But my own feeling is that what we are dealing with here are vast periods of time during which these 2000-year or more ages have been repeated numerous times and are little more than the blink of a cosmic eyelid, and as such we should only consider them as terms of reference appropriate to a particular enquiry and not as 'gospel'. Our Egyptian friends had the humility to place a question mark after each 'suggestion'. I rather think they have the right idea.

To return to the question of genetic mutations associated with an earlier quantum leap, did beings from Sirius actually come down to earth in person to effect these, or were they simply engineered via panspermia? Of that we cannot be sure; well, not for the moment anyway, although I have made my views on the subject known in earlier chapters. However, if the proposed Genome Project goes ahead we may well have the answer to this enigma sooner than we might think, information obtained via *The Gaia Dialogues* providing a very positive clue! The Atlantean settlers obviously took this ancient knowledge with them when they visited those distant shores that were later to become their chief colonies. First Thoth, the priest/teacher, and followed by the five aristocrats who were to act out the ancient story that had been passed down from generation to generation since the time of the original visitation, be that genetic, psychic or otherwise.

We have already considered the possibility of the fourteen pieces of Osiris as relating to certain localities on the body of

Gaia, but the legend may well have a corresponding resonance at another, more practical level. Let us take a hypothetical example and place our scenario in the latter days of the Atlantean civilisation, when it was realised that the return of Sekhmet was imminent. Following through the prophecy in detail, the High Priest and Priestess of the Old Country divided those who carried the Siriun gene into fourteen groups, each of which was despatched to either one of the colonies or some other carefully chosen shore, to ensure the survival of the Siriun inheritance. Let us suppose that one of these groups perished to a man, hence the story of the missing member, although this could also be seen in terms of the loss of the island continent itself. Another suggestion is that the missing phallus, representing the generative factor, symbolises the loss of certain perpetuating energies that are somehow bound up with the spiritual evolutionary development of *Homo sapiens*. The invention of the artificial phallus could therefore be seen in terms of a compensatory *in vitro* fertilisation which allowed a continuing flow of the Siriun energies.

I found the reference to the 'people of the Green Sea' particularly interesting, since, as we have already observed, Osiris is often shown as green and *seated on a throne surrounded by water*. (See illustration on page 76.)

This surely cannot be a coincidence. The truth of the matter probably lies in the fact that all these deities and their legends are purely allegorical, and this is simply one more demonstration of the enactment of a cosmic drama at yet another stratum.

Reincarnatory inferences may be read in the allusion to Tahuti assuming his original form, and Het-Heru recognising him. This suggests to me that the same group of people may reincarnate together each time there is to be some major change in our planet's evolutionary pattern, although they might not always recognise each other immediately. With regard to the later Egyptian interpretation of the myth, as told in the letter, what we could be dealing with here is a change in religious leanings that occurred in another period of time: the worship of one deity giving place to that of another, perhaps an earlier cult that was favoured with a revival. Memphis was, after all, the seat of Ptah, husband of Sekhmet, and their son, Nefer-tem, is frequently portrayed in leonine form.

The contents of my Egyptian friend's letter would appear to imply that the Egyptian tradition favours the idea that the Siriun system relates to the Sekhmet/Hathor/Ra or Amon, or Ra/Shu/Tefnut allocation rather than that of Isis, Osiris and Nephthys. As they point out, Het-Heru, whom we presume to be Sekhmet's gentler persona, was 'the happiest and most gracious of all', and it was only when she became the Eye of Ra that her transformative energies were activated. Using this storyline, the Ra or Amon/Sirius B connection becomes obvious, and assuming Het-Heru to be one and the same as Hathor would serve to connect Sekhmet's gentler persona with Sorghum-Female or Sirius C. This would leave Shu and Tefnut (the Twin Lion gods), or Isis and Osiris as the Egyptians see it, with the blue-white star so readily visible in our night skies. As I have already mentioned in Chapter 5 (page 83), the Siriun hominids are believed to have reached a stage in their somatic evolution (or since they live in a different space-time continuum then us, even surpassed it by now) where the sex differences become less accentuated, to the extent that it would be difficult for an 'outsider' to tell the difference between the males and females. Spiritual refinements tend to dispense with the rougher elements in the male psyche, and produce a corresponding somatic tendency towards a more feminine, gentler, and less macho appearance; a description which, for those disposed to believe in their existence, fits the Crystal People perfectly.

It is my opinion that all these personalities are purely manifestations of the energies of the stellar logoi (the guiding intelligences) of the Siriun system, one of which carries a leonine aspect and the other a highly evolved hominid accent. Emphases of this nature are inevitably the deciding factor as to which evolutionary strains are destined to predominate on any planet within their jurisdiction. However, I must make it clear that much of this is is pure conjecture and only time will tell who is right and who is wrong, as the case may be.

I was particularly impressed by the final paragraph of the Egyptian letter regarding the 'cleverness of humans and their gullibilities and subsequent danger to all life forms around themselves'. Thank the gods for the 'controls of Ra' and his daughter, and may they intervene yet again before we do anything further to ruin the body of Geb or Gaia, or whatever identity we may choose to accord our planet.

The Book of the Dead often refers to Ra and Osiris as one and the same being, or the incarnation one of the other after the fashion of the Hindu Vishnu who was believed to have made several appearances at different periods in the Earth's history. If Ra and Osiris are either soul-mates, or have family in common, then likewise Isis and Tefnut, and Shu and Horus; after all, the latter two were both sky-gods. Or, viewed in the reincarnation context, the implications are obvious: the soul fragments of each divinity assuming incarnation at the physical level in order to convey the experience to the Whole. This would also account for Isis and Osiris as the founders of the dynasties of both Atlantis and Egypt, their 'higher selves' supervising the process from their Siriun abodes.

Whereas the rule of the 'gods' goes back to the reign of Isis and Osiris, the Shemsu-Hor, our Egyptian friends tell us, came much later and drew up their own book of rules. Although generally assumed to be the direct descendants of the original 'gods', or the result of couplings between the Atlantean aristocrats and the indigenous population of Egypt, there could be some connection here between those Frisian sea people whose own land, we are told, sank beneath the North Sea around 5000 BC. Like their Atlantean predecessors, they, too, were very tall, fair-haired and blue-eyed. Could it conceivably be that we are dealing with more than one invasion? After all, Professor Emery assures us that the conquering aristocrats, who arrived towards the close of the fourth millenium BC, came in strange vessels with a high prow, totally dissimilar to anything the Egyptians had at the time. Although Emery sees the hint of a Mesopotamian influence in these craft, they strike me as being more typically Norse, although I must confess to being no expert in such matters. (See *Fig. 14.2* overleaf.)

This and many other riddles of antiquity still remain to be solved, perhaps by some future generation of archaeologists or time travellers. Although much of this enquiry is speculative, amongst the empirical data that is available there is sufficient evidence to imply that we do not as yet possess the whole picture by a long way. However, many amongst us who are prepared to heed the advice and warnings contained in the myths will, no doubt, see the pattern repeating within their lifetimes. As for the Siriun influence, like all real truths, it is there for those who wish to see it. The ancient Egyptians admitted it, as have those descendants of the Old Ones, whose generosity, courtesy and trust have helped to make my task in writing this book an easier one;

Fig. 14.2 The Gebel-el-Arak knife-handle – archaic period.

likewise the Hopi Indians, and other small pockets of Siriun influence that have withstood the onslaught of time.

Encapsulated as we are in the cosmic 'dream sequence' we call the present, our eyes are mostly blinded to the universe beyond our own small domain. And yet, the one thing of which we can be absolutely and utterly certain is that sooner or later death will awaken us from that dream and, like the person who has just witnessed some drama (be it horrendous, romantic, idyllic or agonising) portrayed on the silver screen, we will finally take our leave of this darkened enclosure to return to the comforts of spiritual home. Our exposures to inner time are but the fleeting impressions of the temporarily encapsulated psyche, which are inevitably dissolved in the transition of demise. Although our material experiences may seem very real to us, they are, as we would say in the old Atlantean tongue, *en-u-sta-ri-sta* – but 'a series of dreams'!

Appendix: Egyptian Tables

Early Prehistoric Period

Date BC	Northern or Lower Egypt	Southern or Upper Egypt	Main Sites	Period
c.5000	Faiyum 'A'		Faiyum depression	
		Tasian	Deir Tasa, Mosta-gedda	Neolithic
c.4000		Badarian	el-Badari	Chalcolithic
	Merimda		Merimda	
		Amratian	el-Amra, Nagada, el-Ballas, Hu, Abydos, Mahasna	Early Pre-dynastic
c.3600				

Later Prehistoric Period

Date BC	Northern or Lower Egypt	Southent or Upper Egypt	Main Sites	Period
c.3600		Early Gerzean		Middle and
	Maadi		el-Maadi	Late Pre-dynastic
c.3400		Late Gerzean	el-Gerza, Haraga	Historic
c.3200	The union of Upper and Lower Egypt under one king		Hierakonpolis Memphis Abydos	

Archaic Period (Dynasties I and II)

Approx Date BC	Principal Kings	Funerary Customs	Significant Events
3200	**Dynasty I**		Development of writing, copper tools and weapons
	Menes (Narmer)	Royal burials in main tomb at Saqqara	
	Ity I (Hor-Aha)		Trade with Levant
	Ity II (Djer)		
	Merbiapen (Adjib)	Cenotaphs at Abydos	Expeditions to Sudan
2900	**Dynasty II**		
	Hetep-sekhem-wy	Private burials near tomb or cenotaph of the king	Use of stone in building and for statuary
	Neb-re		
	Ni-neter		
	Peribsen		Religious and political strife
	Kha-sekhem-wy		Pacification of the Two Lands
2660			

Old Kingdom (Dynasties III and IV)

Date BC and Years of Reign	Principal Kings	Main Sites	Funerary Customs	Significant Events
c.2660	**Dynasty III**			
	Sa-nakht		Royal burial in Step Pyramid	Large-scale building and sculpture in stone
19	Neter-khet (Djoser)	Saqqara		
6	Sekhem-khet	Sinai	Private mastabas near Royal tomb	
24	Huny		(Hesi-re, Methen)	
c.2600	**Dynasty IV**			
			Evolution of true pyramid and climax of its development.	Great technical & artistic mastery over most materials
24	Sneferu	Maidum		
23	Khufu (Kheops)	Dahshur		
31	Khafra (Khephren)	Giza	Private burial in mastabas and some rock-tombs	The classic age of the Old Kingdom
18	Menkaure (Mykerinus)	Bubastis		
c.2500				

Later Old Kingdom (Dynasties V and VI)

Date BC and Years of Reign	Principal Kings	Main Sites	Funerary Customs	Significant Events
c.2500	**Dynasty V**			Rise in importance of Heliopolis
8	Weser-kaf		Royal pyramids smaller, but adjuncts decor-	
15	Sahu-re	Saqqara		
11	Ne-weser-re	Abusir	ated with fine	Expeditions
28	Djed-ka-re	Isesi	reliefs	to Punt.
30	Wenis	Heliopolis	*Pyramid Texts*	Private sculpture in wood
			Gradual increase in size of private mastabas (Ti, Mereruka)	and stone of high standard
c.2340	**Dynasty VI**			
15	Teti	Deir-el-Gebrawi		Decentralisation of government
44	Pepy I (Phiops I)	Koptos	Rock-tombs in	
5	Mer-en-re I	Abydos	provincial centres	Rise in feudalism,
90	Pepy II (Phiops II)	Saqqara		leading to anarchy
c.2180				

Middle Kingdom (Dynasties XI to XIII)

(During the Dynasties VII to X the country underwent a period of chaos or collapse.)

Date BC and Years of Reign	Principal Kings	Main Sites	Funerary Customs	Significant Events
c.2080	**Dynasty XI**		*Coffin Texts* Large rock-	Reunion of
51	Menthu-hotep I Neb-hepet-re	Thebes	tomb with pyramid in forecourt	Two Lands
12	Menthu-hotep II S-ankh-ka-re	Abydos		
c.1990	**Dynasty XII**		Royal burials	Development of Literature
30	Amun-em-het I (Ammenemes)	Thebes	in pyramids	Large irrigation schemes in
44	Sen-wosret I (Sesostris)	Lisht	Private burials in mastabas	Faiyum. Re-building on
18	Sen-wosret II	Dahshur	and rock-tombs	all sites. Final
36	Sen-wosret III	Lahun		suppression of
50	Amun-em-het III	Hawara		feudal nobles
c.1785	**Dynasty XIII**		Appearance of anthropoid coffin	Rise of Osiris cult
	A large number of kings. Probably a separate line of rulers in Western Delta forming Dynasty XIV		and shawabti-figure	at Abydos. Subjugation of Nubia. Trade through Byblos with Syria and Aegean. Arrival of the Hyksos
c.1640	**Dynasty XV/XVI**		There is little information avail-able on this period	
	Dynasty XVII			Hyksos driven out

New Kingdom (Dynasties XVIII to XX)

Date BC and Years of Reign	Principal Rulers	Funerary Customs	Foreign Affairs	Significant Events
1570	**Dynasty XVIII**		Nubia and Kush under Egyptian Viceroy	Introduction of bronze and new weapons, horse and chariot
25	Ahmosis			
21	Amun-hotep (Amenophis I)		New dependencies in Palestine & Syria	
19	Tuthmosis I	Kings buried in elaborate rock-tombs at Thebes: separate mortuary temples	Diplomatic relations with Cyprus, Aegean, Anatolia, Babylon	Glass-working
21	Q. Hatshepsut			
54	Tuthmosis III			Trade with
25	Amenophis II			Punt restored
14	Tuthmosis IV		*Fall of Knossos*	
39	Amenophis III	Private burials in rock-tombs at Thebes & elsewhere gradually become less opulent: tendency for self-contained burial in highly decorated coffin. Magic funerary texts written on papyrus rolls ('The Book of the Dead)	Loss of influence in Asia	Akhenaten's failure to impose monotheism
17	Amenophis IV (Akhenaten)			
9	Tut-ankh-amun		Rise of Hittites	
?	Haremhab			
1304	**Dynasty XIX**		Attempt to challenge Hittites in Syria.Treaty between Egypt and Hittites *Fall of Troy*	Appearance of iron weapons Capital moved from Thebes to Pi-Ramesse. Exodus of Hebrews. Great building activity
13	Sethos I			
67	Rameses II			
12	Merenptah			

1181	**Dynasty XX**		Ethnic movements	
2	Set-nakht		in Mediterranean	
32	Rameses III			Army recruits
	and eight other		Eclipse of Hittites	mercenaries
	Ramesides			
			Repulse of	Decline in prestige
			Libyans and	of kingship
			Sea-Peoples	Tomb robberies
				at Thebes
			Loss of Asiatic	
			dependencies	Rebellion
				in Middle
				Egypt
1075				

Late Period (Dynasties to XI)

Date BC and Years of Reign	Principal Kings	Chief Centres	Foreign Affairs	Significant Events
1075	**Dynasty XXI**		Dorian invasions of Greece. Growth	Leadership of Delta
45	Psusennes I	Tanis Thebes	of Phoenicia	Libyan mercenaries
			Rise of Israel	achieve supremacy
940	**Dynasties XXII–XXIII**			Kush independent
21	Sesonchis I	Bubastis	Sack of Temple at Jerusalem	Skill in metal-
36	Osorkon	Tanis		and faience-work
54	Pedubast	Thebes		Rising anarchy in Egypt provokes
		Herakleopolis		intervention of Kush
830	**Dynasty XXIV**		Revival of	
5	Bocchoris	Sais	Assyrian power under Tiglath-Pileser III	Amun-cult dominant at Napata and Thebes. Rebuilding at Thebes and elsewhere

751	**Dynasty XXV**			
35	Pi-ankhy	Napata (Sudan)		
15	Shabako	Thebes	Invasions of Egypt by Assyrians	
20	Shebitku			Antiquarian study
			Sack of Thebes	of the past
26	Taharqa			
664	**Dynasty XXVI**		Expulsion of Kushites	Revival in arts and crafts
54	Psammetichos I	Sais		
			Independence	Eclipse of Amun
15	Necho II	Edfu	from Assyrians achieved	
				Philhellenism
6	Psammetichos II	Saqqara	Excursion into Phoenicia. Trade	Greek mercenaries
19	Apries (Hophra)	Daphnae	with Greece. Anti-	in pay of kings
44	Amasis	Naukratis	Persian intrigues	
525–	**Dynasty XXVII**		Conquest of Egypt	
404	(Persians)		by Cambyses	
404–	**Dynasty XXVIII**			Resistance to
398				Persians weakened
7	Amyrteos	Sais	Eventual liberation	by dynastic
			with Greek aid	squabbles
398–	**Dynasty XXIX**			
378		Mendes	Alliances against	Last flourish of
13	Achoris		Persia	native arts
378–	**Dynasty XXX**	Sebennytos		
341			Repulse of Persian	
19	Nectanebo I	Bubastis	invasion (Phama-	The last native
			barzus) 373 BC	Pharaoh
19	Nectanebo II	Edfu		
341–	**Dynasty XXXI**		Reconquest of	
333	(Persians)		Egypt by Persians	
332	Alexander of Macedon conquers Persian Empire			
332–	Alexander the Great			Egypt Hellenised
304	The Ptolemies			
	– Cleopatra etc.			

Glossary of Terms

Aats   The word also translates as 'districts', but in the magical context relates to states of consciousness, or the wavebands of certain subtle frequencies.

Akashic Records   From the Sanscrit *Akasa*, which means 'soniferous ether' (metaphysics), one of the five elementary principles of nature. The word as borrowed by Pythagoras who applied it to the fifth element of quintessence (the basic four being fire, air, water and earth). He taught that the celestial ether of astral light fills all space. His followers decreed that every action and thought that takes place in the physical world is recorded in the celestial medium (the Akashic Records) and the idea has been observed in metaphysical studies ever since. Pythagoras is believed to have gleaned his information form the Orphean schools, which carried a decidedly oriental flavour, although the concept is believed to predate these by many centuries.

Amentet   The Hidden Place, also translated as 'The Mountain in the West', as alluding to another dimension, or possibly a folk memory of Atlantis.

Anima/animus   The feminine/masculine aspects of the personality. In Jungian psychology the anima is seen as the feminine principle present in the male unconscious, and the animus the masculine principle in the female unconscious. However, opinion has tended to broaden to embrace the concept that each person is imbued with a degree of both, the state of balance between the two being one of the deciding factors as to the mode of outward expression.

Arits   The seven Reception Halls through which the spirit was believed to move after death. The word also appears in other contexts, for example, the Pylon of the fifth division of the hour is also called Arit.

Astrological Ages   Periods of time, generally considered as around 2,160 years or one-twelfth of the solar cycle of about 25,900 years, which is the approximate time required for the point of vernal equinox in precession to travel all around the zodiac. Thus we are at present hovering on the cusp which divides Pisces from Aquarius. Each Age is seen to bring radical changes, especially during its latter days.

Boats of Ra Atet, the Day Boat and Sektet, the Night Boat. Many other boats feature in Egyptian myth and magic, some of which are associated with specific deities while others ferry the spirit from region to region following death.

Blower on knots A priest specialising in the magic of knots and numbers. Knots were highly significant magically, being associated with the binding of energies. In knot magic seven was the master number.

Brain hemispheres The two hemispheres of the brain, which are joined by the *corpus callosum*, have become associated with different kinds of mental activity, such as memory, speech, writing and abstract thought. The left hemisphere, which functions in what I refer to as inner or linear time, is generally concerned with logic, analytical abilities, and day-to-day factual matters. The right hemisphere, which governs creativity, spatial perception, abstract thought, and musical and visual appreciation, tends to function in outer time, or a state of timelessness, hence its strong connection with the supraphysical.

Double Fire Sometimes referred to as the Khet-Khet. The Fire of Solidification, which comes under the rulership of Isis and the Fire of Dispersion, which is ruled by Nephthys. In accordance with the second Law of Thermodynamics, the Law of Entropy, the Egyptians were only too aware of the sequence of arranged, or solidified matter (order) inevitably giving way to entropic disorder or dispersion.

Entropy 1. A measure of the capacity of a system to undergo spontaneous change, thermodynamically specified by the relationship $dS = dQ/T$, where dS is an infinitesimal change in the measure for a system absorbing an infinitesimal quantity of heat dQ at thermodynamic temperature T. 2. The tendency of the energy of a closed system, including that of the universe itself, to become less available to do work with the passage of time. 3. A measure of the randomness, disorder, or chaos in a system specified in statistical mechanics by the relationship $S = klnP + c$, where S is the value of the measure for a system in a given state, P is the probability of occurrence of that state, k is the Boltzmann constant, and c is an arbitary constant. (*Readers' Digest Great Illustrated Dictionary/*, Vol. 1, p. 564.)

For the less scientifically orientated among us, what we are basically being told is that there is a universal law, acknowledged in physics, that decrees both the solidification and the inevitable dissolution of matter – which was personified by the ancient Egyptian goddesses, Isis and Nephthys.

Epagomenal From the Greek *epagomenos* (*epi* – upon, *agein* – to bring). The intercalculated or intercalary days, and the gods worshipped on those days that formed no part of the month of the old solar year.

Genome Project A proposed scientific survey of the peoples of the earth, based on analysis of their personal genetic code. A forerunner of this is the genetic fingerprinting now used by police forces throughout the world, whereby an individual may be identified by his or her DNA.

Hekau Words of power, the knowledge of which is believed to have been given to the ancient Ammonite tribe by the gods, or Neters, who arrived 'from the skies' centuries before the rise of dynastic Egypt. The original knowledge, that was probably concerned with the science of sonics, has been long since forgotten, and what later became known as *hekau* was more concerned with the magical effect of certain words on the psyche in both this world and the afterlife.

Individuation The uniting of the anima and animus (feminine and masculine elements) in the personality to produce a state of stability and balance within the individual psyche.

Inner time Linear time, the time we see on our clocks that is decided by the movement of our planet in relation to the sun, etc.

Karma From Hinduism and Buddhism, usually defined as the principle of retributive justice determining a person's state of life and the state of his or her reincarnations as the effect of past deeds. The concept of karma, which is based on the 'As ye sow, so shall ye reap' principle, can also be seen as a popular metaphysical variation of the 'sins of the fathers' theme, the idea being that we will be required to return to atone for those misdeeds we have perpetrated in former lives (assuming an acceptance of the *linear* reincarnation theory, which your author does not). For example. if we have committed a gross wrong against another, reparation must be made to that person, or any living creature, in fact, in a future life. Or perhaps we, ourselves, may elect to assume the role or mantle of the sufferer. Sometimes, however, our karmic 'sins' are those of omission the things we should have done, but did not. The ancient Egyptians saw this in terms of the 'negative confession' during which the spirit or soul was obliged to say what it *had* accomplished with kindness and correctmess rather than what it had not, the more good deeds it could notch up, the better its chances with Osiris. There is a metaphysical belief that we each enter life with a specified spiritual program, or karmic blueprint of what our spirit has chosen to carry out in that specific life. If, during the course of life's journey, we become 'off track', a form of spiritual frustration may occur which can give rise to psychological or physical problems (somatizations). Of course, it is not uncommon for a spirit to enter incarnation full of hope and the anticipation of an easy fulfilment of its karmic blueprint, only to find the going so difficult once he or she is here, that those good intentions soon fall by the wayside and the test has to be retaken in another life (or time-frame, as I prefer to call it).

Law of Three Requests That occult or cosmic law that designates that all requests from the subtle dimensions are repeated in triplicate. The first utterance alerts the conscious mind, the repeat engages the reasoning faculties and the third makes contact with the psyche or Essence.

Logos (plural – *logoi*) From the Greek: *logos* – speech, word, reason. Cosmic reason, regarded in ancient Greek philosophy as the source of world order and intelligibility. The self-revealing thought and will of God or the gods. In metaphysics, the term logos or logoi is applied to those guiding intelligences behind planets, suns, stars, and all cosmic bodies also called genii. Thus, one may refer to the Solar Logos of our own system (seen by some schools of belief as the Christos), or those logoi who are responsible for the evolution of clusters of stars, galaxies, and all planes or levels of existence throughout the visible and invisible universe. It has now become accepted in some scientific circles that our own planet Earth is a living, highly intelligent, self-regulating entity in its own right, which Professor James Lovelock has chosen to refer to by the old Greek mythological name of Gaia, (*Gaia – A new look at life on Earth* and *The Ages of Gaia* by Professor James E. Lovelock, Oxford University Press). One might therefore see Gaia as the terrestrial logos or genius.

Multidimensional awareness The ability to compute mentally more than one state of reality, or time-frame simultaneously.

Neters Gods. The feminine version is Neterit, but this is seldom used.

Outer time Non-linear time or timelessness, a state which is believed to exist in the subtle dimensions, and experienced when the psyche is freed from the inner time cycle of the physical world. In outer time, all time is believed to exist *simultaneously,* although the psyche or soul is only able to grasp that portion of the whole decreed by its soul-age or field band-width.

Panspermia Professor Fred Hoyle's concept which conceives of alien micro-organisms distributed throughout interstellar space, and penetrating the Earth's atmosphere. This concept is not entirely new. 'It was considered already during the nineteenth century, in particular by British physicist Lord Kelvin. Unfortunately, however, the possibility of understanding biological evolution here on Earth in terms of this concept was not appreciated, with the consequence that scientists became forced away from what is almost surely the correct theory by the rising tide of Darwinism. This was in spite of a valiant effort early in the present century by the Swedish chemist Svante Arrhenius to support the "panspermia" theory (meaning "seeds everywhere") by carefully reasoned arguments.' (Fred Hoyle, *The Intelligent Universe* p. 158.)

Hoyle sees the universe as a living, intelligent entity which scatters its interstellar particles [seeds?] by design, and in an orderly manner. To do justice to his theories in a short summary would be impossible, and those interested are referred to the above-mentioned book.

Pylon   A division of the Underworld, from the *Shat En Sbau*, or 'Book of Pylons', which describes the various sections of the regions over which Osiris presides, the idea being to facilitate the journey of the soul from one region to another. For fuller details, ref. Budge (see Bibliography).

Quantum leap   Any abrupt change or step from one level or category to a quite different one, especially in knowledge or information. Also called quantum jump.

Samyama   From the Sanscrit meaning 'fusion'. The technique of fusing one's consciousness with the consciousness (field) of the object or person about which one wishes to gain information, thus accessing its databanks and current stage of consciousness/awareness, plus the group databanks of its species.

Shape-shifting   1. In shamanism, the process by which a shaman, during an altered state of consciousness or out of the body experience (OOB), assumes the shape, appearance, or contours of his or her totem beast. 2. In magic – the ability of the practitioner to change shape at will during out of the body experiences, in dream state, or in outer time. 3. In psychology – the process by which a teacher or shaman 'changes the shape of or transforms the lives and ideas of individuals, groups of people, or the 'world paradigm'.

Sothis   The old name for Sirius, a large, bright blue-white star approximately eight-and-a-half light years away from the Earth in the constellation of Canis Major, called the 'Dog Star' by the ancient Egyptians who calculated the annual spring floods of the Nile River according to its heliacal rising.

Spirit Fragment Theory   This involves a concept of reincarnation and soul-age which is at variance with the popular belief of a progression of incarnations through linear or inner time. Rather, it conceives of the complete Essence (whole soul) as a hologram which is shattered and its fragments *simultaneously* deposited throughout all periods of time and across the limitless dimensions of this and other universes. Since every piece contains the same image as the whole, a fraction of the essential Self is retained in every life, and it is that connection with the basic Essence, which has given rise to the concept of the 'higher' or Transpersonal Self. We therefore experience some lives as young-soul fragments, and others in intermediate or mature modes. This concept highlights the folly of spiritual snobbery, which is a young-soul failing anyway.

Tuat   The Underworld, as equivalent to the Greek Hades.

Bibliography

Aldred, Cyril, *The Egyptians*, Thames & Hudson, London, 1961.

Bauval, Robert, *The Orion Mystery*, William Heinemann Ltd, London, 1994.

Berlitz, Charles, *Atlantis*, Macmillan Press Ltd, London, 1984.

Bonwick, James, *Egyptian Belief and Modern Thought*, Falcon's Wings Press, Colorado, USA, 1956.

Braghine, A., *The Shadow of Atlantis*, Aquarian Press, Wellingborough, 1980.

Budge, E. A. Wallis, *The Gods of the Egyptians*, Vols. 1 & 2, Dover Publications, New York, 1969.

Budge, E. A. Wallis, *Egyptian Magic*, Routledge & Kegan Paul, London, 1979.

Budge, E. A. Wallis, *Amulets and Talismans*, Collier Books, Toronto, 1970.

Budge, E. A. Wallis, *The Book of the Dead*, Kegan Paul/Trench, Trubner & Co., London, 1901.

Donnelly, Ignatius, *Atlantis, the Antediluvian World*, Low, Marston & Co, London 1884.

Emery, W. B. *Archaic Egypt*, Penguin Books, London, 1961.

Eysenck, Hans & Sargent, Carl *Explaining the Unexplained*, Weidenfeld & Nicholson, London, 1982.

Frazer, James G. *The Golden Bough*, Macmillan, London, 1978.

Goodman, Jeffrey, *The Earthquake Generation*, Turnstone Books, London, 1979.

Hone, Margaret, *The Modern Textbook of Astrology*, Fowler & Co., London, 1975.

Hope, Murry, *The Psychology of Ritual*, Element Books, Shaftesbury, 1988.

Hope, Murry, *Practical Egyptian Magic*, Aquarian Press, Wellingborough, 1984.

Hope, Murry, *Practical Celtic Magic*, Aquarian Press, Wellingborough, 1988.

Hope, Murry, *Atlantis: Myth or Reality?* Penguin/Arkana, London, 1991.

Hope, Murry, *Essential Woman: Her Mystery, Her Power,* Collins/Crucible, Wellingborough, 1991.

Hope, Murry, *Time: The Ultimate Energy,* Element Books, Shaftesbury, 1991.

Hope, Murry, *The Gaia Dialogues,* Thoth Publications, Loughborough, 1995.

Hope, Murry, *The Lion People,* Thoth Publications, Bognor Regis, 1988.

Hoyle, Fred, *The Intelligent Universe,* Michael Joseph, London, 1983.

Iamblichos, *The Egyptian Mysteries,* William Rider & Son, London, 1911.

Ivimy, John, *The Sphinx and the Megaliths,* Abacus Books, London, 1976.

Jacq, Christian, *Egyptian Magic,* Aris & Phillips, Warminster, 1985.

Jung, Carl Gustav, *The Archetypes and the Collective Unconscious,* Routledge & Kegan Paul, London, 1979.

Jung, Carl Gustav, *Memories, Dreams and Reflections,* Routledge & Kegan Paul, London, 1973.

Lamy, Lucie, *Egyptian Mysteries,* Thames & Hudson, London, 1981.

Larousse Encyclopedia of Mythology, Paul Hamlyn, London, 1959.

Lemesurier, P., *The Great Pyramid Decoded,* Compton Russell Element, Tisbury, 1977.

Maspero, Gaston, *The Dawn of Civilization,* The Society for Promoting Christian Knowledge, London, 1910.

Masters, Robert, *The Goddess Sekhmet,* Amity House Inc., New York, 1988.

Mead, G. R. S. *Fragments of a Faith Forgotten,* John N. Watkins, London, 1931.

Mead, G. R. S. *Thrice Greatest Hermes,* Vols. 1, 2 & 3, Theosophical Publishing Co, London, 1906.

Mooney, Richard, *Colony Earth,* Souvenir Press, London, 1974.

Ouspensky, P. D. *In Search of the Miraculous,* Routledge & Kegan Paul, London, 1950.

Robson, Vivianne, *Fixed Stars and Constellations in Astrology,* Cecil Palmer, London, 1928.

Rose, John, *The Sons of Re,* JR-T Books, Warrington, 1985.

Rundle Clark, R. R. *Myth and Symbol in Ancient Egypt,* Thames & Hudson, London, 1959.

Scheuler, Gerald and Betty, *Coming Into the Light,* Llewellyn Publications, St Paul MN, 1989.

Schwaller de Lubicz, R. A. *Sacred Science,* Inner Traditions International, Rochester, Vermont, 1961.

Scrutton, Robert, *The Other Atlantis,* Neville Spearman, Jersey, 1977.

Temple, Robert K. G. *The Sirius Mystery,* Sidgwick & Jackson, London, 1976.

Tomas, Andrew, *We Are Not the First,* Souvenir Press, London, 1971.

Tomas, Andrew, *Atlantis From Legend to Discovery,* Robert Hale, London, 1972.

Waite, A. E. *The Occult Sciences*, Kegan Paul/Trench, Trubner & Co., London, 1891

Weinstein, Michael, *The World of Jewel Stones*, Sir Isaac Pitman & Sons, London, 1959.

West, John Anthony, *Serpent in the Sky*, Julian Press, New York, 1987.

Witt, R. E. *Isis in the Graeco-Roman World*, Thames & Hudson, London, 1971.

Wood, David, *Genesis*, Baton Press, Tunbridge Wells, 1985.

Index